The Day-by-Day COLORING BOOK OF Saints

SOPHIA INSTITUTE PRESS

Manchester, NH

Sophia Institute Press

Box 5284, Manchester, NH 03108

1-800-888-9344

www.SophiaInstitute.com

Sophia Institute Press® is a registered trademark of Sophia Institute.

Day-by-Day Coloring Book of Saints—first six months

ISBN: 1-622828-203

First printing

Saints Inside

SAINTS INSIDE

Mary, the Mother of God

Marian Feast Day

The angel Gabriel appeared to a young Jewish girl named Mary and announced to her that she would bear a son, and that He would be the Son of God. Mary was frightened. She didn't know how she could have a son without being married. Then the angel told her that the Holy Spirit would overshadow her, and that she would give birth to a baby boy. Mary said "yes" because it was God's will. Because of her "yes," she became Jesus's mother. Jesus is God, so Mary became the Mother of God. After Jesus was born, she fed Him, hugged Him, clothed Him, helped Him learn to walk, and picked Him up when He fell. As Jesus grew up, Mary watched over Him, keeping everything that He said in her heart.

One day, Mary and Jesus went to a wedding, and the bride and groom ran out of wine for the guests. Mary said to Jesus, "They have no wine."

Jesus told her, "My hour has not yet come."

But Mary knew that if she asked, Jesus would help the couple. She said to the servers, "Do whatever He tells you."

Jesus instructed the servers to fill to the brim twelve stone jars with water and take them to the head waiter. The head waiter tasted the water. It had turned into an even better wine than what they had run out of! This was Jesus's first miracle. He performed it because His mother asked Him.

For the next three years, Jesus preached the Good News of how much the Father loves us. But then the Jews arrested Him, and the Romans crucified Him. His mother and John, Jesus's beloved disciple, stayed with Him when he was put to death. Mary felt Jesus's immense suffering, and her heart was in so much pain that she thought she might die, too. But she knew that Jesus must do what He had come to earth to do, which was to save us from sin and death. Jesus spoke to Mary from the Cross, "Woman, behold, your son," and to John He said, "Behold, your mother." Jesus gave Mary to John to be his mother. With the same breath He made Mary our mother, too!

We can turn to Mary, and she asks Jesus to help us. He listens to her as He did during His first miracle. Dear Mary, bring me closer to your Son!

Mary, the Mother of God
January 1

Sts. Basil the Great and Gregory of Nazianzus
January 2

Sts. Basil the Great and Gregory of Nazianzus

329–379 and 329–390 • Cappadocia (modern-day Turkey)

Basil and Gregory met when they were in school. Basil was strong of mind, brave, and firm, while Gregory was sensitive, peace-loving, and quiet. Although they were so different, they became close friends, united in their desire to live for God.

Both Basil and Gregory wanted to live lives of quiet prayer, but God had different plans for them. There were many disagreements in the Church at that time about what Christians should believe. Many leaders in the Church taught heresy (a heresy is a false teaching about the Catholic Faith). The most widespread heresy of that time was Arianism—the belief that Jesus was not fully God and not equal to the Father. God called upon both Basil and Gregory to defend His Church and teach the truth about Jesus and the Faith. Basil, strong and firm, defended the Faith through his preaching. He became a priest, later a bishop, and worked hard to serve the poor and teach others about Jesus.

Basil made Gregory a bishop, too, even though Gregory didn't want to be one. Gregory didn't believe he was strong like Basil was. This led to a disagreement between the two of them, since Basil knew that Gregory had the strength of heart and the holiness to be a bishop. But even though Basil and Gregory disagreed, they still remained friends. When Basil died a holy death, Gregory wrote twelve beautiful poems in honor of him.

Soon after Basil died, Gregory was called to use the strength of heart that Basil knew he had had all along. The Emperor Theodosius made Gregory the leader of the Council of Constantinople, which was a gathering of bishops to settle disagreements about the Catholic Faith. In Constantinople, Gregory gave famous speeches about the Trinity, which helped unite the Church. Gregory's homilies were so popular that he made enemies. A mob of Arians broke into the church during the Easter Vigil Mass and attacked him! Gregory escaped but was wounded. To keep the peace, he resigned his post as leader but told the bishops to seek out the truth of the Faith.

Throughout the rest of his life, Gregory penned many sermons about God and the Faith, as well as poems about his life and the life of his friend, Basil. It is through his poems that we learn about the two saints. Sts. Basil the Great and Gregory of Nazianzus, help me to live for God!

St. Genevieve

c. 419–512 • France

When Genevieve was only seven years old, a holy saint named Germain preached in her village. He spied a young girl in the crowd who stood out for her innocence and purity. The girl was Genevieve. St. Germain took her aside and asked her if she would like to consecrate her life to Jesus, and she said "yes." He gave her a medal engraved with a cross and told her to wear it instead of jewels because she belonged to Jesus now.

At the age of sixteen, Genevieve went to Paris and became a nun. She made many sacrifices for God, performed miracles, and told prophecies. Because she was so holy, many people were jealous of her. At that time, Attila the Hun, a ferocious conqueror, threatened to attack Paris. Afraid and jealous, the people blamed Genevieve for the danger, calling her a false prophetess. So Genevieve gathered the women of Paris to pray outside the city wall. God answered their prayers, and Attila the Hun spared Paris and went to another city. Now the people praised Genevieve as their protector.

Years later, another army threatened Paris, and Genevieve once again became the city's protector. Childeric, king of the Franks, surrounded Paris, and the people were starving because they couldn't bring food into the city. Without fear, Genevieve led eleven boats down the river Seine. Legend says that there was a tree along the river whose hidden roots sank ships as they passed. Genevieve said a prayer, and, with a crack, the tree split and fell. Two angry demons hidden inside popped out from the cloven tree and fled. Then Genevieve went from village to village collecting food. When the ships were full, she returned to Paris by night. Childeric was impressed by what Genevieve had done. When he captured Paris, he was merciful to his prisoners at her request.

Childeric's son, Clovis, converted to Christianity and married Clotilda, who would later become a saint herself. Clotilda and Genevieve became friends. Genevieve advised Clovis to build a beautiful church to St. Peter and St. Paul in the middle of Paris. When Genevieve died, she was buried in the church, which was later renamed St. Genevieve's Church. St. Genevieve, carry my prayers up to Jesus!

St. Genevieve
January 3

St. Elizabeth Ann Seton
January 4

St. Elizabeth Ann Seton

1774–1821 • United States of America

Born just two years before the American Revolution, Elizabeth suffered her first great sorrow at the age of three, when her mother passed away. Her father married again, and the wealthy New York City couple raised Elizabeth as a pious Episcopalian (a type of Protestant). She had a deep love for the Scriptures, and her stepmother would take her to perform charitable tasks for the poor.

When she was nineteen, Elizabeth married the rich and handsome William Seton. They had a happy marriage with five children. Their family grew larger when William's father died, and they took in William's six youngest siblings. Tragically, William developed tuberculosis, a deadly illness. He and Elizabeth traveled to Italy for his health, but William soon passed away. They had been married for just under ten years.

In her sorrow, Elizabeth offered everything to the will of God. William's business friends in Italy were incredibly kind, and through them she learned about the Catholic Faith. She converted to Catholicism because she believed in the Real Presence of Jesus in the Eucharist and because she took comfort in knowing that the Blessed Virgin Mary was her mother in Heaven.

When she returned home, her family rejected her because she was Catholic. The laws limiting the rights of Catholics in America had only just been lifted, and Catholics were still not accepted in society. Elizabeth attempted to start a school for young girls to support herself and her children, but parents removed their children from the school when they discovered that Elizabeth was Catholic. So, she accepted the invitation from the Sulpician Fathers, a French order of priests, to start a school for girls in Maryland. This was the first free American Catholic parish school.

Because Elizabeth wished to dedicate her life to the service of God, Elizabeth took vows of poverty, chastity, and obedience and started the first American religious order for women, the Sisters of Charity of St. Joseph. The sisters made special allowances for Elizabeth to continue caring for her children, and they voted her to be their mother superior. From then on, Elizabeth was known as Mother Seton.

Elizabeth suffered further sorrow when two of her daughters passed away, but she continued to live a life of humility and charity until she died at forty-six years of age. St. Elizabeth Ann Seton, bless all those in Catholic education!

St. John Neumann

1811–1860 • Bohemia (modern-day Czech Republic)

More than anything, John Neumann wanted to be a priest. He learned six different languages so that he could preach about Jesus to as many people as possible. But his bishop thought that there were too many priests in Bohemia and would not ordain him. So John had an idea. He would sail to the United States where he knew they needed priests! He arrived in New York with only one extra set of clothes, a dollar in his pocket, and complete trust in God. And his trust in God worked. Only three weeks later, the bishop of New York ordained him a priest.

John faced many challenges in the United States. People did not like his strong accent, and children made fun of him because he was short. Others, who did not like that he always followed the rules, threw mud and stones at him. Still, he called them "friends" and took no offense. Since he was so alone in his work, John longed for community. He joined the Redemptorist Fathers and served as a pastor in Maryland for many years.

When he turned forty-one years old, John became the bishop of Philadelphia. He faced challenges as a bishop, too. His accent still made him unpopular. The United States was also deeply anti-Catholic at that time, and anti-Catholic groups burned down convents and churches. There were, however, many immigrants in Philadelphia who did not speak English. Knowing many languages, John could help them settle into the community and teach them about Christ. He even learned new languages to help them!

John knew that Catholic education was important, and he wanted children to learn about Jesus and the Faith. When he was first made bishop, there were only two Catholic schools in Philadelphia. As bishop, he increased that number to one hundred! He loved to visit the schools and answer students' questions on their studies. He also wrote two catechisms that taught the Catholic Faith.

John served as bishop until he died of a heart attack when he was only 48 years old. After his death, everyone saw how much good he had done and was amazed. St. John Neumann, help me trust in God even if, at times, others don't like me!

St. John Neumann
January 5

St. André Bessette

January 6

St. André Bessette

1845–1937 • Canada

From his childhood, André suffered terrible and constant stomach pains, making him unable to hold down a job. He would jump from shop to farm, trying out different employments. He was fired every time because he was too weak to perform his duties.

When André was twenty-five, his pastor sent him to the Brothers of the Holy Cross. He knew that André was special, and he told the brothers that he was sending them a saint. But the brothers saw that André was too sickly to work and couldn't read or write. They didn't know how he would be able to fulfill the duties of the monastery. They tried to send him away, but André knew he was where God wanted him to be. He begged a visiting bishop for help, and the bishop promised André that he would be able to stay on and take his vows as a brother. And that is how André Bessette became Br. André.

The brothers searched for work that André would be strong enough to do. They sent him to Notre Dame College in Montreal (a school for boys ages seven to twelve) to be the porter. André greeted guests, ran errands, woke up the boys for school, and even delivered mail. He always found time to pray and had a special love for St. Joseph. He would visit the sick and anoint them with oil while praying to St. Joseph. When a terrible epidemic spread throughout the area, André cared for the sick, and many said that he healed them. But André insisted that it wasn't him; rather, it was St. Joseph who had healed them.

Br. André asked the bishop for permission to build a chapel to St. Joseph. The bishop agreed as long as André did not have to borrow money to build it. André had very little money, but he knew that if St. Joseph wanted his chapel built, he would make it happen. First, André built a tiny wooden structure, and then he raised enough money for the roof. Many pilgrims visited the chapel and donated money. André used it to expand the chapel until it was a magnificent church. Br. André became its full-time caretaker, greeting all the pilgrims who visited. Many experienced the healing of St. Joseph.

When Br. André died at the age of ninety-one, over a million people attended his funeral. The church he built is called St. Joseph's Oratory and is the largest church in Canada. Millions of pilgrims visit it every year. St. André Bessette, ask God to heal my body and soul!

St. Raymond Penyafort

1175–1275 • Spain

God gifted Raymond Penyafort with so much intelligence that he became a teacher at the famous University of Barcelona at the young age of twenty. Raymond not only passed on knowledge, he also instructed his students on virtue and serving the poor. Raymond even taught many classes for free so that the poor could attend.

When he was about thirty, Raymond travelled to Italy and first met the Dominicans, an order of friars founded by St. Dominic. Raymond was drawn to how the Dominicans offered their prayer, work, and study to God. Eventually, he joined the Dominican order. Even though Raymond had studied so much, he was humble and asked to be taught as if he was just a beginner. Now he was able to give his time to God and take even better care of the poor, all the while remaining kind and cheerful to everyone he met.

At that time, the island of Majorca had just been converted to Christianity. King James of Aragon invited Raymond to join him on the island and preach to the newly baptized. Raymond saw this as an opportunity to teach the new Christians about God's love for them. But after he arrived, he saw that the king was leading a sinful life. He knew that the king would serve as a bad example to the new Christians, so he threatened to leave Majorca if the king did not repent. King James did not want to change his life, but he also did not want Raymond to leave the island. And so he ordered all the sailors not to let Raymond onto their ships under pain of death. But Raymond trusted in God and would not let the king stop him from doing what was right. He went to the shore of the island, took off his cloak, and laid it on the sea. He tied the edge of the cloak to a large stick, which acted as a mast. Then he made the Sign of the Cross over it and, without fear, stepped onto the cloak—and it did not sink! The winds carried him away on his cloak as if it was a ship. This great miracle convinced King James to change his life and give up his sins.

When Raymond turned sixty, he tried to retire and lead a quiet life of prayer and writing. But only two years later he was elected as leader of the Dominicans. Raymond taught about God's love and served the poor until he died a holy death at one hundred years of age. St. Raymond Penyafort, help me to never be afraid to do what is right!

St. Raymond Penyafort
January 7

Bl. Eurosia Fabris

January 8

Bl. Eurosia Fabris

1866–1932 • Italy

Eurosia Fabris was born into a poor Italian family and did chores for her parents on the farm to help out. She only had two years of schooling, but those two years were enough for her to learn how to read. Her favorite books were the Bible, the catechism, and other holy texts. Eurosia loved spending time with children, and when she was fifteen years old, she taught the catechism to the children of her parish.

Eurosia's mother taught her how to be a seamstress. Eurosia worked hard and was always kind. Many noticed how good and holy she was, and by the time she turned eighteen years old, she had received two marriage proposals. Eurosia, however, did not know if God wanted her to get married, so she refused the proposals.

Only a few years later, one of her neighbors, a young mother, passed away, leaving behind two baby girls. Eurosia did everything she could to help the little girls—she took care of them every day for six months. The girls' father, Carlo Barban—on seeing how good and kind Eurosia was—asked her to marry him. Eurosia prayed long and hard, and she realized that God was calling her to marriage and to have children. She said "yes" and became a wife to Carlo and a mother to the girls. God gave Eurosia and Carlo nine more children. Each child was a gift for them. They wanted their home to be a place where they could share God's love, and so they adopted even more children over time. Everyone called Eurosia "Mama Rosa."

Even though the family didn't have a lot of money, Eurosia always made sure to give to the poor. She also always made time for God in prayer. She was such a witness of God's love to her children that three of her sons became priests, and one of her daughters joined the Sisters of Mercy. In her sixties, when her husband died, she joined the Secular Order of Franciscans.

Soon after, Eurosia told one of her sons that God had revealed to her that she would die in eighteen months. She saw this as a blessing, because that meant she could prepare her soul for death through prayer. She died of pneumonia, and many people came to lay flowers on her coffin in thanks for all the care she had shown them. Blessed Eurosia Fabris, please ask God to bless my family!

St. Adrian of Canterbury

d. 710 • Africa

Adrian was born in Africa sometime in the early 600s. No one knows much about his childhood. We do know that, when he was young, he became the abbot of a Benedictine monastery near Naples in Italy. During that time, he became friends with a Greek monk who would also become a saint, Theodore of Tarsus.

One day, the pope called Adrian to Rome. The Archbishop of Canterbury in England had died, and the pope wanted to appoint Adrian the next archbishop. But Adrian was a very humble man. He did not think he was worthy to be an archbishop. And so he said "no" to the pope. The pope asked him to be bishop two more times. Both times Adrian said no. The second time, he recommended that his friend Theodore of Tarsus should be made archbishop instead of him. The pope agreed on one condition: Adrian would have to go with Theodore to Canterbury. This time Adrian said "yes."

Adrian and Theodore set off for England. They had to travel through the kingdom of the Franks (which is now France) to get there. The mayor for the Frankish king suspected Adrian of being a messenger from the Greek emperor to stir up trouble in his kingdom. While Theodore was allowed to continue on to England, Adrian was kept in the kingdom of the Franks for two whole years. Eventually, the mayor realized that Adrian was innocent and let him go. When Adrian finally arrived in England, Theodore, who was now the archbishop of Canterbury, appointed him abbot of St. Peter's in Canterbury.

Archbishop Theodore and his friend and advisor Adrian travelled all through England to make sure that the churches were united in the Catholic Faith under Rome. Then they also started a school in Canterbury. Adrian was a very educated man. Not only did he know his theology, he knew Latin and Greek, science and literature, mathematics and astronomy. Scholars from all over England travelled to Canterbury to study under Adrian and Theodore. England became known as a place of great learning. Adrian served and taught in Canterbury for almost forty years before he died a holy death. St. Adrian of Canterbury, help me to be humble!

St. Leonie Aviat

1844–1914 • France

When Leonie Aviat was a young girl, her parents sent her to a convent school in Troyes for her education. There she received spiritual guidance from the chaplain of the school, Fr. Bisson, who was a holy man. While still at school, Leonie felt the call to be a nun. She returned home after she graduated from school and told her parents of her calling. Her father became upset. He wanted Leonie to marry. In fact, he had already chosen a rich young man to be her husband! So, Leonie had to wait. As she waited, Leonie visited a factory full of young working girls making eyeglasses. Leonie felt a sudden urge to stay with them, to tell them that their work was important in God's eyes, and to tell them how much God loved them. Now she knew she had found her calling, to serve working women and bring them closer to God.

Leonie returned to the convent on retreat and confided her calling to Fr. Bisson. Fr. Bisson also knew that it was important to help the working girls. Young country girls were swarming to the big cities to work in textile mills. The girls were poor and had nowhere to live or anybody to take care of them if they fell sick. Fr. Bisson and Leonie started a new order called the Oblate Sisters of St. Francis de Sales to serve these working girls. Leonie became a nun and took on a new name, Sr. Françoise de Sales.

Sr. Leonie Françoise de Sales was elected as the mother superior of her order twice. She started a foundation for the young girls in Troyes and stayed with them in the boarding house. She educated them and told them that their work was important. She spoke to them of God's love. Leonie's love and kindness spread to all the girls who lived in the boarding house. If one girl was sick, the rest split her work and gave the sick girl the money earned. Once, a girl came to the building in rags, and another one gave her an entire wardrobe of clothes, even though she was poor herself.

It was time for the order to grow, so Leonie went to Paris to found schools and boarding houses for girls. Sisters of her order founded missions all over the world, as far as South Africa and Ecuador. In 1905, anti-clerical laws were passed in France which disbanded all religious houses. Fearing persecution, the Oblate Sisters of St. Francis de Sales moved their motherhouse to Perugia, Italy, so they could continue to serve working women. Sr. Leonie Françoise de Sales died in Perugia of a fever. St. Leonie Aviat, help me be patient so that I can discover God's will for me!

St. Theodosius the Cenobiarch

423–529 • Cappadocia (modern-day Turkey)

Theodosius's parents greatly loved God and taught Theodosius to love God, too. Theodosius loved God so much that he wanted to give up the world—all that would distract him from God—so he could give God everything. So he left his home and went on a journey to the Holy Land, the place where Jesus had lived. There he visited a holy man who had also given up the world—St. Simeon Stylites, who lived on a platform on the top of a single pillar. St. Simeon blessed Theodosius and blessed his mission to give his life to God.

In the nearby mountains was the cave where the Magi, or the Three Kings, had stayed after they had seen the Infant Jesus in Bethlehem. This was where the angel had visited the magi to warn them that Herod wished to kill Jesus. Theodosius knew that this cave was a holy place, so he settled there to live a life of prayer and sacrifice. He never stopped praying; he stood praying all day, and he stood praying all night. He even tied a rope around his waist and attached it to a tree or a rock to hold him up in case he fell asleep. As a sacrifice to God, he ate only enough to keep from starving, surviving on dates and the wild vegetables that grew in the area. He lived this way for thirty years.

Many men flocked to Theodosius, attracted to his life of prayer and holiness. They wanted to give their lives to God like him. So many men came that Theodosius had to leave his cave and found a monastery near Bethlehem. There, Theodosius and the monks took care of the sick, the elderly, and the mentally disabled, and Theodosius performed many miracles for those who came for help.

The Patriarch of Jerusalem (the leader of the Church of Jerusalem) made Theodosius the leader of the monastic communities in the Holy Land. That is why Theodosius is known as the Cenobiarch, because the word cenobiarch in Greek means "leader of a community of monks." He died a holy death at about one hundred five years of age. St. Theodosius the Cenobiarch, help me to give my life to God!

St. Theodosius the Cenobiarch

January 11

St. Marguerite Bourgeoys
January 12

St. Marguerite Bourgeoys

1620–1700 • France

In her youth, Marguerite Bourgeoys suffered terrible loss. Her father died when she was a child, and her mother died when she was only nineteen. Alone without her parents, Marguerite sought comfort in Mary, her heavenly mother. The desire to give her life to Mary and serve the poor filled her heart.

A local order of nuns was dedicated to educating the poor. At that time, nuns were cloistered, which meant that they could not leave their convent. Marguerite joined a group of young girls associated with the order but did not become a nun herself. In this way, she could educate poor young girls beyond the convent walls.

Ten years later, the founder and governor of Montreal in Canada, Monsieur de Maisonneuve, traveled to France. He was searching for someone to teach the children and native people in his new settlement. Once again, Marguerite felt a deep desire within her heart. She knew that this was God's mission for her. So, she and the governor sailed across the Atlantic Ocean to Canada. After they landed, Marguerite founded the Sisters of the Congregation of Notre-Dame, which was dedicated to educating young girls.

The governor gave Marguerite a stable, where she opened Montreal's first school. Poor girls were sent to her stable-schoolhouse, but Marguerite knew that if she and her group of nuns were truly going to educate the young girls of the new settlement, they would have to go from town to town and teach those who could not travel. But nuns were not allowed to leave the convent, and the local bishop ordered Marguerite and her sisters to remain cloistered.

Marguerite knew that she would have to do something brave to help as many children in the new colony as possible. She returned to France and sought an audience with the king. After the king listened to Marguerite explain how important her work was, he sent her back with a letter declaring royal support for her work. When the bishop saw the king's letter, he allowed Marguerite and her sisters to travel so they could teach all the girls in the colony.

Now Marguerite was living the life that her heavenly mother had shown her. She became like a mother to these young girls and was called the "Mother of the Colony" until she died a holy death. St. Marguerite Bourgeoys, help me accept God's mission for me!

St. Hilary of Poitiers

d. 367 • France

Hilary was born in Poitiers around the year 300. His parents were pagans and gave Hilary a good education. More than anything, Hilary wanted to find out who God was. He had so many questions he wanted to ask Him: Why was the world made? Why was he made? One day he read the Scriptures. He read the psalms and the Gospels. In the Scriptures, he found out who God was, and he found the answers to all his questions. So he and his wife and his daughter Abra—who would also become a saint—were baptized.

The Christians in Poitiers greatly respected Hilary, and in the early 350's, they elected him bishop. This was in the early days of the Church, when some priests and bishops were married. Hilary knew that, as bishop, it was his job to defend the Church. At that time, a false teaching about the Faith was being spread. This false teaching was called Arianism, and it declared that Jesus was not fully God and not equal to the Father. Hilary knew the Scriptures. He knew how important it was to know who God is. He knew how important it was to know who Jesus is—that He is fully God and fully man.

The emperor at the time was an Arian. Hilary stood up against him, and so the emperor had him exiled. During his exile, Hilary wrote many letters and theological works that helped spread the true Christian Faith. His writings would influence many saints, including St. Augustine and St. Jerome. Eventually, Hilary was allowed to return to Poitiers, where he continued to write and govern his people as a good bishop. There he died a holy death.

St. Hilary of Poitiers, help me to learn about Jesus!

St. Hilary of Poitiers
January 13

St. Macrina the Elder
January 14

St. Macrina the Elder

c. 270–340 • Neocaesarea (modern-day Turkey)

Macrina was born, raised, and married in Neocaesarea. Both she and her husband were pagans and did not know about the Good News of Jesus's love. Then one day a man named Gregory arrived. He was the new Christian bishop of Neocaesarea, and Macrina and her husband became his friends. Gregory taught Macrina and her husband about Jesus, and they decided to be baptized Christian. Macrina and her husband had a son named Basil, and they raised him to be strong in his new Faith.

At that time, the Roman emperors persecuted the Christians because they would not worship the emperor as a god. Macrina and her family had to flee terrible persecution under the Emperors Diocletian and Maximian. They escaped from the city to the woods and scrounged and struggled to live in the wild for seven years. They would not have been able to survive if God had not taken care of them. During that time, Macrina's husband died. Some people say that he was martyred, which means that he died for his faith in Jesus.

Finally, the persecutions died down. Macrina and her son returned to Neocaesarea. But now they were poor, and Macrina had to raise her son all by herself. Macrina and Basil begged on the streets for food, and Macrina would tell stories for coins. The city people made fun of her because she was a Christian. Still, her love for Jesus never weakened, and this love was also strong in Basil.

Even though he was poor, Basil became a lawyer and a teacher. He married a holy woman named Emmelia, and Macrina lived with them. Basil and Emmelia had nine children and raised them in the Christian Faith. They were especially kind to the poor, remembering their time living in poverty. Macrina read the Bible to her grandchildren and passed on to them the strength of her faith. She died a holy death surrounded by the love of her family. Her son, Basil, and his wife, Emmelia, and four of her grandchildren—Macrina the Younger, Basil the Great, Gregory of Nyssa, and Peter of Sebaste—all became saints.

St. Macrina, bless my mother and grandmothers!

St. Paul of Thebes

c. 227–c. 341 • Egypt

Paul was a Christian born in Egypt. In Paul's twenties, his parents died, and their inheritance was split between Paul and his married sister. But his sister's husband was cruel and greedy—he wanted the entire inheritance to go to his wife and himself. He knew that Paul was a Christian, and at that time Christians were persecuted for their Faith, and so he reported Paul to the Egyptian officials. Paul fled to the desert in Thebes in fear for his life.

In the desert, he found a cave near a spring and a palm tree. He clothed himself in palm leaves, ate the tree's fruit, and drank the water from the spring. God took special care of Paul in the desert. Every day, He would send a raven to Paul with a single loaf of bread. In this way, Paul survived and lived for many years, dedicating his life to God through prayer.

There was another man who lived in the desert named Anthony, who would one day be known as St. Anthony the Great. Anthony thought that he was the only one who lived alone in the desert. One night, he had a dream in which God told him to visit Paul. When he woke, he went to the cave where his dream had revealed that Paul would be.

Paul and Anthony were happy to meet, and they spent the day talking about the things of God. By this time, Paul was one hundred thirty-three years old. He knew that it was his time to die. So, he asked Anthony to go back to his monastery and bring him a cloak. When Anthony returned, Paul was already dead.

Anthony was not sure what to do. He had not brought anything to dig a grave. But just then, two lions came bounding from the desert. With their sharp claws they dug a grave in the earth for Paul's body. At the sight of this, Anthony rejoiced over how God takes care of His own. He wrapped Paul in the cloak he had brought and laid him in the grave. Then he took the robe woven from palm leaves that Paul usually wore and brought it back to his monastery. From then on, Anthony wore the palm robe twice a year, at Easter and Pentecost, in honor of Paul. St. Paul of Thebes, help me to trust that God will always take care of me!

St. Paul of Thebes
January 15

St. Joseph Vaz

January 16

St. Joseph Vaz

1651–1711 • India

St. Joseph Vaz is known as the Apostle to Ceylon. He was born to Catholic Indian parents in Goa, India, and became a priest. More than anything, he wished to be a missionary in Ceylon (modern-day Sri Lanka). Joseph knew that the Catholics in Ceylon had not seen a priest or received the sacraments in many, many years because the Dutch, who persecuted Catholics, controlled Ceylon. Though he suffered many delays, he was finally allowed by his order to minister to the Ceylonese people. Disguised as a beggar so as not to be caught by the authorities for being a priest, he went house to house, wearing a rosary. One house in particular always received him with warmth and kindness. He revealed to the owner of the house that he was a priest ministering to the Catholic community there that was in hiding.

The Catholics in Ceylon moved Joseph from village to village so that he would not get caught. Eventually, Joseph decided to stay in the nearby kingdom of Kandy. However, Joseph was betrayed and became the king of Kandy's prisoner. When the king saw that Joseph was a religious man who would not harm anyone, he allowed Joseph to say Mass and minister to the local Catholics. But the king still kept him under house arrest, so Joseph was not able to preach wherever he wanted.

Then one day, a miracle happened that changed the king of Kandy's mind about Joseph. The kingdom was suffering because there was no rain and the crops would not grow. So the king tested Joseph. He told Joseph to pray to God to make it rain. Joseph sent a message to the king saying if God willed it, then it would rain. Setting up an altar in the public square opposite the palace, Joseph fell on his knees, praying to God for a rain that would soften the king of Kandy's heart. God answered his prayer. An enormous downpour of rain fell from the heavens, but not a single drop fell on Joseph! The king of Kandy gave Joseph his freedom and allowed him to preach wherever he wanted.

Joseph travelled to many villages throughout the kingdom, spreading the Good News of Jesus's love. He also took care of the sick and saved many lives during a terrible smallpox epidemic in Kandy, winning him further favor with the king. He continued to preach from village to village, until he died a holy death at the age of 59. St. Joseph Vaz, help me to show God's love to everyone I meet!

St. Anthony of the Desert

251–356 • Egypt

When Anthony was a young man, he sat in church one day as the Gospel was being proclaimed from the pulpit: "If you would be perfect, go, sell what you possess and give it to the poor, and you will have treasure in heaven; and come follow me" (Matthew 19:21). The words of Scripture pierced his soul. Anthony knew that Jesus was calling him to perfection.

Anthony sold everything he had, gave the money to the poor, and went to live in a hut all by himself so he could give his life to prayer. Sometimes Anthony felt bored. Other times he worried about whether he was doing the right thing. Sometimes he was tempted to sin. But in the face of every temptation, Anthony poured out his prayers to God, and God gave him the grace to overcome them all.

The desire to find God in even deeper solitude filled Anthony's heart. He searched the desert until he discovered a ruined Roman fort through which a stream flowed. Here was the place he would find deep solitude, Anthony thought, amid the ruins and the water. So Anthony sealed up the entrance to his cell in the fort with stones, and asked a friend to pass him bread through a hole in his cell from time to time so he would not starve.

Once again, Anthony faced temptations. The devil sought to discourage him from his life of holiness. The evil one would send Anthony frightening visions and powerful temptations, but through it all Anthony turned to God in prayer and was given the grace to overcome his trials. Twenty years passed with Anthony alone in his cell in the desert. Finally, he instructed his friends to remove the stones so he could leave his cell. Anthony's fame for holiness had spread far and wide. Men flocked to the desert and asked Anthony to teach them how to be holy. They built monasteries around his cell, and Anthony guided them like a father.

Shortly before he died, Anthony gathered his followers and told them to remain strong in the true Faith and strong in their love for Christ. Then he asked two of his followers to bury him in the desert. Another of his followers, St. Anthony of Alexandria, wrote the story of Anthony's life, and that is how we know about St. Anthony of the Desert. St. Anthony, help me to pray to God whenever I face temptation!

St. Anthony of the Desert
January 17

St. Margaret of Hungary
January 18

St. Margaret of Hungary

1242–1270 • Croatia

Margaret was the daughter of King Bela IV of Hungary, who had fled with his family to Croatia because his enemies, the Tartars, had invaded Hungary. Right before she was born, King Bela promised God that if the Tartars left his country, he would give his next child to the Church. After the Tartars left, the king kept his promise. Margaret was born soon after, and so was sent to live in a Dominican convent at the age of three.

When Margaret was eighteen, the king of Bohemia wished to marry her. Margaret's father, King Bela, also wished this marriage to take place because it would create a strong alliance between the two kingdoms. But Margaret refused. What had started as a promise to God from her father had become a promise Margaret made to God in her heart. Margaret wanted to be a nun and give her love to God alone. When King Bela discovered that Margaret had a true vocation as a nun, he allowed Margaret to remain in the convent.

Margaret gave her life to God in a special way. She offered Him many sacrifices and would spend nights alone, praying before the Blessed Sacrament. When she realized that the nuns assigned her the easiest work because of her royal blood, she chose to do the dirtiest and lowliest tasks with joy and a prayer in her heart. She also worked hard to comfort and care for the poor and the sick. Soon, God called the holy young nun to be with Him in heaven, and she died at the young age of twenty-eight.

St. Margaret of Hungary, help me to love God with all my heart!

St. Germanicus of Smyrna

d. 155 • Greece

Germanicus was an early Christian martyr who lived in the Greek city of Smyrna in the mid-100s. To practice Christianity at that time was dangerous. Christians were put to death because they would not burn incense to worship the Roman emperor. But Germanicus was not afraid to be Christian. He was young and very brave. Germanicus knew that there was only one God in three Persons: Father, Son, and Holy Spirit. He knew that God the Father loved us so much that He sent His only Son to die for our sins.

Many Christians were arrested in Smyrna, and Germanicus was one of them. The Roman consuls tried to force Germanicus to give up his Faith. Germanicus refused. He would not worship an emperor who pretended to be God. And so the Romans threw him to the lions. Without fear, Germanicus stood before the ferocious beasts. One of the consuls saw with pity how young and full of life Germanicus was. He pleaded with the youth and begged him to give up his Christian Faith and deny Christ. He told Germanicus that he was much too young to die.

But Germanicus was not afraid of death. He looked around him and saw the other Christians watching him. They had fear in their eyes, and Germanicus knew he must show them how to die bravely.

Germanicus marched straight up to the lions. He yelled at the fierce beasts, poked them, even dragged them toward him until they attacked. And so he died, a martyr for Christ. All of the onlookers were amazed by Germanicus's brave death. One of them was a Christian who recorded Germanicus's martyrdom in a book so that it would not be forgotten. That is how we know the story of St. Germanicus today.

St. Germanicus of Smyrna, help me live bravely for Christ!

St. Germanicus of Smyrna

January 19

St. Sebastian
January 20

St. Sebastian

285–305 • Italy

Not much is known about St. Sebastian except that he was an early Roman martyr. Legends have arisen about his life and death. The legends say that Sebastian lived during the reign of Diocletian, a Roman emperor famous for savagely persecuting Christians. Sebastian was a member of the emperor's army, but he kept his Christianity a secret so he could protect the Christians who needed help. Because Sebastian was so brave, the emperor made him a member of the Praetorian Guard (the emperor's own personal guard), not suspecting that Sebastian was also a Christian.

Because Sebastian converted so many soldiers to Christianity, Diocletian finally discovered that Sebastian was a Christian. Enraged, the emperor ordered Sebastian to be tied to a tree and shot dead with arrows. Many arrows sped through the air and pierced the bound Sebastian, and so the soldiers left him for dead. A Christian widow named Irene wished to bury Sebastian. When she untied his body from the tree, however, she discovered that he was miraculously alive! She cared for the wounded Sebastian until he was strong and healthy again.

The Christian soldier could not stand by and do nothing while Diocletian continued persecuting Christians. He snuck into the emperor's palace and waited for the emperor to walk by him. He called out to Diocletian and told him that what he was doing was wrong. The emperor was shocked. His soldiers had reported that Sebastian was dead, yet here Sebastian was, unafraid and defending his fellow Christians. But Diocletian was a hard, cruel man. Not even a miracle could change his mind. For the second time, he ordered his soldiers to kill Sebastian. This time they beat him with clubs, and Sebastian died a martyr, a witness to Christ.

Even though Sebastian's story is mostly a legend, he is an example of how we should not be afraid to show our love for Jesus. St. Sebastian, help me to be a witness to Christ!

St. Agnes

Late 3rd Century • Italy

St. Agnes was an early Christian virgin who died under the Roman Emperor Diocletian's violent persecution of Christians.

Born of the Roman nobility and raised a Christian, Agnes had many suitors who wished to marry her. But Agnes was only thirteen. She did not love these men and wished to remain pure, so she refused each and every one of them. Angry at the refusals, the rejected suitors reported her to the Roman officials as a Christian.

Roman soldiers arrested Agnes and tried to force her to give up her Faith. The soldiers even tried to force Agnes to sin against purity, but Jesus miraculously protected her. Even though Agnes was young, she was strong. Nothing could make her deny her love for Jesus. And so she died as a witness to Christ.

The early Christians dearly loved their young, virgin martyr. They buried her body near a Roman road, and Christians would pray at her tomb. Many who prayed there reported miracles that happened through Agnes's intercession.

In Christian art, Agnes is shown with a white lamb. This is because her name, Agnes, means "lamb" in Latin. The snow-white wool of a lamb also represents purity, and Agnes was pure in defending her love for Jesus. To this day, we pray to St. Agnes in the Roman Canon of the Mass. If you listen carefully, you can hear her name in the prayers right before we receive Communion.

St. Agnes, help me remain pure in my love for Jesus!

St. Agnes

January 21

St. Vincent the Deacon
January 22

St. Vincent the Deacon

d. 304 • Spain

St. Vincent lived during Emperor Diocletian's persecution of Christians. Under Bishop Valerius of Saragossa, Vincent was ordained a deacon. A deacon serves alongside a bishop or priest in order to assist with preaching the Gospel and helping the poor. Because Bishop Valerius could not speak well, he had Vincent preach for him to the people.

The Emperor Diocletian ordered his governor and soldiers to persecute the Christians in Spain and to burn their sacred books. Vincent and his fellow Christians knew the soldiers were coming. They hid the sacred books that contained the Word of God so that the soldiers could not treat God's Word with disrespect. When the soldiers arrived, they arrested the bishop and his deacon, Vincent, dragging them in chains to prison. There they remained for a long time, neglected in the dark prison and poorly fed.

Finally, the deacon and his bishop appeared before the governor. Vincent spoke for himself and his bishop with a strong, clear voice. He declared that there was nothing the governor could do to force them to renounce Jesus Christ. Vincent's strong faith infuriated the governor. He wanted to prove Vincent wrong and force him to renounce the Faith. The governor released Bishop Valerius because he was old but ordered Vincent's torture. He did not believe that Vincent would remain true to Jesus through pain and suffering.

Vincent endured the horrible torture. His torturer promised to stop if Vincent would reveal the location of the hidden sacred books so that they could be burned. But Vincent refused. He would die to protect the written Word of God, the very Word he had spent his life preaching to the people of Christ. Vincent remained true to his declaration—nothing could force him to renounce Jesus Christ.

His body broken and bleeding, Vincent was thrown back into prison. Despite his wounds, Vincent had triumphed. He died in prison a glorious martyr for Christ. St. Vincent the Deacon, help me reverence God's Word!

St. Marianne Cope

1838–1918 • Germany

When Marianne Cope was only two years old, her family immigrated to the United States from Germany. Ever since she was young, Marianne knew that God wanted her to be a nun, and she joined the Franciscan sisters. Eventually, she was elected the mother superior and ran the local hospital. Some people criticized her for receiving "outcasts" in the hospital, but Sr. Marianne rejected no one who needed help. God used her time with the sick to prepare her for an important mission He had planned for her.

In 1883, the Hawaiian government sent a letter to Sr. Marianne, pleading that she come to Hawaii and take care of the lepers on the islands. At that time, there was no cure for the terrible disease of leprosy that damaged the flesh. The Hawaiian government had begged many other religious communities to send help, but none had answered the call. But Sr. Marianne's heart leapt at the opportunity to serve the sick in Hawaii in Christ's name. Immediately, she wrote back that it would be her greatest delight to serve the abandoned lepers.

Sr. Marianne and six of her nuns arrived in Honolulu and took charge of the hospital there. They tidied it up and made it a pleasant place to stay. They served the patients with tenderness and love. There were many young girls who had nobody to take care of them because their parents were sick with leprosy; so Sr. Marianne and her nuns started a home for the girls near the hospital.

A few years later, Sr. Marianne heard that a holy priest had fallen ill with leprosy. The priest's name was Fr. Damien, and he would later become a saint. Fr. Damien served the lepers in a settlement colony on the island of Molokai, where the most hopeless cases of leprosy were sent. Sr. Marianne knew that this priest who had dedicated his life to care for others must now also be taken care of. She traveled to Molokai to comfort the dying priest and promised him that his beloved lepers would be looked after.

For the rest of her life, Sr. Marianne cared for the lepers in Hawaii. She worked so hard that eventually she had to use a wheelchair because she had worn her body out. She never caught leprosy herself, and she died a holy death in old age. St. Marianne Cope, help me take care of the sick!

St. Francis de Sales

1567–1622 • France

Francis de Sales was the eldest son of a French noble family. The young Francis was intelligent and handsome, quiet and sensitive. He was brought up to be a gentleman with a fine education, and his father cherished hopes that Francis would someday have an important political career.

Despite all this, when Francis finished his studies, he declared that he would become a priest. Terribly upset, his father refused to accept his decision. He had arranged for Francis to marry a wealthy heiress to help further his son's political career. The bishop of Geneva, however, saw that God was calling Francis to the priesthood. But knowing that honor and position were important to Francis's father, he promised to give Francis an important position in the diocese if he became a priest. Won over by the high honor offered by the bishop, Francis's father gave his approval for Francis to enter the priesthood.

After being ordained a priest, Francis desired to preach the Catholic Faith in the nearby Calvinist territory. Calvinists are Protestants who, at the time, were extremely anti-Catholic. Francis knew it would be dangerous for him to preach to the Calvinists, but he wanted to share the true Faith with them. When he arrived in the nearby Calvinist city, the people shut their doors against him. They threw rocks in his face. A few even tried to assassinate him! All throughout, Francis was gentle and kind. He would pass booklets under the closed doors that explained the truth of the Catholic Faith. Eventually, the people opened their doors to him, and his gentle kindness won many of them over. About forty thousand Calvinists converted to the Catholic Faith.

When the bishop of Geneva died, Francis was made the next bishop. Soon after, he met the widow Jane de Chantal, who would also become a saint. Together they founded the Order of the Visitation. Francis also gave spiritual guidance to many laywomen, advising them on how to live holy lives in the married state. At that time, most people believed that only priests and nuns could be holy in this life. Francis believed that everyone could be holy if he or she lived the way Jesus did. His most famous book, *The Introduction to the Devout Life*, was written for laypeople.

Until his death, Francis was known for his patience, gentleness, and great love. St. Francis de Sales, help me to be gentle and kind to others out of love for Christ!

The Conversion of St. Paul the Apostle

c. 34 • Road to Damascus (modern-day Syria)

Saul (who would later become Paul) was a pious Jew on fire for his faith. He had heard all about Jesus whom the Romans had crucified. Jesus had said that He was the Son of God, and Paul did not believe Him, so he persecuted the Christians. Some Christians were hiding in Damascus, and Saul took off with a party of men to hunt them down. On the road to Damascus, a blinding light flashed from the sky, and Saul fell to the ground.

A voice called out, "Saul, Saul, why are you persecuting me?"

In fear, Saul asked, "Who are you, sir?"

The voice replied, "I am Jesus, whom you are persecuting."

The light of Truth transfigured Saul's heart. Now he saw that Jesus was the Son of God. Now he saw that he must spend the rest of his life spreading the Truth of Jesus to make up for his sins. Saul opened his eyes, but there was only darkness. The light had been so bright that now he was blind. His men helped him rise and led the blind Saul to Damascus.

At Damascus, an angel appeared to a Christian named Ananias and ordered him to go to Saul to heal him. When Ananias laid hands over him, things like scales fell from Saul's eyes, and his sight was restored. Immediately, Saul rose and was baptized. Now he could truly see, both in body and soul.

Saul became a powerful preacher, risking his life to teach about Jesus. Many Jews came to believe in Jesus because of his words. And so Peter and the Apostles accepted Saul. Saul changed his name to Paul, and, for the rest of his life, he traveled from city to city, preaching the Good News of Jesus Christ. Because of Paul, the Christian Faith spread through all the world.

Paul also wrote many epistles to the Christian Churches; these are letters that taught the Christian communities about the Faith and encouraged them in their love for Jesus. These epistles make up a large part of the New Testament, and you can hear them read when you go to Mass. St. Paul, help my heart see the light of Jesus!

**The Conversion of
St. Paul the Apostle**
January 25

Sts. Timothy and Titus
January 26

Sts. Timothy and Titus

d. 97 and d. 96 • Greece

Both Sts. Timothy and Titus were followers of St. Paul. They travelled with Paul as he went from place to place, spreading the Good News that Jesus Christ was God and that He died and rose from the dead to save us from our sins.

Timothy's mother was Hebrew, and his father was Greek. From the way Paul writes about him in his letters, Timothy seems to have been sensitive and a little shy. But that did not stop him from doing important work and preaching to the early Christian Churches so that they would become stronger and more faithful to Jesus. St. Paul wrote to Timothy and said, "So you, my child, be strong in the grace that is in Christ Jesus. And what you heard from me through many witnesses, entrust to faithful people who will have the ability to teach others as well" (2 Timothy 2:1–2).

When Paul was in prison, he asked Timothy to come visit him. He wished to say goodbye to his beloved follower before being put to death. Timothy was also imprisoned for his faith in Jesus, but he was released. Paul wrote two epistles, or letters, to Timothy. You can read those letters in the Bible.

Titus was St. Paul's secretary and interpreter. He also traveled to many early Christian churches to bring news to them. Paul ordained Titus as bishop of the Greek island of Crete, so that Titus could help guide the Church in Crete into a greater and deeper love for Jesus. Paul wrote a letter to Titus that explains how to be a good bishop. Paul wrote to Titus, "Titus, my true child in our common faith: Grace and peace from God the Father and Christ Jesus our Savior. For this reason I left you in Crete, so that you might set right what remains to be done and appoint presbyters in every town" (Titus 1:4–5). You can also read the letter to Titus in the Bible.

Sts. Timothy and Titus, please help me share the Good News of Jesus's love!

St. Angela Merici

1474–1540 • Italy

Angela and her younger sister lived with their uncle, since their parents had died when they were young. The two sisters were close, as they shared the same sorrow, and Angela was heartbroken when her younger sister also passed away. Angela was especially distraught because her sister's death had been unexpected, and so she had not been able to receive the Sacrament of the Anointing of the Sick to prepare for death. In her distress, Angela offered a heartfelt prayer to God, asking Him to guide her in her sorrow. God heard her prayer and granted Angela a miraculous vision of her sister. To her joy, Angela saw that her sister was with the blessed saints in heaven. Now Angela could be at peace since she knew her sister was happy, and she would see her again one day in heaven.

God continued to guide Angela's life, and her relationship with Him grew stronger and deeper. When she turned twenty, Angela opened up a school to teach the girls of the town about their Faith. She taught them all that she could about Jesus and His love for them. Then God granted Angela another miraculous vision to guide her. Jesus told her that he wanted her to start an order of nuns dedicated to teaching the Faith to young girls. Angela's heart leapt with joy at Jesus's command. She brought a group of women together that would eventually become the Order of St. Ursula, named after a virgin saint that Angela particularly loved. The group of Ursulines were so successful that soon the neighboring town asked Angela to start a school for them, too.

At fifty years of age, Angela went on a pilgrimage to the Holy Land, the land where Jesus lived and died. She wanted to grow even closer to Jesus, who had guided her all of her life. On the way there, she was mysteriously struck blind. Yet Angela's heart still yearned to visit all the holy sites of Jesus's life. So she placed her trust in God completely and journeyed on to all the holy places, knowing that Jesus would guide her even though she could not see. On her return, she prayed before a crucifix at the same place where she was struck blind. There her sight was miraculously restored. She rejoiced in God's miracle and knew that she could always trust in Him to guide her.

Angela returned home and, with the Sisters of St. Ursula, spent the rest of her life teaching young girls and taking care of the poor. St. Angela Merici, help me trust in God's guidance!

St. Angela Merici
January 27

St. Thomas Aquinas
January 28

St. Thomas Aquinas

1225–1274 • Italy

St. Thomas Aquinas's nickname was the "Dumb Ox." He was born into a noble Italian family, who wanted Thomas to have a high and important position in the Church. But Thomas was attracted to a life of poverty, study, and service. At nineteen years of age, he joined the Dominicans, much to his family's disapproval. Soon after he joined the Dominican order, Thomas's brothers came with a troop of soldiers and kidnapped him on the road while he was traveling by foot. His family kept him imprisoned in a castle for two years, but during that time Thomas studied theology and memorized large sections of the Bible. Seeing that they could not change Thomas's mind no matter how hard they tried, Thomas's family finally let him go.

Thomas became a student at the University of Paris. He was very smart, but he never showed off. The other students gave him the nickname the "Dumb Ox" because he was big and always quiet and humble. One of his classmates, thinking that Thomas had not understood the day's lesson, offered to explain it to him. Thomas gratefully accepted his help. But then his classmate stumbled over a particularly difficult part in the lesson and became confused. To help his classmate out, Thomas humbly explained the lesson to *him* because he had understood it all along!

Thomas wrote many books, the most famous being the *Summa Theologica*, a long and important work that explains the Catholic Faith. Thomas also loved Jesus in the Eucharist very much. He wrote about the Eucharist with great reverence, and after he was finished, Jesus appeared to him in a vision and told him, "You have written well of the sacrament of my Body." During this vision, Thomas's body miraculously levitated, floating off of the ground. Thomas also wrote many beautiful Eucharistic hymns. We sing two hymns that he wrote, "O Salutaris" and "Tantum Ergo," during benediction of the Blessed Sacrament.

Near the end of his life, Thomas had many mystical visions. These visions filled him with awe and wonder about the mystery of God. He stopped writing because he knew that nothing he wrote could ever compare to God. He said, "I can write no more. I have seen things that make my writings like straw." Thomas became ill, and when the pope summoned him to visit a council, a meeting of the Church, Thomas collapsed on the road and soon after died at about fifty years of age. St. Thomas Aquinas, help me to be a humble student of God!

St. Joseph Freinademetz

1852–1908 • Italy

St. Joseph Freinademetz became a priest to bring the Word of God to others. He knew that there were still so many people in the world who hadn't heard about Jesus. Deep inside Joseph's heart, God had placed a burning desire to bring God's Word to those who did not know Him. Joseph knew that God wanted him to be a missionary.

He joined the Mission House of the Society of the Divine Word and received his mission's cross. This meant that Joseph could now be sent to faraway places and share God's Word. And so Joseph went to China, where there were very few Christians, to share God's Word with the Chinese. He arrived in Hong Kong after a long five-week journey by ship and spent two years preparing for his missionary work. There was so much for him to learn! The language and customs of China were so very different. And Joseph knew that he would have to understand the Chinese people if he was to preach to them in a way that would touch their hearts. But he also knew that he was just a poor servant of God and that God would speak to the Chinese people through him.

Joseph traveled to a new mission in South Shantung, a province with twelve million inhabitants. Out of the twelve million people, only 158 of them were Christians! Joseph knew that he would have to work hard, with God's grace, to spread the Faith in this new place. He prepared a catechism in Chinese for the people, and he also trained many new Chinese priests to share the Word of God. Joseph had such a deep love for the Chinese people that he wrote in a letter to his family, "I love China and the Chinese. I want to die among them and be laid to rest among them."

Some years later, there was an outbreak of typhus where Joseph lived. He went from community to community, taking care of people suffering from this deadly illness. Finally, Joseph also caught typhus and died a holy death, offering his suffering to Jesus. He was buried in China, as he had wished, and many Chinese Christians made pilgrimages to his grave. St. Joseph Freinademetz, help me to share the Divine Word with others!

St. Joseph Freinademetz

January 29

St. Hyacintha

Mariscotti

January 30

St. Hyacintha Mariscotti

1585–1640 • Italy

Hyacintha's baptismal name was Clarice, and when she was little, she had a devout love of God. But her family was rich, and she became spoiled. She liked fine dresses, parties, and pretty things, and she forgot to thank God, who gave her all her gifts. Clarice fell in love with a nobleman, but the nobleman did not love her. In fact, he fell in love with her younger sister! Clarice became gloomy, and she sulked. She was so unbearable that her family sent her to the convent to become a nun. There she made her vows and took on the new name Hyacintha.

Even though Hyacintha had agreed to become a nun, she did not take all her vows seriously. One of the vows a nun makes is to live in poverty, but Hyacintha refused to give up all the riches she was used to. She loved the things she owned more than her promise to God. She had her father send her the finest cloth for her nun's habit, the best foods and sweets, and soft blankets and pillows to keep her room comfortable.

One day Hyacintha became ill, and her confessor visited her. The priest was shocked to see the luxury in her room! He told her that she was committing a terrible sin in breaking her promise to God and that she was hurting other nuns by her bad example. The priest's words had a powerful effect on her. They made her look into her own heart, and she saw that her love of luxury had crowded out her love of God. She promised that she would change her ways.

At first it was hard for Hyacintha to change. She loved all her pretty things and struggled to give them up. It wasn't until she became sick a second time and almost died that she realized how important it was for her to change her ways. When she recovered her health, Hyacintha gave away all her things. Out went her blankets and pillows. Out went her fine habit and delicious sweets. From then on she went barefoot, wore an old habit, and slept with only a single blanket on her bed.

Hyacintha spent the rest of her life dedicated to those in need. She collected money for the poor and those in prison. When plague struck the city, she took care of the sick. Whenever a poor person knocked on the door, she would give that person her own dinner. She loved to pray before the Blessed Sacrament and to the Blessed Mother, and she had the special gift of being able to read other's hearts. She was so loved by those she served that, when she died, crowds of people flocked to her funeral. St. Hyacintha, help me to love God more than what I possess!

St. John Bosco

1815–1888 • Italy

When he was only nine, John Bosco had a powerful dream. A large group of rough boys were fighting and swearing. He jumped into their midst and tried to stop them not only with his words, but with his fists. Suddenly a man appeared, his face shining so bright that John Bosco could barely look at him. The man said, "You will win these friends not by blows, but by gentleness and love." A gentle woman with a sparkling mantle then took John Bosco's hand and showed him fierce wild animals unexpectedly transformed into gentle lambs. She explained that he must do the same thing for her children—and then he awoke. Jesus and Mary had come to John Bosco to show him how to win young people for Christ. The memory of this dream would stay with him for the rest of his life.

Not long after his dream, John Bosco saw a group of traveling circus actors perform amazing tricks. He had an idea. He learned how to juggle and to walk the tight rope, and then started to perform his tricks for others, beginning and ending each performance with prayer. He realized that if he attracted others to him through kindness and fun, they would be willing to hear him talk about God and pray with him.

John Bosco's love for Jesus led him to become a priest. His first assignment was in the city of Turin, which had many slums and prisons. When John Bosco visited the prisons, he noticed many boys there between the ages of twelve and eighteen. These boys reminded him of the rough boys in his dream. John Bosco knew he must do everything he could to keep more boys from going to prison by teaching them about God's love. So he went to the slums and befriended the boys with humor and juggled for them in the streets. The boys came to him to play games and stayed to hear him speak about Jesus. John Bosco started a home for boys who had no other place to live. One of the boys who came to study under John Bosco was Dominic Savio. John Bosco saw that Dominic was very holy, even though he was so young. Dominic died when he was only twelve years old, and John Bosco wrote a short biography of his life. Later, Dominic Savio was canonized a saint.

John Bosco spent the rest of his life working for the boys in his care. He helped find them jobs, improved their working conditions, and gave them places to stay. For John Bosco, kindness was better than punishment in changing the lives of those in need. St. John Bosco, help me bring others to Jesus through gentleness and love!

St. John Bosco
January 31

Bl. Benedict Daswa

February 1

Bl. Benedict Daswa

1946–1990 • South Africa

From a young age, Tshimangadzo Samuel Daswa believed that education and hard work were important. Because his father died in an accident, Daswa took care of his younger brothers and his sister. He had gone to high school, and he taught his siblings to take pride in going to school, too.

When Daswa was a teenager, a friend introduced him to Roman Catholicism. Daswa studied the Faith and learned that Jesus was the Son of God and that Jesus would give him the strength and love to live a good life. Daswa was also inspired by the life of St. Benedict, who had lived by the motto, "Pray and work." When Daswa was baptized, he chose the name Benedict Daswa so that he would remember to pray and work always.

Benedict Daswa became a teacher and a catechist (someone who teaches the Faith). Now he could pass on the gift of education and the Faith to many children. He was a respected leader of the community, becoming the principal of his school and building the first Catholic Church in the area. He married a woman named Shadi, and together they had eight children.

One day, lightning struck several huts in Daswa's village. The villagers still believed in witchcraft and thought that someone had called down the lightning through magic. The village elders summoned a witch doctor to cast a spell to discover who had caused the storm. In order to pay the witch doctor, they demanded money from the villagers. But Daswa knew that it was a sin to practice magic, and he knew that the storm had happened naturally. The witch doctor intended to lie and accuse an innocent person of causing the storm, and that innocent person would be killed. Daswa refused to pay the money because it would be a sin against the Faith and destroy an innocent life.

A few months later, Daswa was driving home on his way back from delivering food to a poor town. A fallen tree blocked the road. When he stepped out of the car, a mob of men, throwing stones, attacked him. They were angry because Daswa had refused to pay the witch doctor. An injured Daswa ran for his life and tried to hide, but the men found him and killed him. Daswa's final words were the same as Jesus's final words on the Cross: "Father, into your hands I commend my spirit." Bl. Benedict Daswa, give me the strength to defend the innocent out of love for God!

Sts. Simeon and Anna

Feast of the Presentation in the Temple

Soon after Jesus was born, Mary and Joseph brought Jesus to the Temple in Jerusalem. They went to offer Jesus to God the Father and to sacrifice two turtle doves because they were too poor to sacrifice a lamb.

That same day, the Holy Spirit brought a man named Simeon to the Temple. Simeon was an old man who had lived a holy life. More than anything, he wanted to see the Messiah, the promised one who was to save Israel. In fact, the Holy Spirit had promised him that he would see the Messiah before he died. The moment that Simeon's eyes fell on baby Jesus, his heart skipped a beat. He knew that this baby was the Messiah that God and all the prophets had promised.

Simeon took the baby in his arms and said, "Now, Master, you may let your servant go in peace, according to your word, for my eyes have seen your salvation, which you prepared in sight of all the peoples, light for revelation to the Gentiles, and glory for your people Israel" (Luke 2:29–32). Mary and Joseph were amazed at the things that Simeon said. Simeon blessed Mary. He told her that Jesus would reveal many people's hearts. He also warned her that a sword would pierce her soul. When he said that, Simeon was warning Mary that she would feel great sorrow over the many things that would happen to Jesus.

At the same time, a prophetess named Anna also approached the Holy Family. She was eighty-four years old and had been a widow for seven years. She lived in the temple both day and night, constantly praying to God. She rejoiced at everything she had just seen and heard. Her heart was full of thanks that she, too, could see the Messiah. She told every person that she met all about the baby Jesus. Sts. Simeon and Anna, help me always to hold Jesus thankfully in my heart!

Sts. Simeon and Anna
February 2

St. Blaise
February 3

St. Blaise

d. 316 • Ancient Armenia (modern-day Turkey)

If you go to church on February 3, your priest might give the blessing of the throats after Mass. He will hold two crossed candles (the candles were blessed during the Feast of the Presentation, which celebrates when Mary and Joseph offered Jesus to God in the Temple) to your throat and say these words, "Through the intercession of Saint Blaise, bishop and martyr, may God deliver you from every disease of the throat and from every other illness: in the name of the Father, and of the Son, and of the Holy Spirit." Not too much is known about St. Blaise, except that he was a bishop and martyr. But there are many legends told about him.

St. Blaise was a doctor who healed the sick and wounded. But he felt called by God to heal a different kind of sickness, the sickness of the soul. Blaise became a bishop so he could heal the soul's wounds by ministering the sacraments and forgiving people's sins.

At that time, Christians were persecuted because they did not worship false gods. The governor arrested Blaise and sent him to jail because he refused to renounce his Faith. As Blaise was put in jail, a distressed woman brought her son to the jail cell. A fishbone was stuck in the boy's throat. The terrified mother worried that her son would choke to death. She begged Blaise for help. She knew he was a holy man and that God would listen to his prayers. Blaise felt compassion for the mother and her boy. He prayed to God for a cure, and God listened to his prayer. The boy was healed, and his mother cried tears of joy.

Despite this miracle, the governor still ordered Blaise to renounce his Faith. Blaise would not deny Jesus, so the governor had him tortured and put to death. Blaise became a glorious martyr for the Faith! St. Blaise, protect me from all sickness, in particular sickness of the throat!

St. Joan of Valois

1464–1505 • France

St. Joan of Valois was the daughter of King Louis XI of France and was born with a humped back. Her father, the king, was ashamed of her. He had wanted a son and did not like seeing her humped back. The king sent her from court to live in a country house so no one could see her. He placed her in the care of a noble couple that did not have children, and Joan brought much joy to the couple's life.

Still, Joan was often sad and lonely because her father was ashamed of her. She would go to the chapel and pray for many hours, and God comforted her in her loneliness. Joan also had a special friendship with Jesus's mother, the Blessed Virgin Mary. Mary spoke to the young Joan in her prayers and told her that she would someday found an order of nuns dedicated to Mary.

When Joan was only twelve years old, the king forced her to marry Louis, the young Duke of Orléans, who was only fourteen years old. Joan's husband also was ashamed of her. He hated being forced to marry, and he also hated the hump on Joan's back. He was often unkind to her, but still Joan did her best to be a good and faithful wife. When her father died, her younger brother took the throne and became King Charles VIII. Joan's husband rebelled against the new king and was imprisoned. Joan begged her brother Charles to be merciful, and he released Louis as a favor to Joan. But even though Joan had had him released from prison, Louis continued to be unkind to her.

Then King Charles VIII died in an accident. Joan's husband, Louis, was next in line for the throne. He became King Louis XII of France, and Joan became queen. Now that Louis was king, he had his marriage to Joan annulled (which meant that their marriage had never been a real marriage). Joan was humble and submitted to the will of the king without complaint.

Even though Joan was hurt, she was also thankful. Now she was free to found the order of nuns that the Blessed Virgin Mary had told her she would when she was a child. She founded the Order of the Annunciation, in which nuns dedicated their lives to penance and prayer and sought also to imitate the life of the Blessed Virgin Mary. Joan took the vows of her order and prayed for the soul of her husband until she died. St. Joan of Valois, help me remember that God will always love me!

St. Joan of Valois

February 4

St. Agatha
February 5

St. Agatha

c. 231–c. 251 • Sicily

St. Agatha was an early Christian virgin who died for her Faith during the Roman persecution of Christians. Like many martyrs during this time, not much is known about her, though Christians since the early years of the Faith have dearly loved her. The people of the seaport city of Catania, in Sicily, claim that St. Agatha was born there. Catania is located on the east side of the volcano, Mount Etna. The Catanians pray to St. Agatha to protect them from the volcano's eruptions.

Legend says that Agatha was very beautiful and that a senator named Quintianus wished to marry her. Agatha, however, had dedicated herself to love of Jesus alone, so she refused to marry the senator.

Quintianus was furious. He was a cruel and selfish man. If he couldn't marry Agatha, then he wanted her to suffer. He denounced her as a Christian to Roman officials and had her undergo painful torture. Agatha prayed to St. Peter for help, and he healed her of her wounds. This only made Quintianus angrier. He had her tortured again. Agatha bravely endured her suffering. She knew that it would soon be over and that Jesus would take her to heaven as a reward for her faithfulness. When she gave up her life for Him, Jesus rewarded her by making her one of the glorious saints in heaven.

St. Agatha, help me be true to my love for Jesus no matter what!

St. Paul Miki

1562–1597 • Japan

St. Paul Miki was the son of a Japanese military leader. His family converted to Christianity when he was a child, and Paul was baptized at five years old. He studied under the Jesuit missionaries in Japan and later became a Jesuit himself.

In that time in Japan, there were many political and religious tensions between the Japanese and the Christians that came from Spain and Portugal. The Japanese lord, Toyotomi Hideyoshi, ordered the arrest of twenty-six Christians at Kyoto. Paul Miki had just completed his eleven-year training as a novice, and he was one of the twenty-six Christians arrested. The arrested Christians had their ears cut off as a sign of disrespect, and they were paraded through the streets of Kyoto. Paul Miki stood out among the crowd. The onlookers recognized him as the son of the nobleman and remembered that he could even have been a Samurai if he wasn't a Christian. Many in the crowd felt pity for the Christians, and some were even converted by their heroic example.

The twenty-six Christians were then marched over six hundred miles from Kyoto to Nagasaki. They were told that if they gave up their Faith, they would go free. But not one of them rejected Jesus. When they reached Nagasaki, they were crucified high on a hill like Jesus was. Paul Miki gave a final sermon from his cross. He declared that he was Japanese born and that he was being crucified because he was a Christian. Then he forgave his enemies, saying "I obey Christ. After Christ's example I forgive my persecutors. I do not hate them. I ask God to have pity on all, and I hope my blood will fall on my fellow men as a fruitful rain."

The twenty-six Christians sang the Canticle of Zechariah from their crosses, pouring their souls into their music for God. The executioners waited for them to finish the song out of respect and then put them to death by the lance. The eyewitnesses in the crowd were impressed by the faith, patience, strength, and peace with which the martyrs met their deaths.

For the next couple of hundred years, Christianity was forbidden and persecuted in Japan. When missionaries returned to Japan, they could not find any traces of Christianity at first. But to their complete surprise, they discovered thousands of Christians around Nagasaki—where the twenty-six martyrs had died—who had secretly kept the Faith. St. Paul Miki, help me forgive my enemies like Jesus did on the Cross!

St. Paul Miki
February 6

Bl. Rosalie Rendu

February 7

Bl. Rosalie Rendu

1786–1856 • France

The terror of the French Revolution swept through France when Rosalie was only three years old. Not only were the rich nobles sentenced to death, but priests and nuns were also sent to the guillotine. Rosalie's parents, simple mountain people, hid endangered priests in their home. At first Rosalie did not know that the men staying with them were disguised priests. A new hired hand named Pierre arrived. She was fascinated by him; he was kind, well-spoken, and holy. One day, she discovered Pierre secretly saying Mass. Pierre wasn't a hired hand after all—he was a priest in disguise. And he wasn't only a priest; he was the bishop! The bishop gave Rosalie her First Communion in their basement in secret, by candlelight.

When the persecution was finally over, Rosalie wanted to help the suffering people in France. When she was only seventeen, she joined the Daughters of Charity of St. Vincent de Paul. She was then sent to Paris to serve in the slums, which were full of the poor and the sick, the oppressed and ignored. In every poor person, Rosalie saw Christ, and she served each one with respect and love. Eventually, she became the superior of her community. She taught her sisters that their work for the poor was also a prayer. Rosalie opened a free clinic, an orphanage, a school, and a home for the elderly. She did all this to fight poverty, neglect, and despair.

Still, there were terrible and violent uprisings in France. The workers set up barricades from which to fight the powerful. The archbishop tried to stop the violence and was killed. Rosalie was terribly sad at the archbishop's death, but she knew his death was not in vain. He had died for Christ. Rosalie would not let the archbishop's death frighten her. Her faith in Christ made her brave and strong. She climbed the barricades herself and tended to the wounded fighters on both sides. Everyone admired her for her courage.

Rosalie made such a difference for the poor in Paris that the Emperor Napoleon III decided to give her the Cross of the Legion of Honor in 1852. Rosalie was humble and wanted to refuse the award. All of her service for the poor had been done for Jesus, not for earthly honors. But the superior general of the order made her accept it. She died a holy death four years later from illness. Bl. Rosalie, please help me to be brave and strong in my service for others!

St. Josephine Bakhita

c. 1869–1947 • Sudan

A nine-year-old girl was walking with a friend in the fields of the Sudan in Africa. Two strange men appeared and ordered the girl to go pick fruit in the forest for them. Her friend they sent away. In the forest, the men seized the little girl, brought her to their town, and made her a slave. She was so frightened that she forgot her name. Because she could not remember her name, the slave raiders called her Bakhita, which means "fortunate one."

But Bakhita did not feel fortunate. In all, she was sold to five different masters. One of her masters was especially cruel and would beat the young Bakhita terribly. Her fifth master was an Italian man named Calixto Leganini, who served as an Italian consul in the Sudan. For the first time, Bakhita felt she might be fortunate because Leganini did not beat her or whip her. When Leganini returned to Italy, he brought Bakhita with him. At the Italian harbor, the wife of one of Leganini's friends, Mrs. Michieli, begged him for one of his slaves. Leganini gave Bakhita to Mrs. Michieli.

Mrs. Michieli took Bakhita home to watch over her daughter. When she and her husband left to manage a hotel in the Sudan, they left Bakhita and their daughter in Italy under the care of the Canossa Sisters of Venice. At the convent, Bakhita's soul was set free. The sisters taught Bakhita about God and His love for her. Bakhita realized that she had been longing for God all of her life, but only now understood that longing. She was baptized into the Catholic Faith and took the name Josephine.

Soon Mrs. Michieli returned to Italy. She wanted to take Josephine Bakhita and her daughter back to Africa. All of her life, Josephine Bakhita had done what her masters commanded out of fear. But now she knew that she should serve no one but God. She refused to leave the convent, and Mrs. Michieli was angry. But the sisters stood by Josephine Bakhita. They declared that since slavery was illegal in Italy, Josephine Bakhita was free to stay if she wished.

Josephine Bakhita stayed at the convent and became a nun. Now she felt truly fortunate because all of her suffering had brought her to God. For the next fifty years of her life, she performed her duties at the convent and served God's poor with quiet humility and love. She even forgave her captors. On her deathbed, her last words were "Madonna," a final prayer to Mary. St. Josephine Bakhita, show me how serving God sets me free!

St. Miguel Febres Cordero
February 9

St. Miguel Febres Cordero

1854–1910 • Ecuador

St. Miguel Febres Cordero was born with crippled feet. He could not walk or stand up. Then one day, when Miguel was five years old, his mother was outside with him in their rose garden. Suddenly he pointed to the roses and cried, "Look at the beautiful woman who is on the roses!" His mother saw no one, but the little boy described a beautiful woman in white, wearing a blue mantle. In great excitement he rose to his feet and, to his mother's joy, walked over to the rose bushes. The beautiful woman Miguel had seen was the Blessed Virgin Mary, and she had healed his feet. From then on, little Miguel could walk.

When he was fourteen, Miguel went to school with the Christian Brothers. The president of Ecuador had invited the brothers to come and teach his people in Ecuador. Miguel loved learning, but even more than that, he knew God was calling him to enter the Order of the Christian Brothers and belong to their teaching mission. Joining the order on the Feast of the Annunciation, in honor of the Blessed Virgin Mary, he was the first man from Ecuador to join the Christian Brothers.

Miguel's students loved him. He was kind and patient, and he treated all students, rich or poor, the same. Miguel saw that the textbooks the children were studying were badly written, and he wanted to give his students the best education possible. So he started writing textbooks himself! He wrote his first textbook when he was only seventeen! It was a textbook on the Spanish language, and it was used all throughout Ecuador.

Miguel taught for thirty-two years in Ecuador. He lived a prayerful and holy life, and he had a great devotion to the Eucharist and to the Blessed Virgin. Then the Christian Brothers sent him to teach in Europe. First he went to France, but the air was so cold in comparison to Ecuador that he got sick. So the brothers sent him to Spain to recover his health. While he was teaching in a school near Barcelona, there was a revolution, and the revolutionaries attacked the school. Miguel took the Blessed Sacrament from the chapel and led schoolboys across the bay to Barcelona where they would be safe. He defended the two most important things in his life: Jesus and his students. The revolution died down, and Miguel and his students were able to return to the school, but Miguel's bad health returned. He received the Last Rites and died a holy death. St. Miguel, bless me in my studies!

St. Scholastica

480–543 • Italy

In the year 480 in Nursia, Italy, twins were born—a girl named Scholastica and a boy named Benedict. The twins grew up together, played together, and loved to talk about the same things. But they also shared something even more important in common. Both were destined to become great saints.

When Benedict was old enough, he went to study in Rome, and Scholastica stayed at home. She missed her brother terribly, but she also knew that she was where God wanted her to be. She knew that He wished her to be His in a special way. Benedict founded a monastery called Monte Cassino, and Scholastica felt called to follow a similar path as her twin brother. So she founded a convent only five miles away from Monte Cassino. Once a year, Scholastica and Benedict would meet at a nearby farmhouse and spend the day talking about what was most precious in their hearts: their love for God.

One day, Scholastica sensed that her time of death was near. She and her brother met at the farmhouse and spent the day talking. When it was time for Benedict to leave, Scholastica begged him to stay longer. Benedict insisted that he must go. He was a monk and had to follow certain rules. He could not spend the night away from his monastery. But Scholastica knew that this was the last time she would see her brother, so she offered a heartfelt prayer to God. All of a sudden, lightning flashed and heavy rain poured from the sky. God had listened to Scholastica's prayer and sent a powerful thunderstorm, making it impossible for Benedict to leave.

"Sister, what have you done?" Benedict cried. He was afraid that breaking the monastery rules would be going against God's will.

"I asked a favor of you and you refused. I asked it of God, and He granted it," she replied.

Then Benedict understood that God loved his sister very much, and He wished Benedict to stay as a special gift to her. They spent the entire night talking about the things of God. The next morning, Benedict returned to his monastery. Three days later, he was praying and saw a shining, white dove rising up to heaven. He knew that the dove was his sister's soul and that she had died and gone to heaven. Benedict had her body brought to the monastery and buried her in the tomb he had prepared for himself. St. Scholastica, help me to trust that God always hears my prayers!

St. Scholastica
February 10

Our Lady of Lourdes
February 11

Our Lady of Lourdes

1858 • France

One day, fourteen-year-old Bernadette was gathering firewood by the river near the French town of Lourdes. Close by was a tall, rocky hill with a natural grotto, like a small cave. The sound of rushing wind surrounded Bernadette, but the trees were still. Only those near the grotto were rustling. Suddenly, a cloud golden with light filled the grotto, and within the cloud was the most beautiful lady Bernadette had ever seen. She wore a flowing white robe with a blue sash and a long white veil, and on her feet gleamed golden roses. She beckoned Bernadette to approach, and the young girl sank to her knees and pulled out her rosary. Together they prayed. When the Rosary was finished, the lady and the golden cloud vanished.

On the following Sunday, the lady appeared to Bernadette as before, and they prayed the Rosary. This time, several of Bernadette's friends also came, but they saw and heard nothing. Soon, reports spread throughout the village about Bernadette's vision. Many thought that Bernadette was pretending or that she was crazy. But that didn't stop Bernadette from visiting the grotto. When the lady next appeared, she asked Bernadette to come visit her every day for the next fifteen days.

Many townspeople followed Bernadette on her visits with the lady, though they could see nothing. Bernadette found the crowds of people disturbing. But when she saw the lady's kind and beautiful face, she forgot everything else. The lady asked Bernadette to pray for sinners, and during one of her visits, she told Bernadette to drink from a nearby spring. Bernadette could not find a spring, so she dug into the ground and drank the muddy water. The crowd laughed at her, but the next day the mud had turned into a clear spring that flowed into the river. The townspeople said it was a miracle, and many who were sick and injured bathed in the spring and were miraculously healed.

Bernadette finally asked the lady who she was. The lady replied, "I am the Immaculate Conception," revealing that she was the Blessed Virgin Mary (the Immaculate Conception is a title given to Mary because she was conceived without original sin). Mary asked for a chapel to be built near the grotto. Today, a great shrine stands above the spring Bernadette found. The water was channeled into a place where people can bathe in it and receive healing. Many people from all over the world travel to this shrine every day to be healed. Our Lady of Lourdes, ask your Son to heal my soul from sin!

St. Ethelwald

c. 740 • England

St. Ethelwald was a holy hermit. He lived on the small island of Inner Farne, off the northernmost tip of England. The two great monks Sts. Aiden and Cuthbert had lived there before him and built small huts of stone and turf where a hermit could live in solitude and pray. Ethelwald lived alone on the island. The sea, wind, and the seals were his everyday companions.

Some monks from the nearby monastery of Lindisfarne came by sea to visit the holy hermit. Together, Ethelwald and the monks spent the day in conversation and prayer. In the evening, the monks said farewell to Ethelwald and boarded their small ship for the monastery. After they had sailed some distance from the shore, clouds gathered, and the wind picked up. A great storm broke. Tall waves and pelting rain lashed and rocked the boat. The frightened monks struggled through the storm, but it was no use. If they continued further, they would sink and drown. They turned to sail back to the small island of Inner Farne, but their hearts sank. It was too far away. They would never make it to the island before the storm overwhelmed them!

One of the monks pointed to the island with a cry. They could just perceive Ethelwald's distant figure watching them from the shore. Ethelwald sank to his knees in prayer. Suddenly the wind ceased, and the waves calmed. The storm had ended! The monks were able to sail back to Lindisfarne. After they landed, they looked back over the sea, and once again the storm began to rage. Gratitude and awe filled the monks' hearts. They realized they had just witnessed a miracle. God had answered Ethelwald's prayer so that they could reach the shore safely.

Later, Ethelwald became the bishop of Lindisfarne and lived a holy life of prayer until he died. St. Ethelwald, keep me safe in the storms of life!

St. Ethelwald
February 12

St. Paulus Liu Hanzuo

1778–1818 • China

St. Paulus Liu Hanzuo wished to follow Jesus in all things. He was born a Catholic in China and learned about Jesus from his parents. Until recently, the emperors had persecuted Catholics in China, but for now, Catholics lived in peace.

Paulus's family was poor, and when Paulus was little, he was a shepherd. As he watched over his goats and sheep from the shade of a tree, he must have thought about how Jesus had been called a shepherd too—the Good Shepherd who watched over His flock, the Church. When Paulus grew up, Jesus called him to be the same kind of shepherd that He had been. He called Paulus to be a priest.

Paulus entered the seminary when he was twenty-four years old. Because he didn't know any Latin, the common language of the Church at the time, his teachers let him complete his studies in Chinese. While he was studying for the priesthood, the Chinese emperor passed a harsh decree against the Catholics in China. Now Paulus Liu Hanzuo and the Chinese Catholics knew they would be persecuted for their Faith as their people had been in the past.

But even though it was dangerous to be Catholic, Paulus knew he must follow Jesus in all things. He finished his studies and was ordained a priest. The emperor had published a special decree against priests, so Paulus knew that he must keep the fact that he was a priest secret. During the day he worked as a vegetable seller, feeding the bodies of the local townspeople. By night, he visited the Catholics in hiding and gave them the sacraments, feeding their souls with the Eucharist. But soon Jesus would call Paulus to follow Him to His Cross.

A local carpenter betrayed Paulus, just as Jesus had been betrayed by Judas, and handed Paulus over to the authorities. After Paulus was imprisoned, he was flogged, just like Jesus had been flogged by Roman soldiers. The Chinese authorities tried to get him to give up his faith in Jesus, but Paulus refused. By his refusal, he knew that he would follow Jesus to his own death and then be raised by Him to heaven. Paulus was executed for the Faith and became one of the Martyr Saints of China. St. Paulus Liu Hanzuo, help me to follow Jesus in all things!

Sts. Cyril and Methodius

826–869 and 815–885 • Greece

Sts. Cyril and Methodius are known as the "Apostles to the Slavs." They were brothers, and Methodius was the oldest of the two. Though they were more than ten years apart, they both shared a deep love for God and became priests. Soon, God would also call them to share the same missionary work.

Prince Rostislav of Morovia asked the Byzantine emperor to send Christian missionaries to his kingdom to teach his people about Jesus. His people were the Slavs and spoke Slavonic. Both Cyril and Methodius could speak Slavonic, so the emperor sent the two brothers to Morovia.

Cyril understood how important it was for the Slavs to understand what was being said to them. He created an alphabet that became the first Slavic alphabet, and then he began the great task of translating the Mass and parts of the Bible into Slavonic. Cyril and Methodius won many hearts to Jesus through their teaching because now the Slavic people could hear and understand the Word of God.

Unfortunately, the two brothers got into trouble with the German bishops, who were angry that the two brothers said the Mass in Slavonic. They believed that the Mass should only be said in Hebrew, Greek, or Latin. They thought what the two brothers were doing was wrong. Because of this conflict, Cyril and Methodius were summoned to Rome. The brothers spoke before the pope and defended their use of the Slavonic language. The pope saw that the two brothers were strong in the Faith and were doing the Slavs good. He supported their mission and approved the Slavonic liturgy.

While the brothers were in Rome, a great sorrow befell Methodius. His dear brother, Cyril, who had shared in his mission and hardships, fell gravely ill. Before his death, Cyril urged Methodius to continue sharing God's love with the Slavic people. Cyril died in Rome, and Methodius was deeply sorrowful, but God gave him the strength to continue his work without his brother.

The pope sent Methodius back to the Slavs as an archbishop. Once again, Methodius said Mass for the Slavs in the Slavic tongue, and he continued to preach about Jesus to them until he died a holy death. Sts. Cyril and Methodius, give me the strength to preach the Word of God to others!

Sts. Cyril and Methodius
February 14

St. Claude de la Colombière

February 15

St. Claude de la Colombière

1641–1682 • France

Claude entered the Jesuit order at the age of seventeen and was ordained a priest. The Jesuits recognized in Claude a gifted preacher and confessor. They saw that his spiritual advice helped others live holy lives. He was sent to the convent of the Visitation Sisters of Paray-le-Monial to be their confessor. Claude said Mass for the sisters, absolved them of their sins, and gave them spiritual advice. At the convent was a nun named Sr. Margaret Mary Alacoque who would later become a saint. Jesus had appeared to her and asked her to spread the devotion to His Sacred Heart. None of the nuns believed in Margaret Mary's visions, however, so she felt lonely and did not know how she could do what Jesus asked of her.

Claude met with Margaret Mary to discuss her visions. He prayed long and hard and listened carefully to Margaret Mary's words. Finally, Claude declared that Margaret Mary's visions were truly from God, and together they spread devotion to the Sacred Heart throughout France.

Not long after, Claude was sent to England to be the confessor to the future queen of Britain. He served the English Catholics, hearing their confessions and guiding their souls. He also continued to guide Margaret Mary through letters, their written words crossing the English Channel, back and forth between the two countries. But the weather in England was cold and wet. Sickness entered Claude's lungs, and before he could leave England to recover, a terrible thing happened. Two anti-Catholic English ministers lied to the British king and told him that there was a Jesuit plot to kill him. Because Claude was a Jesuit and the confessor to the future queen, they accused him of being part of the plot! Of course, this was not true, but that didn't matter. Claude was thrown in prison.

The cold, dank prison made his lungs worse, and now Claude became really sick. Over twenty other Jesuits who had been falsely accused were killed or died in prison. But Claude's life was spared because he was under the special protection of the king of France.

Finally, Claude was released from prison, and he returned to France to recover his health. But the damage had been done. He had become too sick in prison to fully recover. At Paray-le-Monial Claude died a holy death and was united with the Sacred Heart of Jesus in heaven. St. Claude de la Colombière, guide me to live a holy life!

St. Juliana of Nicomedia

d. 304 • Nicomedia (modern-day Turkey)

Born to a wealthy pagan family, Juliana was baptized a Christian in secret because the Roman emperor persecuted Christians. Her father did not know she was a Christian, however, and so he promised her in marriage to the local pagan governor. But Juliana refused to marry the governor because he was not a good man. She loved God alone and had promised Him she would never marry. Furious at her refusal, the governor discovered that Juliana was a Christian and threw her into prison.

The governor had Juliana tortured. He wanted to change her mind and force her to give up the Faith. But none of his tortures worked. While she was in prison, a demon disguised as a beautiful angel appeared to her. The pretend angel tried to coax her into sacrificing to the Roman gods. But because the false angel was tempting her to sin, Juliana recognized him for what he was—an evil demon. She knew that the devil was full of lies. He whispers into everyone's ear that sin is beautiful and fun, but that is a lie. Sin is always ugly and leads to death. Juliana would never believe the devil and his lies. Immediately, she prayed to God for help, crying, "Lord God of heaven and earth, do not desert me, nor permit your handmaid to die." With that prayer, the demon's false beauty was stripped away, and he vanished with a howl.

Juliana had remained steadfast in the Faith. When she prayed to God not to let her die, she was praying that He would never let her soul die in sin. God answered her prayer. She refused to deny the Faith and became a glorious martyr for Jesus. Her soul did not die but was raised to heaven to live with Jesus forever. St. Juliana of Nicomedia, help me to see through the devil's temptations!

St. Juliana of Nicomedia
February 16

Seven Holy Founders of the Servite Order

February 17

The Seven Holy Founders of the Servite Order

c. 1220 • Italy

The wealthy city of Florence was full of busyness and temptation. Many people stopped living their Faith, and false teachings confused those who strove to remain faithful. Seven wealthy and important men in the city were tired of all the turmoil. They decided to form a group and dedicate their lives to prayer. Their names were Buonfiglio dei Monaldi (the eldest and the leader), Alexis Falconieri, Benedict dell' Antella, Bartholomew Amidei, Ricovero Uguccione, Gerardino Sostegni, and John Buonagiunta.

While the men were gathered together to pray on the Feast of the Assumption—the feast that celebrates how Mary was taken into heaven, body and soul—Our Lady appeared to them in a vision. Mary wanted these men to give themselves to her Son, Jesus, even more. She told them that they must withdraw from the city to some solitary place and live only for God.

The seven men listened to their holy mother. At first, they moved to a house called La Carmarzia, right outside the city gates. But that was not far enough because many people visited them and distracted them from their prayers. So they moved to the quiet and deserted slopes of Mount Sernario outside of the city of Florence and founded a hermitage. There they prayed and offered sacrifices to God.

Mary appeared to the seven holy men a second time. She stretched out a black robe and said it would be their habit. Beside her stood an angel holding a scroll that said, "Servants of Mary." Mary told them that she had chosen them to be her servants and that they would follow the rules that St. Augustine had written on how to live a holy life in a monastery. Once again, the seven men listened to their holy mother. They founded the order that was called the Servants of Mary or the Servites. They especially honored the Seven Sorrows of Mary: the prophecy of Simeon; the flight into Egypt; the loss of the Child Jesus for three days; meeting Jesus on His way to Calvary; Jesus's crucifixion and death; Jesus's body being taken down from the Cross; and Jesus's burial.

Mary blessed the order dedicated to her, and it grew quickly and spread throughout the world. Seven Holy Founders of the Servite Order, help me to pray even when my life is full of distraction!

St. Francis Regis Clet

1748–1820 • France

St. Francis Regis Clet was a missionary to China. He was a Vincentian priest and a professor at the seminary. His students and fellow teachers all called him "the walking library" because he knew so much! But even though he was doing important work for God in helping to form His priests, Fr. Francis Clet knew he was supposed to serve God in a different way. He knew that God was calling him to be a missionary. Several times he asked his superiors to let him travel to China and tell the Chinese about Jesus's love for them, and several times they refused to let him go.

Then, when Fr. Francis Clet was forty-three years old, a priest on assignment to China had to withdraw at the last minute. This time, the superiors listened to Fr. Francis Clet's request. They let him go to China in place of the other priest. On the six-month journey to China by sea, Fr. Francis Clet learned Chinese customs and wore Chinese clothes. He would always struggle with the Chinese language, but he did the best that he could. He knew that adopting the Chinese way of life would be the best way to serve the people of China.

Fr. Francis Clet joined two Chinese priests in Hou-Kouang. But it was very dangerous to be a Catholic priest in China. The Chinese emperor especially persecuted Catholic priests and offered large rewards to anyone who turned them in. In that first year, Fr. Francis Clet's two companion priests died, one in prison and one from exhaustion. That left Fr. Francis Clet to serve his region all alone for two years. He ministered to the Christians in China, inspiring them to trust in Jesus in the face of persecution. His faith and zeal brought many other souls to the Catholic Faith. He served the Catholics in China for many years.

The persecution of Chinese Catholics only grew more intense, and the faithful there did all they could to hide their beloved priest. Many times, the authorities came looking for Fr. Francis Clet, and many times the Chinese Catholics warned him just in time for him to escape capture. Then came the day that he was betrayed by a Chinese Catholic who revealed where he was hiding. Fr. Francis Clet had once corrected this man's sinful behavior, and so he betrayed Fr. Francis Clet for revenge.

In prison, Fr. Francis Clet was treated cruelly, but he never complained. With great patience, he offered all of his suffering to Jesus. He was sentenced to death and executed, becoming one of the glorious martyrs who helped bring the Faith to China. St. Francis Regis Clet, help me to tell others about Jesus's love for them!

St. Francis Regis Clet
February 18

St. Barbatus
February 19

St. Barbatus

c. 610–682 • Italy

St. Barbatus ended pagan superstition in Benevento. Benevento was a great city on top of a tall hill in Italy. But the prince of Benevento practiced pagan superstition, and all of his people followed him. They bowed down to a golden viper made by human hands and worshipped a walnut tree.

Barbatus was a Catholic priest in Benevento. He told the people that worshipping false gods was a sin. But the people of Benevento would not listen. Their souls were ensnared by the golden viper and the walnut tree. And so Barbatus prayed and fasted, begging God to change the people's hearts so that they would give up their sins.

Then one day, Barbatus gave a prophecy to the people of Benevento. He told them that enemy forces would attack the city. And soon, Barbatus's prophecy came true. The eastern Roman Emperor Constans II laid siege to Benevento. The terrified people of Benevento knew God was punishing them for their sins. They renounced their pagan superstitions and prayed to God to forgive them.

With his own hands, Barbatus chopped down the walnut tree that the people worshipped as a false God. He melted down the golden viper and turned it into the chalice for the church. He promised the people that God saw that their hearts had changed. God would protect them. Constans II would fail to take the city, and they would be safe.

All happened as Barbatus predicted. Constans II could not take the city and left defeated. During the siege, the bishop of Benevento had died, so now Barbatus was made the next bishop. He served the people of Benevento for many years and died at around seventy years of age. St. Barbatus, help me to worship God alone!

St. Olcan

5th century • Ireland

St. Patrick was walking in the hills and fields of Ireland. The wind carried a weak but unmistakable sound to his ears. It was a baby crying!

He discovered a baby boy sobbing beside his mother's body in the field. He could tell by the mother's clothes that she was not from Ireland but was a stranger from over the sea. Sadly, the mother was dead, so Patrick took the orphan baby into his arms and decided to raise him. Patrick baptized the baby and named him Olcan.

Olcan grew up beloved by Patrick. He followed in Patrick's footsteps and became a priest, preaching about Jesus to the Irish. Finally, Patrick ordained Olcan bishop of Armoy, the village near where Patrick had discovered Olcan as a baby. Olcan founded the monastery of Armoy, and Patrick gave Olcan two relics of St. Peter and St. Paul. These relics were important treasures for Patrick. He gave them to Olcan so that the two great saints would bless Olcan's new monastery.

Soon, Patrick left Olcan to preach all throughout Ireland so that he could bring as many souls to Christ as possible. He left knowing that the monastery of Armoy was in good hands with Olcan. Olcan lived a holy life. Irish tradition says that he blessed a well so that people who bathed in its waters were healed of sickness and their wounds. St. Olcan, watch over me as you were watched over by St. Patrick!

St. Olcan
February 20

St. Peter Damian
February 21

St. Peter Damian

1007–1072 • Italy

Because Peter's parents died when he was a child, his older brother adopted him. But Peter's brother had a hard heart. He mistreated his little brother and cast him out of the house to take care of his pigs. Peter had another older brother named Damianus, who was a priest. When Damianus saw how badly young Peter was being treated, he rescued him and sent him to school. Peter was so grateful to Damianus that he took his brother's name as his last name and called himself Peter Damian.

Peter Damian loved his studies so much that he became a famous teacher when he was in his twenties. But his studies weren't the only thing important to Peter. He also had a deep love for God and the poor. Peter fasted and offered many sacrifices to God. To the poor he gave alms and also a seat at his table during meals. Peter Damian felt God calling him more and more to leave behind his teaching career and dedicate his life to Him in prayer.

One day, two Benedictine monks visited Peter Damian's home. They told him all about their way of life in the monastery. As they talked, Peter heard God's call. He, too, would become a Benedictine monk! He entered their monastery where he prayed and studied Scripture. Soon he was teaching his fellow monks! After some years, he became the prior, which is the leader of the monastery. Peter's rule of the monastery was disciplined and wise. He made sure his monks practiced penances, but he also introduced a short sleep during the day, so they would not become overtired from waking up at night to pray.

Even though Peter Damian did not leave his monastery, he was aware that many priests and bishops outside in the world were living in sin. He wrote letters to the pope, urging him to reform the Church. The pope made Peter Damian a cardinal, which is the second highest rank in the Church. At first, Peter Damian did not want to be a cardinal. If he became a cardinal, he would have to leave his peaceful life in the monastery. But he also knew that he must obey the pope. Soon Peter realized that God wanted to use him to reform the Church.

The new cardinal traveled from diocese to diocese and urged bishops and priests to lead holy lives. He told them that they must practice purity and avoid greed. Peter Damian worked tirelessly to reform the Church for fifteen years. Near the end of his life, he rested at a monastery because he had a fever, and he died a holy death at the end of the evening prayers. St. Peter Damian, help me to lead a holy life!

The Chair of St. Peter

Galilee

One day, Simon (whom Jesus would later name Peter) and his brother Andrew were out fishing. Jesus called out to them and told them to leave their fishing nets and to follow Him. Jesus said that He would make them fishers of men. Simon and the disciples followed Jesus as He healed the blind, the sick, and the lame; He even forgave sins. Because Jesus did all these wonderful things, people talked about Him. Jesus asked His disciples what the people were saying about Him, and they told him that the people thought He was a great prophet. But Simon knew Jesus was more than a prophet. He said, "You are the Messiah, the Son of the living God." Jesus declared that His Father had blessed Simon by revealing to him this truth. Jesus gave Simon the name Peter and proclaimed him the rock on which He would build His Church. Jesus also gave Peter the keys to the Kingdom of Heaven (Matthew 16:13–20).

But even though Peter was especially blessed by God, he was still human, weak and full of sin. At the Last Supper, Jesus told Peter, "This very night before the cock crows, you will deny me three times." Peter could not imagine denying Jesus and said he would die rather than do such a thing (Matthew 26:34–35). That night, Jesus was betrayed by Judas and arrested. Peter followed Jesus and the soldiers to the high priest's house. There a servant recognized Peter as one of Jesus's disciples. Peter was frightened of being arrested also, so he denied knowing Jesus. Two other people recognized Peter, and two more times he denied Jesus. At that moment, a sharp cock crow filled the dark night. Immediately, Peter remembered Jesus's prophesy of his denial. Peter fled in shame and deep sorrow, and the Romans crucified Jesus (Matthew 26:69–75).

When Jesus rose from the dead, He appeared to his disciples many times before He ascended to His Father in heaven. One of these times, Jesus asked Peter, "Do you love me?" Jesus asked Peter this question three times, the number of times Peter had denied him. And every time Peter answered "yes" (John 21:15–17).

Jesus made Peter the first pope, commanding him to feed His sheep, which meant that He was asking Peter to take special care of His flock, the Church. When we celebrate the Feast of the Chair of St. Peter, we think of the chair as a throne, representing Peter's office as pope. We celebrate how Jesus made Peter the leader of His Church on earth. St. Peter, help me to always remain faithful to Jesus!

The Chair of St. Peter

February 22

© Sophia Institute Press

St. Polycarp
February 23

St. Polycarp

69–155 • Smyrna (modern-day Turkey)

St. Polycarp was kind even to his enemies. Born only sixty-nine years after Jesus, he knew St. John, who was the Beloved Disciple and the youngest of the Twelve Apostles. St. John told Polycarp all about what Jesus said and did. He passed down to Polycarp the events of Jesus's life and the truths of the Faith.

Polycarp became the bishop of Smyrna and taught to faithful Christians all that he had learned from St. John. When Polycarp was an old man, the emperor was persecuting Christians because they did not believe the emperor was God. Polycarp knew that soldiers were hunting him down because he was a Christian, so he hid in a farmhouse. There he had a vision that his pillow burst into flames. Polycarp knew that the vision predicted his martyrdom. He would die as a witness to Christ!

Soldiers discovered Polycarp's location and came to arrest him. When they arrived at the farmhouse, Polycarp was unafraid. He went outside and greeted the soldiers kindly. He even invited them inside and offered them food and drink. After they had eaten, the soldiers arrested him.

Officials sought to convince Polycarp to offer incense to the emperor and worship him. Polycarp refused. Furious, the officials threw Polycarp into the stadium to be burned alive, just as Polycarp's vision had shown him. Polycarp heard a voice from heaven say, "Be strong, and show yourself a man, O Polycarp!" Other people heard the voice, too, but they could not see where it came from.

The crowd collected fuel and sticks and piled it around Polycarp. The soldiers set the sticks alight with their torches. But then something happened that made the crowd gasp in amazement. Instead of burning Polycarp to a crisp, the fire fanned into an arc, forming a flaming wall that surrounded the old man. While this miracle did not touch the hearts of the persecutors, it gave courage to the Christians who were watching. Polycarp's persecutors realized that the execution was not going the way they wished. They did not want the crowd to be won over by the miracle. The executioner ordered that Polycarp be killed by the sword, and Polycarp died as a witness of his love for Jesus. But the Christians who watched wrote down all that they had seen, so that future Christians would have courage.

St. Polycarp, please help us to be kind to those who persecute us, just like you offered food and drink to those who came to arrest you!

Bl. María Ascensión Nicol y Goñi

1868–1940 • Spain

Sr. María Ascensión disembarked with her fellow nuns at the harbor in Lima, Peru. She and four of her sisters had just endured many months of tumultuous waves and seasickness as they sailed across the ocean from Spain. But their journey was not over yet. They had to march through the forest to reach Porto Maldonado, where they would serve the native Peruvians and teach them about Jesus. The five nuns trekked twenty-four days through the tall green forest, the air alive with bird calls and the constant humming of life. As they hiked, Sr. María Ascensión reflected on what had brought her to Peru.

As a little girl at her boarding school in Spain, her life had been forever changed by the Dominican nuns who taught there. When she graduated, she knew that she, too, was called to be a nun. She made her vows and worked as a teacher at the same school, but inside her heart was a deeper desire to serve the poor in faraway lands. Then the Spanish government snatched away their school, and the Dominican sisters no longer had anyone to serve. Immediately, they wrote to the Americas and offered themselves as missionaries for Christ. And now Sr. María Ascensión and her fellow nuns were trekking through the hot forest, and her heart rose with excitement at each step. She was on a great adventure to bring Christ to others. She was a missionary of service and love.

When the sisters finally reached the camp, they set up a school for girls. Sr. María Ascensión knew how important it was for girls to learn how to read and write. Her heart flooded with joy as the young girls grasped each new word and their world grew larger because of it. The native peoples embraced the sisters. Through their love, these holy women brought many souls to Christ.

Sr. María Ascensión felt closer to God in the Peruvian mountains than she ever had before. She saw Christ especially in the young people, the poor, and the women, all those in most need of her care. To better fulfill her mission, she founded the Dominican Missionaries of the Rosary. Her new order would focus on missionary work. She was appointed as the first superior of her congregation and remained so for the rest of her life. Bl. María Ascensión, inspire me to go on adventures for Christ!

Bl. María Ascensión Nicol y Goñi

February 24

St. Walburga
February 25

St. Walburga

710–777 • England

When Walburga was eleven, her father, later known as St. Richard the Pilgrim, left for Rome on pilgrimage, leaving her in the care of the nuns at the monastery of Wimborne. She grew up at the monastery and became a nun whose intelligence was matched only by her humility.

Walburga's uncle was St. Boniface, who preached the Catholic Faith to the Germans. Her two older brothers, Willibald and Winibald, had become monks and joined their uncle in his missionary work. But Boniface needed more help, so he asked the abbess of Wimborne to send nuns to aid him in his mission. Among those sent was Walburga. The ship with the nuns from Wimborne set sail, and during the journey a terrifying storm overcame the ship. Thunder, rain, and angry waves threatened to swallow it whole. The sailors despaired, sure that the dark waters would be their grave. Then they saw the brave figure of a woman kneeling on the deck. It was Walburga in prayer. She begged God to spare their lives, and immediately the waves calmed, and the sun broke through the clouds. The sailors rejoiced; and after they landed, they proclaimed the miracle they had witnessed to all.

Walburga became the abbess of the German abbey of Heidenheim, where her brother Willibald was the abbot. Together the monks and nuns served the people of Heidenheim, and the Catholic Faith in Germany grew deeper and stronger. When Willibald died, Walburga had him buried in Heidenheim abbey and became the abbess of both the monks and the nuns. When Walburga died, Winibald lovingly had his sister buried beside their brother. The people of Heidenheim visited the two tombs, and many who prayed there were healed of illnesses and wounds.

Almost one hundred years later, a local bishop decided to repair the parts of Heidenheim monastery that had started to crumble. The workers were careless and desecrated St. Walburga's tomb. That night, St. Walburga appeared to the bishop in a vision. She scolded him for allowing her tomb to be treated with such disrespect and warned him that he should be reverent with the bodies of the saints. Immediately, the bishop ordered Walburga's body to be reburied in the Church of the Holy Cross, which from then on was known as St. Walburga's. All three siblings, Walburga, Willibald, and Winibald, are recognized as saints. St. Walburga, help me be reverent toward everything that is holy!

St. Porphyry of Gaza

347–420 • Greece

Born in Greece, St. Porphyry would journey far to dedicate his life to the Cross. When Porphyry was twenty-five, he set off for Egypt to become a monk. There he lived a life of prayer and sacrifice. But in his heart arose a desire to journey yet again, this time to the Holy Land to visit all the places where Jesus had walked on this earth. In Jerusalem, Porphyry paid a visit to the relic of the true Cross, which was a piece of wood from the Cross on which Jesus had died. His heart full of the mystery of Jesus's death and resurrection, Porphyry retired to a cave to live a simple life of prayer.

Five years later, Porphyry's legs were stricken by a terrible disease. Though every step was painful, he stumbled and dragged himself back to Jerusalem, this time to pray for healing. At Golgotha, where Jesus had been crucified, Porphyry collapsed in prayer. There he had a vision: Jesus descended upon him from His Cross, saying, "Take this Wood and preserve it." When Porphyry awoke, his legs were healed! His heart burst in gladness over Jesus's great mercy. Now he knew he must dedicate himself to Jesus's Cross. He returned to Jerusalem, became a priest, and was later made the custodian of the relic of the true Cross, which meant that he was appointed to preserve and watch over it just as Jesus had asked.

But soon, Jesus had another mission for Porphyry. The bishop of Gaza in Egypt died, and Porphyry was made bishop in his place. Gaza was a pagan city full of temples to false gods. Christians were treated badly there and were even forced to build their churches outside the city walls. Now that Porphyry was bishop, he had to protect its small Christian community. He also knew that he must do all he could to bring the pagan souls to Christ. But he would need help.

Porphyry traveled to the magnificent city of Constantinople, where the emperor and empress lived. He pleaded with the Empress Eudoxia, and she convinced her husband to destroy all the pagan temples in Gaza. She even gave Porphyry enough money to build a new church. Everything happened as the emperor decreed, and a great Christian church was built in Gaza, bringing Jesus's Truth within the city walls. Porphyry watched over his flock in Gaza until his death. St. Porphyry, help me to love the Cross of Jesus!

St. Porphyry of Gaza
February 26

St. Anne Line
February 27

St. Anne Line

1563–1601 • England

Born Protestants in England, Anne, her husband Roger, and her brother William all became Catholics. Converting to Catholicism was a very brave thing for them to do. Elizabeth I was the queen of England, and she persecuted Catholics (as her father, Henry VIII, had before her). The reason the queen persecuted Catholics was that she had declared herself the leader of the new church Henry VIII had started, the Church of England. All of her subjects had to be part of her church to prove their loyalty to her. But even though Anne, her husband, and her brother were loyal English subjects, they were loyal to God first. They knew that the Church that Jesus founded was the Catholic Church.

Both Roger and William were caught for being Catholics and banished from England. Anne Line was left behind all by herself. But this did not frighten her. Instead, she chose to risk her life to run a safe-house for priests. The priests would come to the safe-house and say Mass. But one day, too large a crowd came to Anne's house for Mass. It was the feast of Candlemas, also known as the Presentation of Jesus in the Temple. A neighbor was suspicious of the large crowd and notified the authorities. Constables burst into Anne's home. In the confusion, the priest was able to escape, but Anne was sent to prison.

At the time of Anne's trial, she was so weak with fever that she had to be carried to court in a chair. But even though her body was weak, her spirit was strong. She told the court that she did not regret hiding priests, but only wished she could have hidden more. The court sentenced her to death by hanging. Anne Line and two other female English martyrs, St. Margaret Ward and St. Margaret Clitherow, were all brave women in England who died to protect Catholic priests. St. Anne Line, watch over the souls of priests!

St. Villana de' Botti

1332–1361 • Italy

When Villana de' Botti was thirteen years old, she ran away from home to a nearby convent and asked if she could become a nun. But the nuns refused, and a disappointed Villana returned home. Villana's father was upset when he found out that she had run away. To make sure that Villana did not run away again, he arranged Villana's marriage to a rich husband.

After her marriage, Villana changed. She became vain, lazy, and wasteful of her riches. She wore sparkling gems and the fanciest of dresses. And the more beautiful she grew on the outside, the more rotten she became on the inside. She lived in luxury but never gave a thought for the poor or thanked God for her wealth. But even though Villana had forgotten God, God did not forget her. He gave Villana a special blessing so that she could see how full of sin her soul had become.

One evening, as she was dressing for a party, Villana put on her most sumptuous gown, studded with pearls. She went to her mirror to admire how beautiful she must look. Instead, the mirror gave her the greatest shock of her life. In the mirror's reflection stood a richly gowned woman with the head of a demon! In a flash, Villana realized that the mirror did not show her what she looked like on the outside, but on the inside. Her soul was so full of sin that she was as ugly as a demon. Villana tore off her gown and put on her plainest dress before rushing to the church. There she immediately made a confession.

Villana was truly sorry for all of her sins. She joined the third order of the Dominicans and read the Bible and the lives of the saints every day. In penance, she offered many sacrifices and knocked on the doors of the rich to beg for money for the poor. She learned that she could give herself to God no matter what her state in life, and she became a better wife to her husband by loving God first. As she grew holier, she would fall into religious ecstasies during Mass, which meant that she was so transported by joy at the presence of Jesus that she became unaware of everything else around her. Many people made fun of Villana for her sudden change. But through her kindness and patience, the holy beauty of Villana's soul shone through. The people who made fun of Villana soon realized that she was a living saint. On her deathbed, Villana asked that Jesus's Passion be read aloud to her from the Bible. When the words of Jesus's death on the Cross were read aloud, Villana followed Jesus and passed away from this life to her new life in heaven. St. Villana, please help me care more for beauty on the inside than beauty on the outside!

St. Villana de' Botti

February 28

St. David
March 1

St. David

c. 520–c. 601 • Wales

David wandered throughout the island of Britain proclaiming the Word of God from shore to shore. He founded many monasteries, and all his monks lived lives of great sacrifice to purify their hearts for Jesus. They worked hard in the fields, prayed all day long, ate only bread and vegetables, and drank only water. But David's strict rules did not discourage his monks; instead, more and more men wanted to join his monasteries.

David was an eloquent preacher. Legend says that one day, while he was preaching, the crowds were so great that the people could not hear him. And so the earth groaned under David and lifted him high in the air. Where once there had been flat ground, there was now a hill, on top of which stood David. A pure white dove fluttered from the heavens to rest on his shoulder. David was so high up that his voice carried far. Now all the crowds could hear him! His powerful words won many hearts for Jesus that day. Because of David, the Catholic Faith grew strong in Britain.

David's last words to his fellow monks were, "Be joyful, keep the Faith, and do the little things." His tomb became a destination for many pilgrims.

St. David, help me to do even the smallest thing with joy and faith!

St. Angela Guerrero

1846–1932 • Spain

Young Angela Guerrero worked in a shoe shop in Seville. Her health was frail, but the work was simple and quiet. The shop owner was a good and kind lady. Together with her workers she would pray the Rosary and read aloud the lives of the saints. All day, Angela would pray, laugh, and stitch shoes, the air full of the musty scent of leather. This life of work and prayer brought Angela closer to God.

When Angela was nineteen, she asked the Carmelite sisters if she could join their order. But they refused because Angela's health was too weak to live their life of hard work. Three years later, Angela once again tried to become a nun. This time, she joined the Sisters of Charity, who tried to help her become strong and healthy. But soon, Angela had to return to her quiet life in the shoe shop, too weak to live the life of a Sister of Charity.

But Angela did not give up. She knew that Jesus wanted her to be a nun. She and three other women, all from poor families like hers, decided to start their own order under the guidance of a priest. They rented a small room in Seville and from there offered care and support to the city's poor and sick. They wore habits of brown cloth, and Angela took on the name Mother Angela of the Cross. Only a year later, the bishop approved her new order, and her sisters became known as the Sisters of the Company of the Cross.

The sisters took care of the poor and the sick that no one else would care for. More sisters quickly joined, and soon twenty-three convents were founded. Despite her poor health, Mother Angela lived a long life in the service of God, taking care of His poor, hungry, ill, and abandoned.

St. Angela, help me never to give up doing what Jesus calls me to do!

St. Angela Guerrero
March 2

St. Katharine Drexel

March 3

St. Katharine Drexel

1858–1955 • United States of America

Katharine Drexel was the daughter of a wealthy banker in Philadelphia. Her mother had died soon after her birth, and her father remarried a few years later. Her father and stepmother were strong in their Catholic Faith and believed that they should use their great wealth to care for those in need. Katharine would watch her father pray for half an hour every day, and her stepmother would open their house a few times a week to distribute food and clothing to the poor.

Raised as a young heiress, Katharine received her education from private tutors, toured Europe, and entered into high society. But when she nursed her stepmother for three years through terminal cancer, Katharine realized that money could not protect her from pain and suffering. She grew close to Jesus in the Eucharist. He gave her a deep love for the poor and oppressed. Katharine's father took her on trips through the western states, and she saw firsthand the suffering and poverty of the Native Americans. Katharine knew she had to do something to help.

She went to visit Pope Leo XIII in Rome and asked that he send missionaries to help the Native Americans. She was surprised when the pope told her that she should become a missionary herself! Katharine listened to the pope and joined the Sisters of Mercy in Pittsburgh, Pennsylvania. Philadelphia society was shocked! The newspapers ran the headline, "Miss Drexel Enters a Catholic Convent—Gives Up Seven Million." People couldn't believe that Katharine would give up her wealth to serve the poor.

But Katharine was now able to serve the people she knew God was calling her to help. She founded the Blessed Sacrament Sisters and used her fortune to fund its work. The nuns opened schools for Native American and African American children. Katharine paid for the printing of a catechism for the Navaho children. But not everyone liked how Katharine served these neglected people in the community. A member of an evil, racist organization threated Katharine and her sister's lives, but God protected them. Only a few days later, the headquarters of the man's organization were struck by lightning and burned to the ground.

Later in life, Katharine suffered a heart attack, so she had to give up the leadership of her order. For her last eighteen years she could barely move because of a serious illness. She spent the rest of her life in deep prayer in front of the Blessed Sacrament and died a holy death. St. Katharine Drexel, help me to serve the poor and oppressed!

St. Casimir

1458–1484 • Poland

St. Casimir was the son of the king of Poland and had a great love for Jesus. As a young boy, he would think of how Jesus had suffered and died for him on the Cross, and so Casimir would also offer up his own sufferings to Jesus. Even though he was the king's son, he was humble. He did not wear fancy robes, but only simple clothes so as not to show off. Late at night, courtiers would find him on his knees in prayer before the doors of the church. When he did fall asleep, Casimir stretched out on the floor instead of a soft bed.

When Casimir was not even fifteen years of age, some of the noblemen in Hungary asked him to be their king. The Hungarian king, Casimir's uncle, had died without an heir, and different nobles supported different men to be the next king. The king of Poland ordered Casimir to go to Hungary and fight for the kingship. Casimir obeyed his father and led an army to Hungary; but when he arrived, it became clear that he could not win. Casimir did not want to spill his soldiers' blood in vain, so he ordered the retreat, even though he knew this would anger his father. The king punished his son by imprisoning him in a nearby castle for three months. From then on, Casimir refused to participate in war.

Casimir made a promise to God to remain unmarried so that he could dedicate his life entirely to Him; however, the king tried to arrange a marriage for Casimir with the daughter of Emperor Frederick III. While Casimir obeyed his father as his king, he would not break a promise he had made to God, an even higher King. He refused the marriage and spent the next twelve years of his life in prayer and serving others.

At the king's court, Casimir always urged his father to rule with justice. He noticed that often people forgot to take care of the poor. Casimir would quietly point out this neglect to his father so that the poor could be taken care of throughout the kingdom. Because of his service to them, the poor loved him, and he was known as the "Father of the Poor." When Casimir was only twenty-five years old, he grew ill and died a holy death. St. Casimir, help me to serve Jesus before all others!

St. Casimir
March 4

Pope St. Lucius

d. 254 • Italy

St. Lucius was the twenty-second pope. The twenty-first pope, Pope Cornelius, had been sent into exile because of terrible persecution from the Roman Emperor Gallus. In exile, Pope Cornelius had died, suffering from deprivation. Pope Lucius was elected to replace Pope Cornelius. The new pope must have wondered if he, too, would suffer the same fate as Pope Cornelius.

The Roman emperor continued his fierce persecutions, and the day came when Lucius was banished from Rome. His heart must have been heavy as he left his city and the flock of souls he watched over. He must have been afraid that he, too, would die like Pope Cornelius, alone and neglected. But most of all, he must have trusted in God's mercy. He knew that God would never abandon him.

Indeed, God mercifully spared Pope Lucius's life. The Emperor Gallus suffered a violent death and was replaced by a new emperor, who allowed Pope Lucius to return to his flock in Rome! Pope Lucius rejoiced when he returned to his city, the heart of the Catholic Church. He thanked God for His great mercy in restoring him from exile.

While Lucius was pope, a debate arose in the Church. There were many Catholics whose courage had failed them under Roman persecution. They had denied Jesus because they feared the death of the body more than the death of the soul. Now they wanted to confess their sins and return to the Church. Many people in the Church, however, cried out that those who denied Christ should not be forgiven. But Pope Lucius's exile had taught him to trust in God's mercy. He knew that God forgave sinners if their hearts were truly sorry. And so Lucius taught that the blood of the martyrs had earned pardon for those Catholics who had turned away from Christ, so long as they were now sorry for their sins and performed penance. Pope Lucius died a holy death, watching over his flock, the Church.

Pope St. Lucius, help me to trust in God's mercy!

St. Colette

1381–1447 • France

Colette's parents were sad because they did not have a child. They prayed to St. Nicholas, the patron saint of children, for a baby. Soon after, a baby girl was born to them. They named her Nicoletta, in honor of St. Nicholas, and called her Colette for short.

When Colette's parents died, she decided to give her life to God. At first, she wanted to live in a small cell in prayer all by herself. But God had other plans for her. While she was praying, she saw a vision of St. Francis of Assisi kneeling before the Lord. The saint said, "Lord, give me this woman for the reform of my order," and the Lord nodded approval. Now Colette knew that God wanted her to reform the Franciscan order. But Colette also knew how difficult this would be. She would much rather stay in her small cell in peace. She refused to leave her cell, and in punishment for her refusal, Colette was struck blind and deaf. When Colette decided to obey the Lord, her sight and hearing were restored.

So, Colette set about restoring the Franciscan order. She received the approval of the pope and was sent to reform a community of Poor Clare nuns. The nuns regarded Colette with suspicion. They did not understand why this new nun thought she could change things in their community. But then a great miracle happened that showed the nuns that God was with Colette.

A farmer's wife had given birth to a stillborn baby. The distraught father had brought the baby to the parish priest and begged him to baptize the baby. But the priest pointed out that the baby was already dead and, therefore, could not be baptized. The farmer begged and begged. He would not leave the priest alone. In frustration, the priest told the farmer to take the baby to the nuns. Maybe they could do something for him!

The farmer took the priest at his word and carried the baby in his arms to Sr. Colette. Colette gazed at the sorrowful father, took off her black veil, and gave it to him. She told him to wrap the baby in her veil and return to the priest. When the priest saw the farmer and his little black bundle, the two started arguing once again. But suddenly their words were interrupted by a wail. The baby underneath the veil was crying! Immediately, the priest baptized the baby.

News of Colette's miracle spread and made it easier for her to reform the Franciscan communities until she died a holy death. She reformed seventeen monasteries, and her nuns were known for their dedication to lives of poverty and fasting. St. Colette, bless the women I know who are pregnant!

St. Colette

March 6

Sts. Perpetua and Felicity
March 7

Sts. Perpetua and Felicity

d. 203 • Africa

The woman pointed to a jar on the ground and said, "See that pot lying there? Can you call it by any other name than what it is?"

"Of course not," her father said.

She responded, "Neither can I call myself by any other name than what I am—a Christian."

The woman's name was Perpetua, and she was a noblewoman of the city of Carthage. Her husband had most likely recently passed away, and she had a little baby boy. Her mother was a Christian, and her father was a pagan. When Perpetua turned twenty-two, she decided she would be baptized a Christian, like her mother. Her father was scared and furious. The Emperor Severus persecuted Christians because they did not worship the emperor as a god. Perpetua's father pleaded and argued with his daughter, begging her to give up her Faith. But she refused. Soon Perpetua was arrested and thrown into a crowded prison—dirty, hot, and dark. But the worst suffering for her was being separated from her baby boy.

In prison, Perpetua met another Christian woman, a pregnant slave girl named Felicity. The noblewoman and the slave girl became close friends. It did not matter that one was noble and the other a slave; they were the same because they were Christians, and both loved Jesus more than their own lives.

The horrible condition of the women's jail cell was difficult to bear. Two kind deacons paid the guards to allow Perpetua and Felicity into a better part of the jail. Perpetua's mother and brother brought her baby boy to her. Holding her little boy in her arms brought peace to her heart. Perpetua's father came to visit her in prison twice, kissing her hands and begging her to give up her Faith. But even though Perpetua loved her father, she loved Jesus more. She could not reject the One she loved more than her own life.

Two days before the execution, Felicity gave birth to a little girl, and another Christian woman in Carthage adopted her. Perpetua wrote about the birth in her diary, where she recorded all that happened that led to both of their martyrdoms. Then came the day when Perpetua and Felicity bravely showed how much they loved Jesus. The two women were taken out to the arena and gave each other a kiss of peace before they were put to death by the sword, becoming glorious martyrs for the Faith. Sts. Perpetua and Felicity, help me to love Jesus more than anyone else!

St. John of God

1495–1550 • Portugal

When John was only eight years old, he was kidnapped from his home in Portugal and abandoned in the streets of Spain, where he wandered hungry and alone. A kind farmer took him in, and the grateful John worked hard on the farm. He worked so hard, in fact, that when he grew older, the farmer wanted John to marry his daughter. But John did not want to get married, so he ran away and joined the army.

For many years, John was a soldier and lived a sinful life. Sometimes his conscience troubled him. Memories of his early life with his parents, who had loved God and taught their son to be good, came back to him. He knew that they would be disappointed with how he lived his life. So John returned to Portugal to find his parents, but he learned the sad news that both of them had died. He then left behind his life as a soldier because he knew his life was empty. He was starting to realize that only God could fill his emptiness.

Looking for a way to serve God, he first went to Africa, hoping to become a martyr. But he returned soon to Spain at the advice of a priest. Next, he started a religious bookstore and traveled from town to town selling books as cheaply as possible so that everyone could afford to read about God. It was during his time as a bookseller that the Infant Jesus appeared to John in a vision. Jesus gave him the name "John of God" and bid him to go to Granada. At Granada, John heard a powerful sermon from a holy priest that inspired in him a deep sorrow for the sins of his past life. John's sorrow was so deep that he ran out into the public square and confessed his sins with loud cries, begging forgiveness. He would not stop lamenting his sins, and so people thought he was crazy and sent him to the Royal Hospital. There the holy priest visited John and told him that he should serve others instead of worrying over past sins that God had already forgiven.

And serving others is what John did. He rented a house and turned it into a hospital; he opened homeless shelters; he fed the hungry; and he clothed poor children. One day the Royal Hospital caught on fire. No one dared to approach the blazing flames—except for John. He rushed into the fire and rescued all the patients. Another time, a young man was drowning, and John dove into the river to rescue him. Soon after, John caught pneumonia from the cold water. The city officials all gathered around his bed to thank him for serving Granada's poor. He died a holy death, and the city honored him with a beautiful burial. St John of God, help me love God and serve others more!

St. John of God
March 8

St. Frances
of Rome
March 9

St. Frances of Rome

1384–1440 • Italy

Ever since she was little, Frances wanted to be a nun, but her father arranged her marriage to a wealthy and noble young man named Lorenzo. Her mother-in-law threw her into a whirlwind of banquets and responsibilities. Frances found this life empty and difficult. She longed to serve God in some way. One day, she was crying alone in the garden when her sister-in-law Vannozza found her. Frances confided her secret desire to serve God, and Vannozza exclaimed that she felt the same way! The two girls decided to pray together and go out into the city to care for the poor and sick. Frances's mother-in-law was upset and tried to get Lorenzo to stop his wife. But Lorenzo loved and respected Frances and supported her work with the poor.

Frances and Lorenzo had a loving marriage, and she bore him four children. When Lorenzo's mother died, Frances took charge of the household and gave food and wine to the poor. When her father-in-law went to the wine cellar for a glass of wine, he found the casket empty. He furiously scolded Frances for giving away all their good wine. Calmly, Frances said a prayer, and when she accompanied him to the cellar, wine flowed freely from the casket. From then on, her father-in-law allowed Frances to perform all of her charitable work, because he knew that God was with her.

Then sorrow came to Frances. A plague struck Rome, and one of her sons and her daughter grew sick and died. A terrible civil war divided Italy; Frances's husband left to fight, and her oldest son was taken hostage. Frances knew that she must serve God even when her heart was heavy. She turned her house into a hospital and gave shelter to the homeless. Her guardian angel appeared to her and helped her. It is said that he would light up her path as she walked through the dark streets, bringing food to the hungry.

The war ended, and Frances's husband and son returned. While her son was grown and healthy, her husband was wounded and broken, and Frances spent years nursing him back to health. With Lorenzo's permission, Frances started an order of Benedictine women called the Oblates of Mary, who were dedicated to serving the poor. Lorenzo never fully recovered from his wounds, and, after his death, Frances joined the Oblates and became their superior until she died a holy death. St. Frances of Rome, help me remember to serve others even when I am sad!

St. John Ogilvie

1579–1615 • Scotland

John Ogilvie was born in Scotland to a Calvinist father (a type of Protestant) and a Catholic mother, who died when he was three. John was raised a Calvinist and sent to Germany to study. But his mother must have been praying for him from heaven, because he not only became a Catholic while he was away, he became a Jesuit priest! He spent eleven years at the Jesuit seminary, deeply studying the Faith and growing in virtue.

After he was ordained, John begged his superiors to send him to Scotland, even though he knew it would be dangerous for him to return home. Most of the Scots were Calvinists, and they were so anti-Catholic that much of Catholicism in Scotland had been wiped out. The few Catholics that remained had no one to care for them and give them the sacraments. John Ogilvie knew it was God's mission for him to serve the Catholics in his home country, to give them the sacraments and the hope they so desperately needed.

John returned to Scotland disguised as a horse trader. In secret, he traveled from city to town all throughout Scotland. In secret, he said Mass at Catholic homes. He served the Catholics in this way for only ten months before he was betrayed. A spy had snuck in among the Catholics and reported that John Ogilvie was a Catholic priest.

The Scottish authorities imprisoned John Ogilvie. They tortured him by keeping him awake for nine whole days. But John Ogilvie did not give up the names of the Scottish Catholics who had helped him. And he refused to give up his Faith, so he was sentenced to death. From the gallows he pulled out his rosary and flung it far out into the crowd. It is said that the person who caught it later became a Catholic. John Ogilvie became a glorious martyr for Jesus.

St. John Ogilvie, help me serve the Catholics in my home community!

St. John Ogilvie
March 10

**Sts. Mark Chong Lu-Bai
and Alexius U Se-Yong**

March 11

Sts. Mark Chong Lu-Bai and Alexius U Se-Yong

1795–1866 and 1845–1866 • Korea

During the 1800s, Catholicism was outlawed in Korea. Catholic missionary priests and Korean converts were hunted down and put to death. Among these brave Korean martyrs were Sts. Mark Chong Lu-Bai and Alexius U Se-Yong.

Mark Chong Lu-Bai was a teacher in Korea. One day, he saw two priests put to death for teaching the Catholic Faith to the Koreans. The calm and peaceful way they approached their death inspired Mark Chong Lu-Bai. He wanted to learn more about this Jesus for whom they so willingly died. There were no books written in Korean about Jesus, so he found some books about Him written in Chinese. The more he read, the more his heart sang within him. This Jesus had suffered and died for the whole world. This meant that Jesus had died for him, too, and for the people in Korea.

Even though it was dangerous, Mark Chong Lu-Bai was baptized into the Catholic Faith. He became a catechist and taught the Faith to other Koreans. One of the converts he taught was the young Alexius U Se-Yong. Alexius U Se-Yong was a wealthy nobleman. His family was opposed to his conversion, but his heart was so on fire for Jesus that he left his rich family to work with the Catholic missionaries. To help the missionaries, he translated a catechism into Korean so that the people could read about the Faith.

But then a terrible persecution broke out, and Mark Chong Lu-Bai and Alexius U Se-Yong behaved in two very different ways. Mark Chong Lu-Bai was offered the chance to escape, but he did not take it. He knew that God wanted him to serve the persecuted Koreans who were unable to leave. He was caught by his neighbors and family, who beat him terribly before they sent him to prison. Through it all, Mark Chong Lu-Bai remained strong in his Faith. Alexius U Se-Yong, however, did not have Mark Chong Lu-Bai's strength. His fear was stronger than the fire of love in his heart. When the persecutors arrived, he gave up his Faith and denied Jesus.

Afterward, Alexius U Se-Yong was sorry. His fear had made him do a terrible thing. He rushed to his bishop, confessed his sin, and received forgiveness. Then he was arrested and imprisoned with Mark Chong Lu-Bai. Together they were tortured and executed along with other Korean Catholics and became glorious martyrs for the Faith. Sts. Mark Chong Lu-Bai and Alexius U Se-Yong, please help my heart be full of love for Jesus!

St. Seraphina

1238–1253 • Italy

St. Seraphina was a young girl who joined her suffering with Jesus's suffering on the Cross. Young Seraphina's family was poor, but, even so, Seraphina would give the little she had to those poorer than she was. She worked hard at home, cooking and sewing to help her mother and father. But when Seraphina was still very young, her father died. This tragedy was made worse when Seraphina was struck with a paralyzing illness. She could not move and had to be carried around on a wooden board.

Then Seraphina's mother also died, and Seraphina had to depend on others to take care of her. Because she was so misshapen and had sores, all her neighbors avoided her, except her one friend Beldia, who would visit and bring her food. Seraphina's loneliness was as painful as her illness. The only comfort she had was her crucifix. She realized that she was called by Jesus in a special way to suffer as He had on the Cross. And so, Seraphina offered up her great pain to Jesus.

In her readings, Seraphina learned about the life of Pope St. Gregory the Great and how he had suffered terribly later in life. From then on, she prayed to St. Gregory, asking him to give her the patience to endure her sufferings. He became her friend in heaven.

One day, St. Gregory appeared to Seraphina in his resplendent papal garments. He told her that her suffering would soon end and revealed to her the day of her death. This filled Seraphina with great joy. Soon she would be joining Jesus and St. Gregory in heaven!

At fifteen years old, Seraphina died peacefully on March 12, the day that St. Gregory told her she would. The whole city attended her funeral, knowing that her suffering had made her holy. Afterward, people discovered beautiful white violets growing in the place where she had lain. St. Seraphina, help me join my sufferings with Jesus's suffering on the Cross!

St. Seraphina
March 12

Bl. Françoise Tréhet
March 13

Bl. Françoise Tréhet

1756–1794 • France

The terrible violence of the French Revolution broke out. The poor people of France demanded deliverance from heartless poverty. But their fury went too far. The wise Sr. Françoise Tréhet knew that the revolution would bring terrible suffering to France. Not only were the royalists (those loyal to the French king) being put to death, but also those who were Catholic, because the revolutionaries did not believe in God. But Sr. Françoise Tréhet did not run away or hide. She continued to tend to the sick in her care. It didn't matter if the sick person was a revolutionary or a royalist; all sick persons were equal in her eyes because they were children of God.

The revolutionaries arrested Sr. Françoise Tréhet and dragged her to court. They accused her of giving royalists medical help. She stood tall and proclaimed in a ringing voice that all royalists and revolutionaries were her brothers in Christ, and she would refuse her help to neither. The judge demanded that she proclaim, "Long live the Republic!" But this Sr. Françoise Tréhet refused to do. She knew that she could not give her loyalty to a government that did not believe in God and persecuted people of faith. Her allegiance belonged to the King in heaven. And so, she kept silent, even though she knew that she would die. The judge sentenced her to death by the guillotine.

The day of her execution had come. On the way to the guillotine, Sr. Françoise Tréhet sang the beautiful hymn to Mary, the "Hail Holy Queen." Her voice was clear, sweet, and unafraid. She knew that soon she would be joining Jesus and Mary in heaven. The singing nun became a brave martyr for Jesus.

Bl. Françoise Tréhet, please help me to care for all the children of God!

St. Leobinus of Chartres

d. 558 • France

When he was young, Leobinus spent his days watching sheep and working the fields. But Leobinus wanted more out of his life. He wanted to learn. So he struck a special deal with the monks at a nearby monastery: he would work for them during the day, and they would teach him at night. And so the monks let Leobinus join their monastery.

The busy days flew by for Leobinus. The work was hard, but he was happy. His heart was hungry for more and more knowledge. He would study late at night by candlelight. The shining light would wake up the monks sleeping nearby. They grumbled in irritation. Didn't this young new monk know that they had to wake up early for their prayers? Leobinus placed a screen around his candle so that its light would no longer disturb them, and he persevered in his studies late into the night.

Soon he went to study at the monastery of St. Avitus of Perche, a man renowned for his wisdom and holiness. But a local war broke out, and outlaw soldiers captured Leobinus. They tortured him, trying to get him to reveal the location of the monastery treasures, the golden chalices and ornate vestments used for saying Mass. Leobinus refused to reveal the location of the sacred vessels. The soldiers threw him in the river and left him, believing he was drowned. With his last remaining strength, Leobinus struggled to the shore. He recovered his health in time.

Leobinus grew wise with all of his learning. Even more important, his time in the monastery in prayer had made him holy. He was ordained a priest and became an abbot, which is the leader of a monastery. Finally, he became the bishop of Chartres, known for his gift of miraculous healing. He served as bishop until the end of his days. St. Leobinus, help me to persevere in my quest for holiness!

St. Leobinus of Chartres

March 14

St. Louise de Marillac
March 15

© Sophia Institute Press

St. Louise de Marillac

1591–1660 • France

Louise was orphaned as a little girl, and at the age of fifteen, she dearly wanted to become a nun. She applied to the Capuchin nuns in Paris, but they turned her down. Louise felt lost. She did not know what God wanted her to do. On the advice of her spiritual director, she allowed her uncle to arrange a marriage to the handsome and ambitious Antoine LeGras. Louise grew to love her husband, and they had a son named Michel. But in a quiet place in her heart lived the fear that she had ignored God's call to be a nun.

During the feast of Pentecost (which celebrates the Holy Spirit's descent upon Jesus's disciples), Louise received a vision that showed her serving the poor and living in a religious community in the future. She was told not to doubt God's will for her and that she should remain with her husband for the present. This vision gave Louise peace. Soon after, she met a priest who would become her spiritual advisor. His name was Vincent de Paul, and he would also one day become a saint.

A few years after her vision, Louise's husband died of illness. Louise spent her days in prayer, attending Mass, and taking care of her son. Fr. Vincent de Paul invited Louise to help him organize the charitable groups he had started. Louise took charge of many humble young women and taught them how to take care of the poor. She invited them into her home and guided them in their spiritual lives. She told the women, "Love the poor, and honor them as you would honor Christ Himself."

This group of women became the Daughters of Charity, nuns who served the poor. The sisters would visit the poor in their homes, at the hospitals, and at orphanages. Louise de Marillac served with the Daughters of Charity until her death. St. Louise de Marillac, help me to be dedicated to the vocation Jesus gives me!

St. John de Brébeuf

1593–1649 • France

A large, cheerful priest landed in the wilds of New France, which is now known as Canada. His name was John de Brébeuf, and he was a Jesuit missionary to the Native American Huron tribe. He had been to New France once before and had studied hard to learn the Huron language, but wars and strife had sent him back to France. Yet he had never forgotten the Huron people. They were children of God whose souls needed the saving waters of Baptism. Now he had returned, and he was here to stay.

John de Brébeuf lived in a small hut in a settlement among the Hurons. The weather, wild beasts, illness—all these were great dangers to him and the Jesuit missionaries. Not only that, the Hurons viewed the priests with suspicion, and their lives were in constant danger. Because the Jesuits were strangers, the Hurons would blame them if there was no rain or if their people got sick. Still, John de Brébeuf's missionary efforts flourished.

John de Brébeuf knew that the best way to explain Jesus's love to the Hurons would be to speak the way they spoke. He composed the Huron Carol, the oldest Canadian Christmas carol, so that the Hurons could celebrate Jesus's birth, too. He translated the catechism in the Huron language so that they could learn all about the Catholic Faith. Many Jesuit missionaries learned the Huron language because John de Brébeuf was there to teach them. Soon, there were Huron Christians in almost every village, so John de Brébeuf and his fellow Jesuits would travel from village to village, teaching the Hurons about Jesus and washing their souls clean with the waters of Baptism.

After many years serving the Hurons, John de Brébeuf was captured by the Iroquois tribe. The Iroquois and the Hurons were at war, and the Iroquois hated not only the Hurons, they also hated Christians. They attacked the settlement and captured John de Brébeuf, his fellow priests, and all the Huron converts. Then the Iroquois tortured John de Brébeuf in terrible ways. The Iroquois were impressed with his bravery, because he would not cry in pain but offered all of his suffering to Jesus. The Iroquois put John de Brébeuf to death, and he became a glorious martyr for Jesus. St. John de Brébeuf, help me to offer up my suffering to Jesus!

St. John de Brébeuf
March 16

St. Patrick
March 17

St. Patrick

387–461 • Britain

When Patrick was sixteen years old, Irish pirates spotted him on the British coast and kidnapped him. They took him to Ireland and sold him as a slave to the chieftain Milchu, who put him to work watching over his flock of sheep both day and night. The dark night and the cry of the wolves frightened the defenseless Patrick. He would say a hundred prayers in the daytime and as many at night. Strength and courage filled his heart. He knew that God was with him and would keep him safe.

One night, after he had been a slave in Ireland for six years, a voice in the darkness told Patrick that a ship was ready to take him home. Knowing that this voice was an angel from God, Patrick ran away from the chieftain Milchu and traveled two hundred miles to the nearest coast. There a ship was waiting that took him back to Britain. His parents must have feared that he was dead and were overjoyed to see Patrick again. At home, Patrick learned more about God and continued to pray. Then one night, he had a dream that forever changed his life. In the dream, he received a letter from Ireland and heard the Irish people cry out, "We appeal to you, holy servant boy, to come and walk among us." When he awoke, Patrick realized that God was calling him to return to Ireland and be a missionary.

Patrick became a priest and returned to Ireland. He knew the Druids and their false religion were powerful in Ireland. But he also knew that God was with him and would keep him safe as He had before. God performed many miracles through Patrick to show the Irish people that He was the one, true God. A Druid celebration in which fire was forbidden fell on the same night as the eve of Easter. Patrick lit a bonfire to celebrate Easter Eve, and the Druids were unable to put it out, no matter how hard they tried. Nor could they do anything to hurt Patrick. Patrick performed many other miracles. He even raised people from the dead in Jesus's name, so that the Irish people could believe in God's power.

Patrick traveled all throughout Ireland, baptizing and preaching the Good News of Jesus's love. Many legends sprang up about Patrick. One of these legends is that he banished all the snakes in Ireland, casting them from a cliff, just the way he banished paganism from that green island. Another is that he left his footprints on a stone where he stood. These legends show just how much the Irish people love St. Patrick. St. Patrick, help me trust that God will always keep me safe!

St. Cyril of Jerusalem

315–386 • Israel

Cyril was very knowledgeable, loved to write, and knew his Bible by heart. First Cyril became a deacon, then a priest, and finally was ordained bishop of Jerusalem. While Cyril was bishop, the Church was struggling against heresies, which are false teachings about the Catholic Faith. At that time, certain Church leaders taught that Jesus was not fully God and not equal to the Father, which is called the Arian heresy. Not only that, but the Roman emperor also was putting pressure on the Church to accept this false teaching about Jesus.

Three years after Cyril was ordained bishop, a sign appeared in the sky. A flashing cross made of light shone bright over the city of Jerusalem. It stretched from the place where Jesus suffered His Agony in the Garden and was betrayed and arrested, to Mount Golgotha, where Jesus was crucified. The cross shone and flashed for many hours, and everyone in the city could see it. The frightened people ran to the churches and into their homes, but they also praised God for this great sign. Bishop Cyril wrote a letter to the Roman emperor and told him about the flashing cross. He explained that the cross was a sign from God that Jesus was the Son of God and equal to the Father.

Cyril spent the rest of his life caring for the Church in Jerusalem. He suffered greatly, being sent into exile many times for defending the true Faith. He wrote about God's merciful love and wrote many lectures to teach others how to become Christians. He died a holy death after watching over his flock and teaching them the truth that Jesus is the Son of God, fully God and fully man.

St. Cyril, help me always to honor Jesus!

St. Cyril of Jerusalem
March 18

St. Joseph
March 19

St. Joseph

Biblical Figure

Jesus was the Son of God, but He needed someone to protect Him and take care of Him when He was a little boy. God the Father chose St. Joseph to be Jesus's protector and watch over Jesus's mother, Mary, because Joseph was a good man.

Joseph and Mary were engaged to be married when the Angel Gabriel appeared to Mary and told her that she was to be the mother of God. When Joseph discovered that Mary was pregnant, he did not believe that the baby was God's Son. But because Joseph was a good man, he decided to break his engagement with Mary quietly and not let anyone know what had happened.

One night, while Joseph was sleeping, an angel of God appeared to him in a dream. The angel told Joseph that Mary's baby was conceived by the Holy Spirit and that Joseph was to name the baby Jesus. Overjoyed, Joseph took Mary into his home and watched over her as her husband. He now knew that he had an important responsibility: he was to love and protect the Messiah, the Chosen One of God.

Then the Roman Emperor Caesar Augustus declared a census (which means that everyone had to be counted so that the emperor would know how many people he ruled over). Joseph was from Bethlehem, so he and Mary had to travel there to be counted. Joseph was worried. Mary was ready to give birth. What if she gave birth on the road? How was he to take care of her?

They made the long journey from Nazareth to Bethlehem, but, to Joseph's dismay, all the inns in Bethlehem were full, and they had nowhere to rest. But Joseph did not give up. He knew that God the Father would help him take care of Mary and the baby. He took Mary to a stable, and there she gave birth to Jesus. Joseph's heart filled with love as he gazed on the baby in the manger.

Soon after, an angel again came to Joseph in a dream. This time, the angel gave a warning: King Herod wanted to kill Jesus, and so Joseph must flee to Egypt. Joseph's heart grew heavy. How was he to take care of Jesus and Mary in Egypt, so far away from home? But, once again, he knew that God the Father would help him. The Holy Family fled to Egypt and lived there under Joseph's watchful care. They returned to Nazareth when King Herod had died and the angel told Joseph it was safe. There Joseph worked hard and took care of Jesus and Mary. He played with Jesus when He was little, and he watched Jesus grow up. Every day Joseph counted himself blessed to live with Jesus and Mary. St. Joseph, please watch over me!

St. Cuthbert

c. 635–687 • England

A young Cuthbert was watching sheep in the green fields near the great stone monastery of Melrose. As he gazed into the clear blue sky, he beheld a magnificent vision: the soul of the holy Aiden, bishop of nearby Lindisfarne, was being carried up to heaven by shining angels. The stunned Cuthbert soon discovered that the saintly bishop had died that very night. In his heart, he knew that God was calling him, through this miraculous vision, to live a life like Bishop Aiden. He knew he was being called to become a monk.

Before Cuthbert could follow his calling, however, the neighboring king attacked the Northumbrian land on which Cuthbert lived. War broke out. All able-bodied young men fought to defend their land. Cuthbert also fought in the war, which only ended after four long years. Free at last, Cuthbert arrived with his horse and his spear at the monastery of Melrose to become a monk.

Cuthbert developed a reputation for his holiness and learning. He was appointed the prior of Lindisfarne, the great monastery over which St. Aidan had once been bishop. There Cuthbert worked with great love to accomplish his work. His love for God brought tears to his eyes every time he heard Mass, and his love for others brought many souls to Jesus. After twelve years, Cuthbert yearned to lead a quiet life of prayer so that his love for God could grow pure and perfect. He retired to the small island of Farne, off the coast of Lindisfarne, where he built a small round hut out of stone and turf.

For many years, Cuthbert lived in quiet prayer on the desolate island of Farne. But he was not finished walking in St. Aidan's footsteps. Cuthbert was elected bishop. At first, Cuthbert refused to leave his island. He did not want to become bishop and carry worry and responsibility. But when a group of men arrived at the island, begging him to become bishop, Cuthbert could not say "no." So he left his island to become bishop of Lindisfarne, as St. Aiden had been before him.

Cuthbert was not bishop for long. After two years of serving God in his new office, he knew he would soon die. He returned to his island at Farne to die a holy death. Cuthbert was buried at his monastery at Lindisfarne, and his tomb became the site of so many miracles that he became known as the "Wonder-worker of England." St. Cuthbert, help me to answer God's call, no matter what happens!

St. Cuthbert
March 20

St. Nicholas of Flüe
March 21

St. Nicholas of Flüe

1417–1487 • Switzerland

Born to a peasant couple, Nicholas of Flüe entered the army when he was twenty-one years old and distinguished himself in battle. Even as a soldier, he never forgot God. When defeated enemies took refuge in a nearby convent, he convinced the army to spare the convent and those inside. Later, he married and had ten children, five girls and five boys. He gained positions of honor by becoming a captain in the army and then serving as a judge. But worldly success did not satisfy him. All the worries and cares of his life were distracting him from what was really important.

At the age of fifty, he went out to the meadow to take care of his cattle. Seizing a quiet moment, he sat on the ground and began to pray from the depths of his soul. Deep in prayer, he experienced a vision: a pure white lily sprouted from his mouth and gave the sweetest of fragrances. Then, to his dismay, his horse devoured this most beautiful lily! Nicholas of Flüe rose from his prayer, the message of the vision dawning in his heart. He understood that the world with all its cares and worries was devouring all his heavenly treasures, just like his horse devoured the lily. He knew that if he wished to pursue what was most important, a close relationship with God, he would have to leave the world behind. And so Nicholas of Flüe went home and received permission from his wife and children to become a hermit.

Deep in a rocky gorge, Nicholas of Flüe built a hut of branches and leaves. There he lived for nineteen years eating no food except the Most Holy Eucharist. He went without a cap or shoes even in wintertime. He lived a life of prayer and sacrifice and received many mystical visions. His reputation for holiness reached far and wide and many went to him seeking his wisdom. His wise advice even saved lives. Once, a great political dispute arose between the leaders of Switzerland. Civil war threatened, which would have meant much bloodshed for the people. The Swiss leaders wished to try one thing more to avoid war: they went to Nicholas of Flüe for help. His wise counsel calmed the leaders and brought them to a solution that did not involve bloodshed.

Nicholas of Flüe died at the age of seventy, surrounded by his wife and children. St. Nicholas of Flüe, help me store up treasure in heaven!

St. Nicholas Owen

c. 1562–1606 • England

Born in a time when King Henry VIII persecuted the Catholics in England, Nicholas Owen grew up in a family that remained strongly Catholic: two of his brothers were priests, and he himself served Catholic priests. It was dangerous to be a priest in England. Priests had to travel with stealth from Catholic home to Catholic home to say Mass. If a priest was caught, he would be sent to the Tower of London and executed.

The first priest that Nicholas Owen served was Edmund Campion, who would be martyred and become a saint. When Edmund Campion was arrested, Nicholas Owen defended his innocence and so was also arrested. Later, the English authorities let Nicholas Owen go, deciding he was harmless, but Edmund Campion they executed. Nicholas Owen was heartbroken. He decided he would do everything he could to keep other brave priests from ever getting caught. So he devised a plan.

With his master carpenter skills, he built hiding places for priests in Catholic homes. These hiding places were called priest holes, and they were artfully disguised. Nicholas would build priest holes behind pretend fireplaces, underneath staircases, inside closets, and in false walls. Sometimes he would build a priest hole inside of another priest hole to trick pursuers into thinking that they had discovered the secret hiding place. All alone, he would work through the dead of night, so that only he and the owner of the house would know where the secret priest hole was hidden.

Then another priest that Nicholas Owen served was arrested and imprisoned in the Tower of London. Nicholas Owen was determined that this priest would not suffer the fate of Edmund Campion. And so he organized the priest's escape by stringing a rope over the moat surrounding the Tower of London. Climbing down this rope, the priest escaped! For eighteen years, Nicholas Owen served the priests who came to England, and he himself entered the Jesuits as a lay brother. Finally, he was captured by the English authorities, who gleefully celebrated that they had at last caught the man who had gotten in their way of catching priests. They tortured Nicholas Owen, but he revealed nothing to them, neither the location of priests nor the location of his priest holes. He died from his tortures and became a brave martyr who had saved the lives of hundreds of priests. St. Nicholas Owen, help me to use my skills to serve Christ's Church.

St. Nicholas Owen
March 22

St. Turibius Alfonso de Mogrovejo

March 23

St. Turibius Alfonso de Mogrovejo

1538–1606 • Spain

Turibius was a professor of law at the famous University of Salamanca. He was such an excellent teacher that King Philip II of Spain made him the chief of the Church courts in Spain. Turibius was a just man and his work impressive. When it was time to appoint a new bishop in Lima, Peru, both the pope and King Philip thought Turibius would be the best choice. At first Turibius resisted. After all, how could he become a bishop? He was a lawyer, not a priest! But the pope told Turibius that he should become the bishop of Lima, and Turibius understood that it was God's will for him to obey. He first became a priest and then was appointed bishop.

And so he set sail for Peru. Because the Americas had only been discovered by the people of Europe less than one hundred years earlier, both North and South America were called the New World. Now Turibius saw that God's mission for him in his life was to serve the people in the New World and bring them to Jesus.

The new bishop landed in South America and walked six hundred miles on foot to Lima. On the way, he preached to the natives and baptized them. This was to be an important way for him to reach the people. Three times as bishop he walked on foot all over Peru, braving the desert, the hot dust and sun, wild animals, and unfriendly natives. Because many people from Spain came to South America, there were soldiers, and even clergy, who abused the native people. Turibius defended the natives. He rooted out corruption in the clergy and saw that no one took advantage of the South American people.

What Turibius wanted more than anything else was to teach the South American people how much God loved them and how Jesus had saved them from their sins. Turibius knew how important it was to speak the native language so he could talk directly to the people. He had a catechism made in three languages: Spanish, and the native Quechua and Aymara languages of the South American people. His words won over many hearts, and he baptized over one million people. Two of those he baptized would also become great South American saints: St. Rose of Lima and St. Martin de Porres. Because of Turibius, many souls who never would have heard of Jesus became brothers and sisters in the Catholic Faith. When Turibius grew ill and knew he was about to die, he gave all of his possessions to the poor and died a holy death. St. Turibius, help me accept God's mission in my life!

St. Catherine of Sweden

c. 1332–1381 • Sweden

St. Catherine of Sweden was the daughter of a holy woman named Bridget, who also became a saint. Ever since she was young, she wanted to follow her mother's holy example and dedicate her life to God. When she was given in marriage at the young age of twelve, she convinced her young, noble husband to live celibate lives for God together.

Bridget went on pilgrimage to Rome, and Catherine accompanied her. While they were away, Catherine's husband died. Catherine vowed never to remarry. She remained with her mother in Rome and dedicated her life to prayer and sacrifice.

Many men wanted to marry Catherine because she was young and rich. But she refused all their offers. There is a legend that a deer would come to Catherine's defense whenever an unchaste man tried to convince her to marry him. With horn and hoof, the deer would chase the man away.

When the saintly Bridget died, Catherine took her body home to Sweden to be buried. There she became head of the religious order her mother had founded, the Brigittines. She governed the nuns with great wisdom and skill, and returned to Rome to gain papal approval for her mother's order. She returned to Sweden with a letter of approval from the pope and soon died a holy death.

St. Catherine of Sweden, help me to dedicate my life to God!

St. Catherine of Sweden

March 24

The Annunciation of the Lord
March 25

The Annunciation of the Lord

Marian Feast Day

There was a young Jewish virgin named Mary who lived in a little town in Galilee called Nazareth. Mary was betrothed to a good man named Joseph. Like Mary herself, Joseph was a descendant of King David, from whose house it was prophesied the Messiah would be born. Long ago, God had promised the Jewish people that the Messiah would be born from a virgin and save the people from their sins. The Jewish people were patiently waiting for God to keep this promise.

One day, the Angel Gabriel appeared to Mary. He greeted her with the words, "Hail, full of grace! The Lord is with you." (Do you recognize these words? They are the words we use at the beginning of the Hail Mary prayer.) The angel's appearance was so strange and wondrous that Mary knew he was no earthly creature. She was frightened and troubled. She did not know why the angel had come to her and was greeting her this way. But the Angel Gabriel told her that she should not be afraid and that she would conceive in her womb a son, and He would be the Messiah that God had promised His people.

This Mary did not understand. Since she was unmarried, she did not know how she could have a son. The angel explained that the Holy Spirit would come upon her, and the power of the Most High God would overshadow her, so that the son she was to have would be the Son of God. He also told her that her cousin Elizabeth, who was too old to have children, would also give birth to a baby boy, because nothing was impossible for God.

Mary thought about the Angel Gabriel's words. She knew that if she agreed to what he had told her, her life would never be the same. After all, who would believe that the child she carried in her womb would be God's Son? Not only that, she knew the Messiah was destined to suffer, and if her son suffered, then she would suffer, too. But Mary loved God with her whole heart. The Angel Gabriel had called her full of grace because God had filled her soul so completely with His grace that she had never sinned. She desired more than anything else to show her love for God by doing His will. She said to the angel, "Behold, I am the handmaid of the Lord. May it be done to me according to your word" (Luke 1:38). With that the Angel Gabriel left her, and everything happened the way he told her it would. Hail Mary, help me to say "yes" to God's will!

St. Castulus

d. 288 • Italy

Diocletian was a cruel emperor who mercilessly persecuted Christians. But he did not know that Christians were living inside his own palace, right under his nose. His personal servant, Castulus, and Castulus's wife, Irene, were baptized Christians! Because they lived in the palace, Castulus and Irene could watch Diocletian's movements and warn the Christians in hiding whenever the emperor's soldiers were coming.

Even though it was dangerous to be Christian, Castulus could not keep his love for Jesus to himself. He would preach the life of Jesus to his fellow Romans. His words of love and mercy swayed the hearts of many who listened. Those who desired Baptism would follow Castulus to the secret hiding places where Christians gathered. There, Castulus would present them to Pope St. Caius for Baptism.

Not only did Castulus know the Christian hiding places, he himself would find safe locations for the hidden Christians to gather and celebrate Mass. According to legend, he even hid Christians in the emperor's own palace, because he knew that was the last place the emperor would look for them! With pounding hearts, he and Irene would make sure that the halls were clear of the emperor and his soldiers. Then they would lead the secret group of Christians to an out-of-the-way room where they could worship together in peace. Other times, Castulus and Irene would hide Christians in their own home.

But then, a fallen away Christian betrayed Castulus and reported him to the Roman authorities. Castulus was mercilessly tortured, but no matter how much pain he suffered, Castulus did not give up his Faith. Finally, he was buried alive in a sandpit, and Castulus offered up his last breath to Jesus. Irene wept at the news of her husband's death, but she knew that she and Castulus would be reunited by Jesus's love in heaven. She, too, would become a martyr for Christ. Sts. Castulus and Irene, help me bring others to worship Jesus!

St. Castulus
March 26

St. John of Egypt
March 27

St. John of Egypt

c. 305–394 • Egypt

As a young man, John wanted to be close to God. But he knew that he could not learn how to be close to God on his own. He needed someone to teach him.

At twenty-five years of age, John went to a hermit in the Egyptian desert and asked him to teach him how to be close to God. The hermit took John in as his student and gave him a special task. He stuck a dry stick in the ground and ordered John to water the stick every day for a year. Water was precious in the desert, and the stick was dry and brittle. John did not understand why he was ordered to water something that was dead and would not grow, but he obeyed his master. Every day, John poured water over the dry stick. After the year was over, the hermit inspected the stick—and then threw it away! But the hermit's lesson had not been meaningless. He had trained John in obedience. The hermit knew that if John could be obedient without needing a reason, then John would also learn to be obedient to God. It is only by obeying God that one can then become close to Him.

When the hermit died, John was ready to strike out on his own. He visited monastery after monastery in the desert, but he did not find the place where he could live the life God wanted him to live. After five years of praying and wandering, he carved three cells in a rock at the top of a tall hill. The first cell he slept in, the second cell he worked in, and the third cell he prayed in. He sealed himself up in his cells but left a small window in one of them so that other people could visit him and bring him food and water. Sometimes he struggled with his path in life, but whenever he did, he would submit his will to God's in obedience, the obedience he had learned from the hermit, and so he grew close to God.

Visitors would come to hear John preach and ask his wise advice. Because of John's holy obedience, God performed miracles through him. Once, he healed a blind woman and appeared to her in a vision. Another time, the emperor came to visit him, and John told him he could trust in God and would have victory over his enemies.

John grew old and knew he was about to die. He asked that no one visit him for three days. Then he sealed off the little window in his cell. In three days' time, his cell was opened, and those that found him saw that John had peacefully died in prayer. Now John was close to God in heaven. St. John of Egypt, help me to be obedient to God so I can grow closer to Him!

Bl. Jeanne Marie de Maillé

1331–1414 • France

Ever since she was a little girl, Jeanne Marie wanted to be a nun. But her father died when she was young, and her grandfather forced her to marry a rich husband, the Baron Robert de Sille. But even though the baron was a good man, Jeanne Marie knew that God did not want her to get married.

On the very day of her wedding, Jeanne Marie's grandfather passed away. Jeanne Marie's new husband took this as a sign from God that Jeanne Marie was meant to dedicate her life to God. When Jeanne Marie asked the baron if she could consecrate her virginity to God, he gave his permission. Not only that, he was a religious man, and together he and Jeanne Marie used their home and fortune to serve all those who turned up at their door for help. They used their fortune to serve the poor and became partners in doing God's work.

Then war broke out between France and England, and the baron and his men rode off into battle. The French suffered terrible losses, and the baron returned home with life-threatening injuries. Before Jeanne Marie could properly tend to him, the English surrounded their home and took the baron away as a prisoner. Jeanne Marie sold all of her things and came up with the money to secure the baron's release. But Jeanne Marie's joy in his return was short-lived, for soon after, the baron died of his injuries.

Jeanne Marie's fate turned from bad to worse. Her dead husband's relatives blamed her for helping the baron give his fortune to the poor. They cast her out of the house and refused her any of her widow's inheritance. She returned home but left soon after because her mother tried to force her to remarry. Now Jeanne Marie, who used to be rich and give to the poor, became poor herself.

But Jeanne Marie saw this change in her fortunes as an opportunity to live her life the way she knew God was calling her to live it. She became a lay Franciscan and moved into a little room in a church. Dressed in an ash-gray habit, she would go out and tend to the sick and God's poor. The rest of her time she spent in prayer, finally able to give herself completely to God the way her soul desired. She died a holy death, her soul rich with the love of God. Bl. Jeanne Marie de Maillé, help my soul grow rich with God's graces!

Sts. Jonas and Barachisius

March 29

Sts. Jonas and Barachisius

d. 327 • Persia

King Sapor of Persia ordered that all monasteries throughout his country be destroyed and Christians hunted down. In the Persian city of Hubaham, a group of Christians were arrested and their faith tested as officials tried to force them to worship the sun, moon, water, and fire. Two brothers, Jonas and Barachisius, heard of the imprisoned Christians. They were Christians, too. They wanted to encourage the imprisoned Christians to remain steadfast in their faith so they would not lose their souls by denying Jesus.

So the two brothers journeyed to Hubaham. There they spoke to the Christians in prison, reminding them of their place in heaven and encouraging them to be brave. Because of the brothers' words, nine of the imprisoned Christians remained faithful and were martyred for Christ. Jonas and Barachisius rejoiced that these brave souls were now in heaven. But the Persian official in charge was furious with Jonas and Barachisius for encouraging the Christians. Immediately, the two brothers were thrown into prison. The Persian official knew it would be a victory for him if he could get the two brothers to deny their Faith.

First, the Persian official separated the two brothers and plotted cruel torments to weaken their spirits. Jonas he had beaten and cast out into the cold night air to spend the night by a frozen pond. Barachisius was also beaten and hung upside down in prison by the ankle. The Persian official went to Barachisius and lied, saying that his brother Jonas had given up the Faith. But Barachisius would not be fooled. He declared that his brother would never deny Jesus Christ. The next morning, the Persian official ordered Jonas brought to him and asked how he had spent the night by the frozen pond. Jonas responded that he had awoken with the sun, feeling refreshed because he had been allowed to suffer for Christ. The official then lied and said that Barachisius had denied his faith in Jesus in the night. But Jonas would not be tricked. He said that his brother loved Jesus too much to deny Him.

The Persian official saw that nothing he could do would convince Jonas and Barachisius to give up their faith in Jesus. And so he had the two faithful brothers put to death. Jonas and Barachisius joined their fellow martyrs in heaven in the glorious company of Jesus. Sts. Jonas and Barachisius, help me encourage others to remain faithful to Jesus!

St. Peter de Regalado

1390–1456 • Spain

When Peter turned ten years old, he knew he wanted to become a Franciscan friar. While his father had died when Peter was little, his mother had raised him to love Jesus and to pray often. The love of God that she taught him is what helped him discover God's will for his life so early on. Only three years later, the wish of Peter's heart was fulfilled when the Franciscans allowed him to enter their order.

Peter was dedicated to fasting and praying. He ate very little bread and drank only water. He offered this sacrifice for love of God and the good of sinners. He inspired his fellow Franciscans to lead lives of sacrifice and prayer as well, and he helped promote reforms in the order that promoted the pursuit of a holy life. In time, he became the leader of all the Spanish Franciscans.

Even though Peter himself ate very little, he did not let the poor go hungry. He would give bread to every hungry person who stopped by the monastery door. At first his fellow brothers were worried. What if they ran out of bread? Then the brothers themselves would not have anything to eat. But no matter how much bread Peter gave away to the hungry, the brothers never ran out of bread. This was a miracle! Peter also performed other miracles. He could bilocate, which means he could be in two places at once, and he would have visions during prayer.

After Peter de Regalado died, his tomb became a place of pilgrimage. Pilgrims from around the world came to pray at the grave of this holy Franciscan. St. Peter de Regalado, please help me to feed the hungry!

St. Peter de Regalado
March 30

Bl. Natalia Tułasiewicz

1906–1945 • Poland

Bl. Natalia Tułasiewicz's life of love overcame the spiritual darkness of World War II. Natalia was a teacher and belonged to the secret Polish resistance against Hitler. Hitler was an evil dictator who wanted the German Nazis to rule the world. He did not believe that life or God was important, and he mercilessly killed all those who did not belong to the German race or believe in the same things he did. He specifically targeted the Jewish people, but he also killed Catholics. Many despaired because they thought that Hitler was going to win the war. But Natalia knew that evil could not win. She knew that God's love had already defeated everything evil. God's mission for her was to be love in the world, bringing Jesus's love to those who lived in fear and despair.

When Nazi soldiers took over Poland, they forced a group of Polish women to leave their homes to perform heavy labor in Germany. When Natalia heard this news, her heart cried in sympathy for these poor women. She knew their lives would be hard, and they would be in grave danger. Worse, she was afraid that they would believe that God had abandoned them. So she volunteered to join these women with a secret mission in mind: she would preach to them about the love of Jesus, giving them words of comfort and hope.

The women worked hard in miserable conditions, but in spare moments, Natalia's bravery and her words of love restored their hope and strength. But the Nazis discovered Natalia's secret mission of love. They did not want women full of hope and strength; they wanted them weak and afraid. And so the Nazis arrested Natalia and sent her to a women's concentration camp in northern Germany. But this did not stop Natalia from continuing her mission of love. Her words about Jesus brought comfort to the women of the concentration camp, the women most in need of hope.

Two years had passed since Natalia had left for Germany. It was Good Friday of Holy Week. Natalia climbed onto a stool in the women's barracks, and in a clear, loud voice she proclaimed the death and resurrection of Jesus. Her words reminded all who listened that Jesus had endured suffering like theirs. But even in Jesus's death, evil did not triumph. Jesus rose from the dead, and if they loved Him, so would they. On Easter Sunday, Natalia was sent to her death in the gas chambers. On the same day Jesus rose from the dead, Natalia, too, shared in Jesus's resurrection and joined Him in heaven. Bl. Natalia Tułasiewicz , help me live a life of love!

St. Gilbert de Moravia

d. 1245 • Scotland

St. Gilbert de Moravia was a holy bishop who fought a dragon, according to legend. Gilbert was the bishop of Caithness. He knew that worshipping God is the most important thing we can do. He built the Dornoch Cathedral as a sacred place of worship, so that all the people of Caithness could gather to give their hearts and minds to God. Gilbert also knew that to love God means to love your neighbor, so he built many dwelling places for the poor.

Gilbert de Moravia is most famous for his legendary defeat of the dragon of Dornoch. A terrible dragon lived in the forest near the city of Dornoch. It had a long neck like a salamander and breathed fire. Every day, it would travel the same path to the city of Dornoch and stick its neck into windows to gobble up young maidens. No one dared face the dragon for fear of its powerful teeth and breath of fire.

When Bishop Gilbert heard news of the dragon, he was determined to kill it to protect his people. He put on his steel cap and armed himself with bow and arrow. Then he traveled to the city of Dornoch and investigated the path on which the dragon journeyed to-and-fro from wood to city. The path was well-worn from the dragon's claws and its great, long tail. Gilbert devised a plan. He had a deep trench dug following the path, with peepholes carved in the walls. Then he went down on his knees and waited, with a prayer to God in his heart.

Soon a great lizard of a dragon emerged from the wood, long neck arched and dragging its long tail behind him. The bishop drew his bow and waited for the dragon to come close enough for his aim to be true. Then his arrow flew into the air and pierced the dragon's hide. With a great howl of pain, the dragon blasted the peephole with its scorching breath. But the bishop was not there! He had scurried down the trench and was now at the next peephole. Again he waited for the dragon to come within range and then loosed an arrow. Again the dragon blasted the peephole with flames. But the bishop was too quick for the dragon and had made it to the next peephole safely. In this manner, Bishop Gilbert shot arrow after arrow until the dragon succumbed to its wounds and fell down dead. The people rejoiced that their holy bishop had defeated the dragon that had plagued the city of Dornoch.

The legend of St. Gilbert de Moravia shows how bishops should protect the Church from the dangers of sin and the devil. St. Gilbert de Moravia, protect me from all evil!

St. Gilbert de Moravia

April 1

St. Francis of Paola
April 2

St. Francis of Paola

1416–1507 • Italy

A married couple in the little town of Paola was sad because they did not have any children. They prayed to St. Francis of Assisi for help, and soon a son was born to them whom they named Francis, in honor of the great saint who had helped them. When he was only thirteen years old, the young Francis decided to live a year with some Franciscan monks, and, soon after, he became a hermit. He sought out a hidden-away cave on the seacoast and dedicated himself to a life of solitude, prayer, and sacrifice.

After Francis had lived alone in the cave for about six years, two men—who were inspired by his life of holiness—joined him. Francis built three tiny rooms in his cave so that all three of them could lead lives of prayer. Soon more men came, and Francis built a monastery and chapel. At that time, the Italians had grown very worldly, and no one fasted for Lent any longer. Francis decided that he and his monks would serve as an example for the Italians and fast the year round. In that way they would serve as an inspiration for the people to fast at least during Lent. Because of his holy life, God blessed Francis with the gift of miracles: he once healed a blind man and even foretold events in the future.

Francis had a great love for animals, much in the same way as his namesake, St. Francis of Assisi. There is a legend told about Francis that once he had a pet trout that lived in a pool. One day, a hungry, neighboring priest saw the trout, caught it, and popped it into a frying pan. When Francis saw that his favorite trout was missing from the pool, he sent his followers to bring back the trout before the priest ate it all up. When the lifeless trout was placed back in his hands, Francis slid the trout back into the pool, and the fish wriggled back to life! While this story is only a legend, it shows how Francis dearly loved all of God's creation.

Francis was so famous that when the king of France was dying, he called for Francis to be with him at his deathbed. The new king also greatly honored Francis and asked his advice every day on how to run the kingdom. Francis wanted to return to Italy, but the new king of France would not let him go. Francis spent the last three months of his life alone in a cell preparing himself to meet God and die a holy death. St. Francis of Paola, help me to make sacrifices for the love of God!

St. Benedict the African

1526–1589 • Sicily

Benedict was the son of slaves in Italy, though he had been born free. One day, a low and ignorant man yelled hateful words to Benedict, insulting the color of his dark skin. Those cruel words hurt Benedict. But then he remembered how cruel soldiers and the ignorant crowd had hurled insults at Jesus on the Cross. Jesus had not gotten angry or used His divine power to punish those who had insulted him. Instead, He not only forgave His enemies, He died for them.

And so Benedict decided to follow Jesus's example. He restrained his anger, even though he was hurt, and the low, ignorant man went away. A Franciscan hermit had witnessed Benedict's patience and forgiveness. He saw that Benedict had a holy soul. The hermit asked him if he, too, wanted to become a Franciscan and dedicate his life to the love and service of God. Benedict's heart filled with joy as he realized that God the Father was rewarding him by calling him to follow Jesus in a special way.

Benedict became a Franciscan friar and started off as the friary's cook. He loved the tastes and smells of the kitchen and serving food to his fellow friars, and cooking became a great joy for him. He did not stay a cook long, however, and soon became the master of the novices, which means that he looked after all young men that were new to the Franciscan community. Even though Benedict never learned how to read, he became known for his wise understanding and deep spirituality—so much so that he eventually became the superior of his religious community.

All throughout his advancements, Benedict's love for cooking remained. In his later years, he would return to the kitchen to cook for his fellow friars. In this, he followed Jesus's example; even though Jesus is the Son of God and God Himself, He served others when He was here on earth, even washing His Apostles' feet during the Last Supper. So Benedict served his fellow friars although he was their leader, performing the loving task of cooking their meals.

At the age of sixty-three, Benedict passed away in a holy death. He was so beloved by his community that the king of Spain ordered a magnificent tomb to be built for the humble friar who had followed Jesus's example all of his life. St. Benedict the African, help me to follow Jesus as closely as I can!

St. Benedict the African
April 3

St. Isidore of Seville
April 4

St. Isidore of Seville

c. 560–636 • Spain

Before Isidore was born, a barbarian people called the Visigoths had taken over Spain. The Visigoths were Arians, which meant that they did not believe that Jesus was God. They fought with the Catholic Church and tried to convince the Spanish people to become Arians. The Church in Spain was in trouble, since people did not know what to believe. God sent St. Isidore to help His struggling Church.

Isidore had three other siblings—Leander, Fulgentius, and Florentina—who also became saints. His oldest brother, Leander, was the archbishop of Seville. Leander educated Isidore, and Isidore was a quick and intelligent student. When Leander died, Isidore succeeded him as archbishop.

Isidore believed that it was important that all the people in Spain, including the Visigoths, were united. He knew that education was one of the best ways to accomplish this, so he wrote an encyclopedia that passed on the knowledge of many ancient thinkers and philosophers. He wrote so much in his encyclopedia that it was twenty books long! Isidore became so famous for his knowledge that people called him the "most learned man" of the age.

But, as a bishop, Isidore knew that education in the Faith was the most important knowledge. He spent his life teaching the truth that Jesus was both fully God and fully man. Because of him, Arianism disappeared from Spain.

St. Isidore, help me learn about God!

St. Vincent Ferrer

1350–1419 • Spain

St. Vincent Ferrer preached about Jesus to all who would listen. He became a Dominican at an early age and first preached in the city of Barcelona. The city was suffering from a terrible famine, and he did his best to serve the poor and hungry. He predicted that ships would come soon bringing grain so that the city would not starve. Many people doubted Vincent's words. But that very evening, two ships full of grain arrived. Vincent's prediction had come true, and so, many more people began to listen to Vincent preach the Word of God.

During Vincent's lifetime, the Church was divided because it didn't know who the true pope was. Vincent moved to France and tried to heal this division. But he was unsuccessful and grew tired. He realized that he was not supposed to be involved in Church politics. He wanted to go back to preaching to all those who would listen.

While Vincent was still in France, he fell ill to a sudden fever. Vincent was so sick, he thought he would die. Jesus appeared to him in a vision, along with St. Dominic—the founder of his order—and St. Francis, two saints who were great preachers. Jesus healed the dying Vincent of his fever, and Vincent felt the strength return to his body. Vincent knew that Jesus had cured him for a great mission. He must go out and preach to others so they could be sorry for their sins and receive God's mercy.

For twenty years Vincent traveled all through Europe, preaching to believers and non-believers alike. He told them that they must repent of their sins and give their hearts to Christ. This was the only way that they would be with Jesus in heaven someday. Many miracles accompanied Vincent's preaching. He healed the sick, and, even though he spoke only Spanish, people of all languages could understand what Vincent said.

Whenever Vincent traveled, he went by foot instead of on a horse. Because he was humble, he wore poor clothes. At night he slept on a mat on the floor, and during the day he fasted, eating only one full meal a day. Vincent often tended to sick children. He did all of these things out of love for God. Through his preaching and example, he converted thousands and thousands of souls to Jesus until his death.

St. Vincent, help me speak about Jesus to all who will listen!

St. Vincent Ferrer
April 5

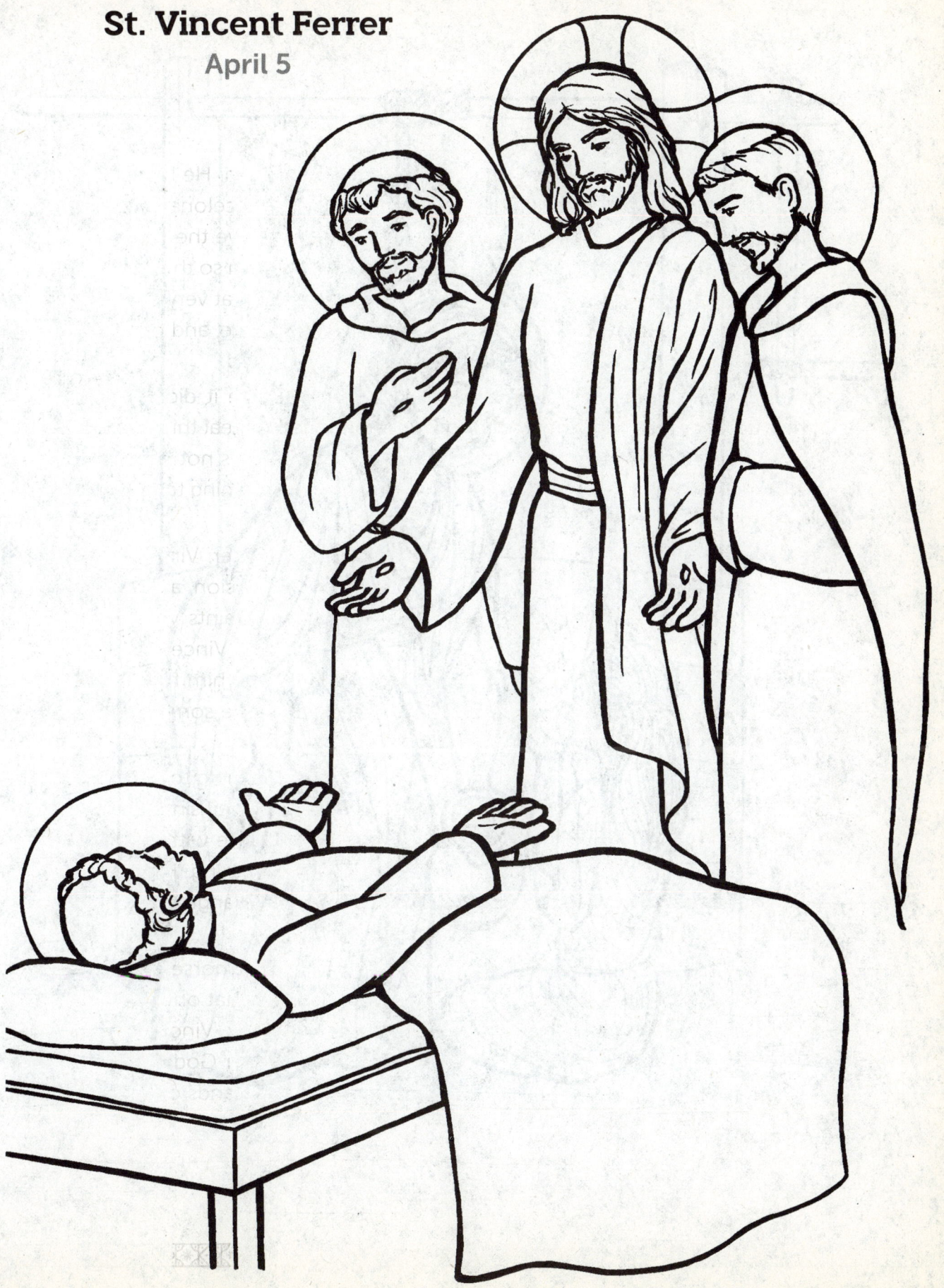

St. Galla of Rome
April 6

St. Galla of Rome

d. 550 • Italy

A little over a year after being married, Galla's husband died. Even though she was young and wealthy, Galla refused to marry again. She wanted to give her life to God and to serve others. So she came up with a plan. She made her appearance as ugly as she could so that her suitors would stop courting her!

Pleased that her ploy had worked, Galla founded a convent and a hospital near St. Peter's Basilica on Vatican Hill. Many good women joined Galla at the hospital and the convent, and together they served the poor and the sick in the city of Rome.

One day, Galla met a little girl who could not hear and could not speak. Her heart felt pity for the girl, and the Holy Spirit moved Galla to help her. Galla said a prayer to Jesus and blessed some water. Then she gave the girl a glass of the water to drink.

As the girl tasted the cool, clear water, she was healed of her ailments. Her ears picked up noises, loud and faint. Her tongue loosened. She haltingly pronounced sounds.

Galla smiled and began to tell the girl that it was Jesus who had healed her. And so, the first words that the little girl heard were about the loving God who had died to heal her of her sins.

Galla continued to serve the poor and the sick until she herself became sick with cancer. She offered her suffering to Jesus and died a holy death.

St. Galla, help me to listen when God asks me to help others!

St. Jean Baptist de La Salle

1651–1719 • France

When Jean Baptist was very young, his grandmother would read to him about the lives of the saints. By learning how much the saints loved God, Jean Baptist learned to love God, too. He learned to love God so much that, when he grew up, he left his hometown of Rheims for Paris to study to be a priest.

While he was gone, Jean Baptist's parents died, and he returned home to take care of his younger brothers and sisters. But even though he had returned home, he knew that God still wanted him to be a priest. He worked hard in his studies, and when his siblings were old enough to take care of themselves, he was ordained to the priesthood.

Soon after, Jean Baptist helped start a school for poor boys. He knew that if the boys were left to themselves, no one would teach them about Jesus. They needed someone to teach them to love Jesus the way he had been taught when he was young. He started the new school because he knew it would be the best way for him to save the boys' souls.

One of the hardest parts of running his new school was that the teachers themselves did not know how to teach. So Jean Baptist started a new order, the Institute of the Brothers of the Christian Schools, dedicated to teaching the poor and also to educating teachers.

Jean Baptist was not only concerned for the poor boys, but all of the city's poor. When a terrible famine struck Rheims, no one had enough to eat, and the poor suffered the most. Because Jean Baptist's parents had been rich, he had inherited much wealth when they died. Because of the famine, Jean Baptist sold all of his property and used the money to buy bread for the poor. He gave bread to the boys in his school, and soon a long line of hungry people formed outside of his doors. He handed out bread to all the people in line. When his money finally ran out, Jean Baptist begged at the doors of the wealthy, asking them for money for bread.

Jean Baptist de La Salle dedicated the rest of his life to teaching the city's poor and supporting his teachers until he died a holy death. St. Jean Baptist de La Salle, help me to teach others about Jesus!

St. Jean Baptist de La Salle
April 7

St. Julie Billiart
April 8

St. Julie Billiart

1751–1816 • France

Seven-year-old Julie Billiart loved playing school. She would gather all the young children of the town and teach them. But she did not teach them math, science, or French; instead, she taught them the catechism, which she had learned by heart even though she was so young. Her love for God was so strong, that, only two years later, she promised Jesus she would never marry and would give her life entirely to Him.

At age sixteen, Julie worked on a farm to make money for her family. The other workers would gather to hear her speak about Christ. They saw that Julie was a special, holy soul, and they called her the saint of their little town of Cuvilly. Then something happened that brought terrible suffering to young Julie. Her family's shop was robbed, and the criminals shot at her father. The terrifying sound of the pistol-shot sent Julie into shock, and she was paralyzed from the waist down. For the next twenty-two years, she was confined to her bed. Julie saw her bedridden state as an opportunity to grow closer to God, and she prayed for many hours of the day. The village children would gather at her bedside, and she taught them the catechism, just as she had when she was a little girl.

It was the time of the violent French Revolution, when authorities persecuted Catholics. But Julie was unafraid and spoke out about the Faith. In fear for her life, her friends hid her on a hay cart and carried her to a place of refuge. There Julie befriended a noblewoman named Françoise, who was also hiding from the authorities. The two women discovered that they shared a deep love for God and a desire to help the poor children of France. Together they founded the Sisters of Notre Dame, whose purpose was the care of children. A year later, a priest instructed Julie to pray for the healing of her body. God answered Julie's prayers, and she was finally able to walk again! Julie was grateful for God's great mercy and knew that she would have to use the newfound strength of her limbs for His service.

And that is what she did. After the French Revolution ended, Julie founded fifteen convents and made the long journeys necessary to visit them as often as she could. The sisters would gather around her as she offered them words of guidance and encouragement in the care of children. Her deep life of prayer strengthened her in her work until she died a holy death. St. Julie Billiart, help me to spread Jesus's message to those around me!

St. Casilda of Toledo

d. 1050 • Spain

Casilda's father was the emir (which is a Muslim ruler) of the great Spanish city of Toledo, at the time when the Muslims occupied Spain. Her mother had passed away from a mysterious illness when Casilda was only a child. Casilda had a kind and generous heart. There were many Catholics in her father's prison who were ill and hungry. She pitied their suffering and wanted to help them.

And so Casilda hid bread and medicine in the folds of her long gown. Then she carried the forbidden items to the prisoners right under the noses of the guards! The prisoners were grateful to the kind Casilda. They would tell her about their Faith and share their love of Jesus with her. The prisoners' words stirred her heart, and she began to wonder if she should become a Christian.

One day, a guard, suspicious of her trips to the prison, stopped Casilda as she was carrying the bread and medicine in her gown. The guard pulled her hand from her skirt so that its contents came tumbling out. Casilda closed her eyes, afraid that she had been discovered. But when she opened them again, she gasped. Instead of bread and medicine, beautiful roses had tumbled from her skirt and were strewn across the floor. The guard sent her on her way because he did not see any harm in roses. Casilda said a grateful prayer in her heart to God who had protected her.

Soon after, Casilda fell sick with the same mysterious illness that had taken her mother away from her. When her father sent his own doctors to look after her, she refused to let them see her. Instead, she made a pilgrimage to the Catholic shrine of San Vincenzo in northern Spain, known for its miraculous, healing spring. When she bathed in the spring she was healed. Now Casilda knew that the Catholic Faith was the true Faith, and she was baptized. She found a quiet place nearby and lived a solitary life of prayer and contemplation, well beloved by the local townspeople. It is said that she lived to be 100 years old.

St. Casilda of Toledo, help me bravely come to the aid of those who are less fortunate than myself, for the love of Jesus!

St. Casilda of Toledo
April 9

St. Michael de Sanctis
April 10

St. Michael de Sanctis

1591–1625 • Spain

Ever since Michael was a little boy, God flooded his soul with special graces. He was only six years old when he told his parents that he wanted to be a monk. Although he knew that he was too young to enter the monastery right away, little Michael wanted to prepare himself to live the life of a monk. And so he would offer great sacrifices to Jesus for the forgiveness of his sins and the sins of others. Some of his sacrifices were so strict that his parents had to make him give them up. Michael listened to his parents, because he knew obedience was also a way to prepare to be a monk.

While he was still young, Michael's parents passed away. He offered the great sorrow he felt as a sacrifice to God. Now more than ever he knew he had no reason to be in the world and that he was called to be a monk. But Michael was still too young to enter the monastery, so he had to learn patience. He worked as an apprentice to a merchant until he was twelve and then tried to enter the monastery in Barcelona. But the monks would not take him.

He returned home and waited patiently for three more years. Then he tried again. This time he went to the Monastery of St. Lambert in Saragossa, and his prayers were answered. The monks received him into the monastery, and Michael felt peace flooding his heart. Finally, he was where he was meant to be.

Michael's early life of sacrifice, obedience, and patience had prepared him to live the life of a monk, and he gave himself over to his prayer and work. At Mass, he would gaze at Jesus in the Eucharist with great love. He wanted to give his whole heart to God. Soon he felt called to even deeper sacrifices, and he joined the Discalced Trinitarians, an order known for their strict rules and life of sacrifice. With them, he was ordained a priest. He continued to live his simple life of prayer, work, and sacrifice, and twice he was made superior of his monastery.

His love for Jesus grew and grew. At the consecration of the Mass, Michael's love for Jesus would overpower him so that he could see nothing else around him except Jesus in the Eucharist. He led such a holy, simple life that the other brothers in his order called him a living saint until the day of his death. St. Michael de Sanctis, help me live a life of sacrifice, obedience, and patience!

St. Stanislaus

1030–1079 • Poland

When Stanislaus was bishop, King Bolesław II ruled over Poland. The king cared more about wealth and power than doing what was right. Bishop Stanislaus condemned the king's sinfulness, and the king became his enemy.

According to legend, Bishop Stanislaus purchased a plot of land for the Church from a farmer. But when the farmer died, the king wanted revenge against Bishop Stanislaus and took away the land. The king knew that Bishop Stanislaus could not prove that he had paid for the land since the farmer was dead, so he claimed that the farmer had never sold his land to Bishop Stanislaus and that it belonged to the farmer's sons.

Bishop Stanislaus was not worried. He told the king that, in three days, he would prove that he had purchased the land.

The king smiled. He did not believe Bishop Stanislaus.

Bishop Stanislaus prayed and fasted. On the third day he went to the farmer's grave. He ordered men with shovels to dig up the earth. Then, to everyone's amazement, the farmer rose from his grave and told the king that he had sold the land to Bishop Stanislaus! The king was furious, but he had no choice but to return the land.

Bishop Stanislaus continued to condemn the king's sinfulness, and he ultimately excommunicated King Bolesław II because the king's sins harmed his people. To excommunicate someone means to cut him off from the Church so that they can no longer receive the sacraments. An excommunication can be lifted when that person repents of his sin. But King Bolesław II did not want to repent. He ordered his soldiers to kill Bishop Stanislaus. Not a single one of his soldiers obeyed the king's order. They would not lift a sword against the holy bishop.

The king was furious. He decided he would kill Stanislaus himself. He found the bishop as he was saying the Holy Mass and struck him down. Bolesław II fled the country because of his evil act, and Bishop Stanislaus became a martyr for defending the Faith. St. Stanislaus, help me to stand up against injustice.

St. Stanislaus
April 11

St. Teresa of the Andes
April 12

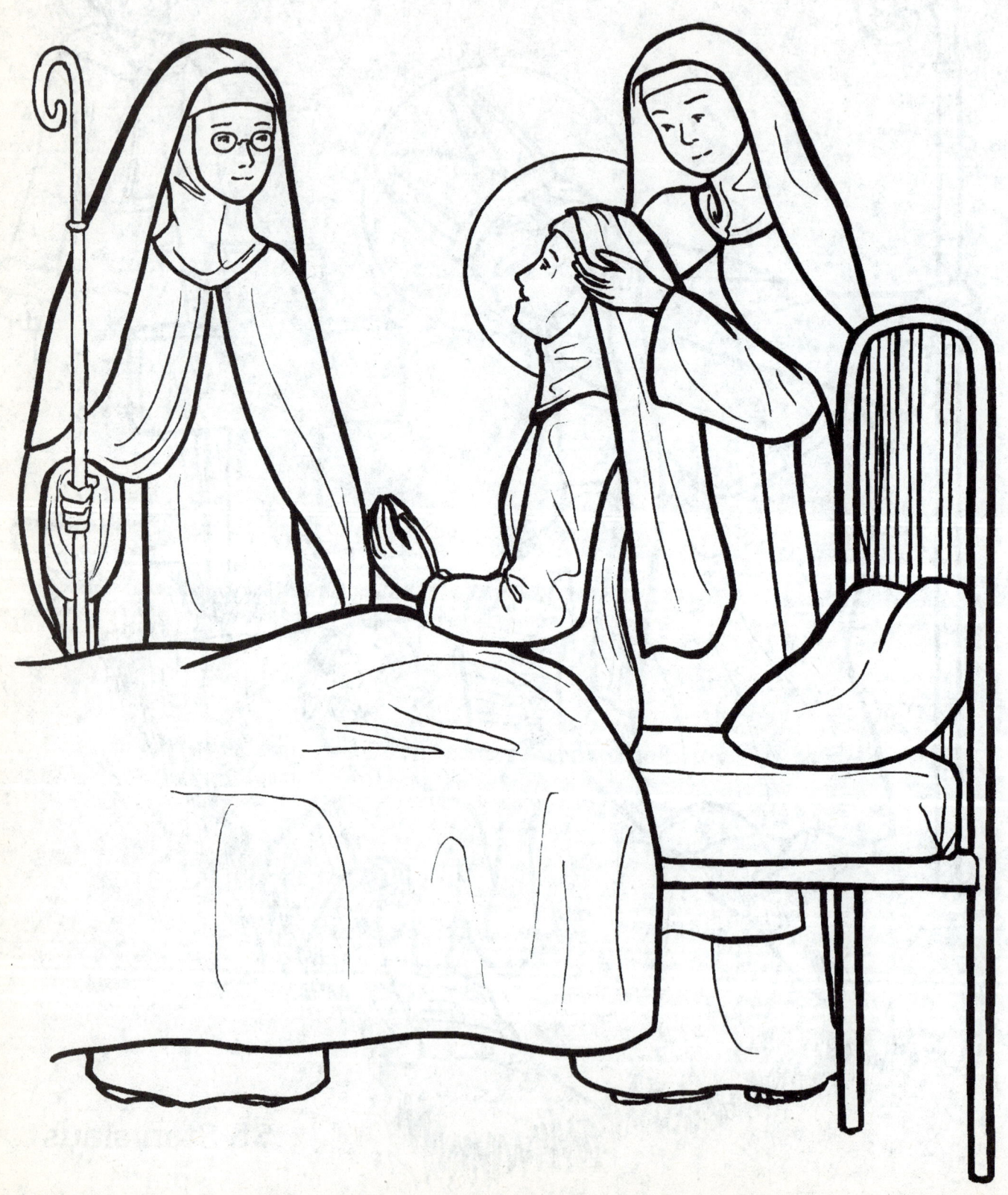

St. Teresa of the Andes

1900–1920 • Chile

St. Teresa of the Andes was baptized Juana Enriqueta Josefina de los Sagrados Corazones Fernández Solar, but she was called Juanita for short. Juanita came from a large family and was an energetic, happy child. She loved tennis, horseback riding, climbing the beautiful Chilean mountains, and swimming the ocean. She had many brothers and sisters whom she would play with, laugh with, and argue with. In fact, Juanita could be vain and stubborn and would get into many silly arguments with her younger sister, Rebecca. But she also showed a deep love for Jesus and Mary. When she was little, her older brother showed her how to pray the Rosary, and from then on she prayed the Rosary every day.

When Juanita was fourteen, she read the autobiography of St. Thérèse of Lisieux, *The Story of a Soul*. The story of the young saint's life touched her heart, and she knew she wanted to live just like Thérèse and become a Carmelite nun. Juanita promised God that she would dedicate her life to Him.

At nineteen years old, Juanita entered a Carmelite convent. Saying goodbye to her family was hard for her, but she knew that she was entering a life of even greater happiness. She took the name Teresa after St. Thérèse of Lisieux. Teresa started her new life joyfully. The mother superior allowed her to write many letters to her family and friends, recognizing that the new novice's letters would help others walk the path of holiness. But soon her life as a nun would come to an end. She told her confessor that Jesus had revealed to her the day of her death and that she only had a month to live. The priest was astonished; he did not understand how she could know when she would die.

On Good Friday, Teresa had a burning fever. The doctor diagnosed her with typhus, a deadly disease. All the sisters at the convent were saddened to know that their joyful young novice was soon to die. Teresa's superiors allowed her to make her final vows to become a nun early, since she was in danger of death. After great suffering, Teresa died a holy death a week after Easter, only three months before her twentieth birthday. That year, Teresa's little sister Rebecca entered the same convent, believing that God had called her to take her sister's place. St. Teresa of the Andes, help me live my life with joy in the love of God!

Pope St. Martin I

d. 655 • Italy

Pope St. Martin I was the seventy-fourth pope. He was the head of the Church during a time when the emperor of Constantinople and many Church leaders were trying to spread a false teaching about Jesus. This false teaching declared that Jesus was fully God but was not also fully human. Pope Martin knew this teaching was false. He knew that Jesus had revealed to us that He is the Second Person of the Trinity and is both fully God and fully man. Because he was head of the Church, Pope Martin knew that it was his responsibility to instruct all Christians on the truth about Jesus.

Pope Martin held a council and declared that Jesus was fully God and fully man, and he condemned the false teaching being spread about Jesus. Now this made the emperor of Constantinople angry. He felt that Pope Martin was challenging his authority. He ordered his soldiers to arrest the pope and bring him to Constantinople. The soldiers went to Rome, and Martin humbly let them arrest him without a fight. He did not want any blood spilled defending him. The soldiers mistreated him on the ship to Constantinople—they did not give him proper food or clothing, and he became weak. All this Martin endured silently and patiently, knowing that he suffered for Jesus.

When the ship arrived at Constantinople, the soldiers left Pope Martin on the ship's deck for hours. Curious onlookers mocked the pope and shouted insults at him. Then he was thrown in prison and suffered from cold, hunger, and thirst. Finally, Pope Martin was dragged in chains before the emperor. But even though he was weak and frail, he was still strong in his Faith and his determination to stand by the truth. Pope Martin did not waver. He refused to support false teachings about Jesus. Furious, the emperor made Pope Martin suffer even more. He stripped the pope of most of his clothes and had his soldiers drag him in chains through the city streets before sending him back to prison. There the pope suffered alone, hungry, and cold for many more days.

The emperor then exiled Pope Martin to a small island which was undergoing a terrible famine. The pope was still weak from all he had endured in prison. He did not have any friends with him on the island, nor did he have enough food to live on. He died of his suffering four months after his arrival on the island and became a glorious martyr for Jesus Christ. Pope St. Martin I, help me humbly endure my suffering for Jesus!

Pope St. Martin I
April 13

Bl. Peter González
April 14

Bl. Peter González

1190–1246 • Spain

Peter's uncle was an important bishop who oversaw Peter's education. When Peter was a young man, his uncle secured for him a prestigious Church position which would give Peter much influence and honor.

Peter rode on horseback to the city where he would be given his new and important position. He sat tall and proud on his horse. Crowds of onlookers gathered to watch the young man pass by.

Suddenly, Peter's horse stumbled, and Peter was launched headlong into the mud! The onlookers laughed to see the fine young man's clothes all muddy.

Peter flushed. He felt humiliated. But he also felt something else—he realized that he had been too proud. His fall from the horse had taught him the lesson that he should strive to be humble and not worry if other people laughed at him.

Peter gave up his important position and decided to become a humble Dominican friar. He preached to the poor in the city, and many people converted to the Faith because of his words. He also preached to the king of Spain and his court. One time, his words restrained soldiers from pillaging a city they had defeated.

But the people Peter most loved to preach to were Spanish and Portuguese sailors. Sailors had a rough and dangerous life. Many would spend months at sea and did not spend their time thinking about God. Peter would go to the harbor and the docks and preach to them. He treated them with respect and kindness. The sailors listened to Peter and invited him onto their ships so they could hear him preach even more. In this way, he won their hearts for Christ. Peter González was beloved by the Spanish and Portuguese sailors until his death.

Bl. Peter González, help me to be humble!

St. Hunna

d. 679 • France

Hunna was a noblewoman who loved God. She was married to Huno of Hunnawetyer, and together the couple used their wealth to serve the poor. Because God had blessed her with riches and land, Hunna knew that she should help her struggling neighbors when they needed her.

No act of service was too humble for Hunna.

Among her many good works for the poor, she helped struggling women do their laundry. These poor women had many worries and little help; their days were spent feeding their families and caring for their children. Hunna knew that doing the time-consuming task of laundry would bring these women some relief.

And so Hunna would don her simplest dress and go to work scouring, scrubbing, and rubbing tunics and smocks by the river. Above her, hanging laundry fluttered in the sun and the breeze.

Hunna's love of God and the poor was an important example to her son. His name was Deodatus, which is Latin for "given by God." When Deodatus grew up, he entered a monastery and also became a saint.

Hunna must have been so proud of her son. Together they lived in the service of God until the end of their days.

St. Hunna, please help me serve those who are struggling!

St. Hunna

April 15

St. Bernadette Soubirous
April 16

St. Bernadette Soubirous

1844–1879 • France

Bernadette Soubirous was born in France, the eldest of nine children. Ever since she was little, Bernadette suffered from bad health. Because she often had to stay home sick, she could barely read and write.

When she was fourteen, Bernadette was gathering wood on the bank of a river near a natural grotto, or cave. As she took off her shoes to cross a stream, she heard a rustling like the wind. But the trees and the river were completely still. Only the bushes near the grotto were moving. There she saw a beautiful lady all dressed in white with a blue girdle about her waist and a long rosary hanging over her arm. She gestured for Bernadette to pray, and together they said the Rosary.

Bernadette continued to visit the grotto, and large crowds of people followed, even though they could not see the lady. During one of her visits, the lady instructed Bernadette to drink from a spring near the grotto. Bernadette could find nothing but muddy water and had to scratch at the dirt in order to drink. The crowds laughed at Bernadette's muddy face, but they were amazed to find that later in the day the water had turned into a clear spring. A man who had been blind for twenty years washed his eyes with the water and was healed! A woman brought her sick son to the spring, and he also was healed. Many, many miracles happened at the spring.

When Bernadette asked the lady who she was, she responded, "I am the Immaculate Conception," revealing that she was the Blessed Virgin Mary. After the apparitions, people flocked to Bernadette because she had seen Our Lady. Bernadette did not like all of the attention, and, to avoid it, she went to live at a school run by the Sisters of Charity of Nevers and was granted permission to join the sisters.

At the convent, Bernadette cared for the sick in the infirmary. Her ill health returned, and she suffered terribly but never went to the spring for healing. Bernadette saw her suffering as something she could offer up to God. She said before her death, "To obey is to love! To suffer in silence for Christ is joy! To love sincerely is to give everything, even grief." Bernadette died a holy death at thirty-five years of age. St. Bernadette, help me to be patient when I am sick!

St. Robert de Turlande

d. 1067 • France

Robert's mother, when she was pregnant with baby Robert, was wandering in the forest one day when the time came for her to give birth. She delivered Robert there among the quiet trees and the open air. A neighbor predicted that Robert would one day become a hermit, since he had been born in the solitude of the forest.

Early in life, Robert's parents gave him to the Church to be educated, and he was ordained a priest. Robert had a great love of God in his heart. His devotion while saying Mass so touched other souls that many of them became truly sorry for their sins. Robert's love for God overflowed into love for his neighbor. He would care for the sick and wash the sores of the poor. Many healing miracles stemmed from his touch.

Inside of Robert's heart awoke a desire to grow closer to God in silence. But the cares and daily duties of his church chased away all the quiet moments he needed. He did not understand why God had given him such a deep longing for solitude if he was meant to live a busy parish life. Seeking answers, Robert made a pilgrimage to Rome to ask God's guidance on how he should grow closer to Him.

Not long after, a knight named Stephen approached Robert to ask for his advice on how to live a holy life. Robert advised the knight to give up the world and become a knight for Christ. But Stephen replied that he would only have the strength to give up the world if Robert gave up the world with him. Robert realized that God was answering his prayer through the knight's words. God wanted Robert to show Stephen how to give up the world. And so Robert, Stephen, and one of Stephen's fellow knights traveled to a ruined chapel in an empty field. There they started a hermitage, where they lived in silence and prayer and dedicated their lives to serving the poor. Here, Robert hoped he and the knights could worship God in prayerful solitude.

Robert and the two knights lived such holy lives that they attracted numerous followers. Soon, Robert used donations to build a Benedictine monastery so that he could give his followers a place to live. He oversaw the construction of the grand Abbey of La Chaise-Dieu. This abbey became a place where Robert and his monks could worship God in prayerful solitude. There were three hundred monks at La Chaise-Dieu when Robert died a holy death. St. Robert de Turlande, help me learn to pray to God in solitude!

St. Robert de Turlande

April 17

© Sophia Institute Press

St. Athanasia

April 18

St. Athanasia

c. 790–860 • Greece

As a young girl, weaving at her loom, Athanasia was graced by a mystical vision. A bright star descended from the heavens and rested on her breast. This mystical experience filled Athanasia with a deep love of God and the desire never to marry, so as to give herself to Him alone. Her parents had a different plan for her, however, and when Athanasia was sixteen, they forced her to marry a soldier. Yet her husband was killed in battle only sixteen days after their marriage.

Once again, Athanasia was forced to marry, this time by imperial decree, as the emperor ordered that all single women of marriageable age must marry soldiers. Still, God was with Athanasia. Her new husband was a deeply religious man who desired to become a monk. Together they agreed to lead lives dedicated to the service of God. Later, Athanasia's husband went to a monastery where he soon passed away.

Athanasia gathered a group of women to live in monastic community and became their mother superior. Although she was their leader, she was humble. She did not allow the women to serve her, but rather served them instead. She lived a life of great sacrifice, fasting for God and even sleeping against a hard rock.

One day, when Athanasia was at prayer, a man with troubled eyesight approached her and begged her to pray for him. Athanasia instructed him to have patience and faith in the Lord. Then she placed her hands over his eyes with a prayer. When she removed her hands, the man's eyes were healed! Athanasia's fame for her miracles and wisdom grew so great that she was troubled. She did not like attention for herself but only wanted people to pay attention to God. And so she left her hometown of Aegina for Constantinople to live the life of an anchoress, which meant she would spend her days alone in prayer, never leaving her cell.

Athanasia lived as an anchoress for seven years. Even though she never left her cell, she did receive visitors during certain parts of the day. Even the Empress Theodora II would sit outside the window of her cell and ask Athanasia for spiritual advice. Near the end of her life, Athanasia received a vision instructing her to return to her hometown of Aegina. After her return home, she became ill and died a holy death three days later. St. Athanasia, help me to know God better through prayer!

St. Gianna Beretta Molla

1922–1962 • Italy

Gianna Beretta was the tenth of thirteen children. Her family was very devout and passed on to Gianna the gift of the Catholic Faith. Together as a family they prayed a daily Rosary, attended daily Mass, and consecrated themselves to the Sacred Heart.

As a child, Gianna spent much of her time outdoors and loved to go hiking and skiing. She also felt a special call to serve others. She was active in her Catholic youth community and did volunteer work to take care of the poor through the St. Vincent de Paul Society. Her call to serve others was so strong that she went to medical school to become a doctor. When she opened her own clinic, she was most drawn to serving mothers, children, the poor, and the elderly. Gianna viewed her practice of medicine as a mission from God.

After much prayer, Gianna realized that she was called to the vocation of marriage. She wanted to raise a Christian family where her children could learn to love God and become holy. She married Pietro Molla, a Catholic engineer, and had three children. The happy couple called their children their "treasures."

When Gianna became pregnant a fourth time, the doctors discovered that Gianna had a deadly tumor in her uterus. To get rid of the tumor, the doctors gave Gianna three options. The first two options would get rid of the tumor, but they would also cause the death of her unborn child. The third option would remove the tumor and leave her child unharmed, but that would make giving birth dangerous. Gianna was a strong Catholic and a doctor dedicated to saving lives. She knew that the life of her unborn child was sacred and precious to God. She bravely chose to only remove the tumor and save the life of her child, despite the potential danger to her own life.

When the time came for Gianna to give birth, she heroically told the doctors to save her child's life over her own if they had to. She gave birth to a healthy baby girl and was so happy to see her! Sadly, Gianna died a week later due to complications from her pregnancy, even though the doctors tried very hard to save her.

Gianna Beretta Molla was canonized on May 16, 2004 and stands as a witness to life and the importance of family. Pietro Molla attended her canonization and is the first husband to attend the canonization of his wife. St. Gianna Beretta Molla, bless all the pregnant mothers that I know!

St. Gianna Beretta Molla
April 19

St. Agnes of Montepulciano
April 20

St. Agnes of Montepulciano

1268–1317 • Italy

Agnes's parents saw that even during her early childhood, Agnes was especially graced by God. They did not want to keep her from God's calling, so they allowed her to enter a convent in their hometown of Montepulciano when she was only nine years old.

A few years later, a lord wanted to start a new convent some thirty miles away and invited a group of nuns in Montepulciano to help found it. Among the nuns sent was Agnes. There she lived a life of such holiness that she became the abbess at the young age of twenty.

God graced this young nun with the gift of miracles. She healed those who suffered injuries, and many times she multiplied loaves of bread the way Jesus had multiplied the loaves and fishes. Agnes was especially dedicated to the Eucharist, and she even had a vision in which she received Communion from an angel. She would spend long hours in prayer and ecstasy before the Blessed Sacrament, and sometimes she would be so consumed by her worship of God that her feet would float above the ground.

All throughout her life, Agnes experienced visions. In one of them, Mary appeared with the Baby Jesus in her arms. The Baby Jesus wore a cross around His neck and was so beautiful and loving that when the Blessed Virgin Mary passed Him into Agnes's arms, Agnes's heart had never before felt so joyous and full. The Baby Jesus warned Agnes that He would soon depart from her vision, but Agnes did not want Him to leave. His loss would be like the loss of a precious treasure.

Agnes knew that she could not keep Jesus from leaving, but she did want something of His to keep with her forever. Her fingers clutched the cross that the Baby Jesus wore and lifted it from His neck. The Blessed Virgin Mary and the Baby Jesus disappeared, and Jesus's departure was so painful that Agnes fainted. When she woke, she saw that she still grasped Jesus's cross in her hands. She was overjoyed that Jesus had let her keep His cross!

In the last ten years of her life, Agnes was called back to lead the convent at Montepulciano. There she suffered from a terrible illness, which she offered up to God. Many a time she must have been comforted by her memory of Jesus and how precious a gift it had been to hold Him in her arms. She died a holy death at the age of forty-nine. St. Agnes of Montepulciano, help me to hold Jesus in my heart with the same love with which you held Him in your arms!

St. Anselm

1033–1109 • France

Anselm's mother loved God and taught Anselm to love God, too. Anselm wanted to enter the monastery, but his father did not want him to become a monk because he wanted Anselm to pursue a life of politics. When Anselm tried to join a monastery at the age of fifteen, the monks would not accept him because they did not want to anger his father. And so, Anselm left behind for a while his desire to enter the monastery.

After his mother died, Anselm left home, wandering throughout France for three years. He ended his journey at the Abbey of Bec. There he studied for many years, and his desire to be a monk returned. He joined the abbey and, in time, became its abbot. He wrote many wise books about God, and the abbey became famous as an important place of learning.

As the abbot of the Abbey of Bec, Anselm would travel to England on Church business. When the archbishop of Canterbury in England died, the English Church officials wanted Anselm to replace him. But the king of England didn't want Canterbury to have another archbishop because he wanted the Church's wealth and land for himself. Anselm himself did not want to be archbishop of Canterbury because he did not want to give up his peaceful life and fight with the English king.

During one of Anselm's visits to England, the king fell terribly ill. He thought he was going to die and was afraid for his soul. The Church officials saw their chance. They surrounded the king and begged for Anselm to be named archbishop of Canterbury. The king gave his permission. This was what the Church officials had been waiting for! They found Anselm, brought him to the king's bedside, and pressed the bishop's staff into his hands. Then they dragged him off to the church while singing solemn hymns. Eventually, Anselm agreed to become archbishop and received approval for his consecration from the pope.

In time, the king recovered from his illness, and Anselm had to spend the rest of his life as archbishop defending the Church of Canterbury from the king's control, and later on from his son's. Twice Anselm was exiled by the king because he would not give in to the king's commands. Anselm remained faithful to the pope and defended the English Catholic Church until he died a holy death. St. Anselm of Canterbury, help me to do what God wants, even if it is not easy!

St. Anselm
April 21

St. Opportuna

d. 770 • France

Opportuna dearly loved her brother Chrodegang, who was a bishop, and they both sought to live holy lives serving God. When Opportuna entered the convent of Monasteriolum, it was her brother, Bishop Chrodegang, who gave her the veil as she said her final vows to become a nun.

Opportuna was wise and kind. When elected as the abbess of her convent, she became like a true mother to all the nuns in her charge. At times she had to correct her nuns to help them lead holy lives, but her corrections always consisted of firm words instead of punishments.

There is a legend that a farmer stole a donkey from the sisters of Monasteriolum. Not only is stealing wrong, but it is especially wrong to steal from holy women dedicated to serving God. Opportuna went to the farm and saw the farmer with the convent's donkey. She asked the farmer to return what he had stolen. But the farmer refused. Not only that, he claimed that the donkey she saw was his and that maybe her donkey had run away.

Opportuna knew that the farmer was lying, but she also knew she could not force him to return the donkey. And so she prayed to God and asked Him to take care of the matter as He willed.

The next morning, the farmer went to his field, but there was something different. He sifted the soil and saw that his field had been sown with salt. Now nothing would grow in his field! The farmer realized that God had punished him for stealing from the sisters of Monasteriolum. Sorry that he had done wrong, the farmer not only returned the donkey to the sisters, he gave them the field as well.

One day, Opportuna received a heartbreaking vision. She saw that her dear brother, Bishop Chrodegang, was on the road to visit her, but that he would never arrive because he would be waylaid and murdered. She was too far away to do anything to save him. All she could do was wait. The terrible news of her brother's murder arrived, and she had his body buried in her convent.

Chrodegang's death was a blow from which Opportuna never recovered. She offered her sorrow to God, but she grew weaker and weaker and eventually fell ill. On her deathbed, the Blessed Virgin Mary appeared to her to give the sorrowing nun comfort. Opportuna died a holy death, knowing that she would soon be reunited with her brother in heaven, and together they would worship Jesus with all the angels and the saints. St. Opportuna, help me to give all of my sorrows to Jesus!

St. George

c. 300 • Israel

St. George was a soldier from the Holy Land. He lived during a time when Christians were persecuted by the Roman emperor. Not much is known about him, but we do know that he died in defense of his faith in Jesus Christ. A wonderful legend about St. George teaches us about the fight between good and evil. It is the legend of St. George and the dragon.

St. George was traveling on horseback when he saw a beautiful maiden weeping. He reined his horse to a halt and asked the maiden why she was so sad.

Through her tears, the maiden explained that a terrible dragon plagued her city, poisoning the pond with its foul breath and eating its people. To stop the dragon from destroying the city, the people cast lots to decide who should be sacrificed to the dragon. The lot had fallen on the maiden, who was the king's daughter and therefore a princess. The king, in great sorrow, had his daughter dressed in her wedding garments and taken to where the dragon came for its prey.

Now she was waiting for the dragon to come and eat her.

St. George was horrified at the princess's story. He promised he would defend her in the name of Jesus Christ.

No sooner had he said those words than he spotted the dragon in the distance. It sped toward them, a red light gleaming in its hungry eyes. St. George raised his shining sword and thrust at the dragon with all his might. He slew the dragon and chopped off its head.

St. George then returned the princess to her father, who received the princess with the greatest joy. Because St. George had defeated the dragon, the king and all his people were baptized and became Christian.

This story shows us how important it is to defend good against evil: the dragon represents sin and the evil one, while the maiden is the Church. We must all fight against evil to safeguard our Faith.

St. George, please help me defend the Catholic Faith!

St. George
April 23

St. Fidelis

April 24

St. Fidelis

1577–1622 • Prussia (modern-day Germany)

Fidelis was a skilled lawyer, but he grew unhappy with the law. He saw that other lawyers did not care about justice or the poor and the needy. They only cared about power and money. God filled Fidelis's heart with the call to serve others, so Fidelis decided to give up law and become a priest.

At that time, many Catholics in Switzerland had converted to Calvinism (a Protestant religion). Sadly, Calvinists and Catholics used to fight each other, even to the point of taking each other's lives. Even though it would be dangerous, Fidelis wished to preach to the Calvinists and bring them back to the true Faith of Christ. Fidelis was not afraid of death. He once told a fellow friar that he prayed to God for the grace to die a martyr. He knew that if he died a martyr he would be giving his life for God, whom he loved more than anything else, and that he would go straight to heaven.

Fidelis bravely entered the Protestant country and preached the Catholic Faith. His words were unafraid and true. They spoke to the hearts of the people, and many of them converted to Catholicism. This made the Calvinist leaders angry. They plotted to kill Fidelis to stop him from preaching and converting the people.

During Lent, Fidelis preached with a special fire for the Faith. When Easter came, he knew that his prayer to die a martyr's death would soon be answered. He confided to his companions that he would die soon. He preached a goodbye sermon, went to confession, and said Mass. Then he set out for another town. His companions noticed that he looked especially cheerful.

When he reached the next town, Fidelis preached at the church. Outside, a group of Calvinists gathered to threaten him. Someone shot a musket, and the people inside the church trembled in fear. They begged Fidelis to be careful, but he responded that he would joyfully give his life for Christ.

Fidelis returned to the road but was quickly surrounded by a large crowd. They threatened him with death if he did not give up his Faith. Fidelis refused, and a man struck him down. Weakly, Fidelis rose to his knees and stretched his arms in the shape of the cross. He prayed aloud for God to forgive his enemies. Then he died a martyr's death by the sword. God had heard Fidelis's prayer to be a glorious martyr for the Faith, and Fidelis went straight to heaven.

St. Fidelis, help me to be faithful to Christ!

St. Mark the Evangelist

Biblical Figure

Mark was not a direct follower of Jesus but was instead a disciple of St. Peter. Peter affectionately referred to Mark as his son when he sent greetings by letter to the churches. Peter told Mark all about Jesus, and Mark wrote down what Peter told him. Like all the authors of Scripture, Mark wrote under the inspiration of the Holy Spirit. His Gospel is one of the four Gospels about Jesus's life in the Bible. The Gospel of Mark is the first and shortest Gospel. You will often hear the priest read from the Gospel of Mark during Mass.

While Mark might not have been a disciple when Jesus was alive, he did know about Jesus. There was a young man who followed Jesus when He was arrested in the Garden of Gethsemane. Scripture describes him in this way: "Now a young man followed [Jesus] wearing nothing but a linen cloth about his body. They seized him, but he left the cloth behind and ran off naked" (Mark 14:51–52). This young man only appears in Mark's Gospel, and many believe that this was Mark himself!

Mark's mother was also an important leader in the early Christian community in Jerusalem. There was a time when Herod arrested Peter for preaching about Jesus. An angel rescued Peter, casting off his chains and leading him past the guards. The first place Peter went when he was freed was to the house of Mark's mother, where Christians were gathered in prayer.

Mark was also the cousin of St. Barnabas, a fellow traveler with St. Paul. Mark accompanied Paul and Barnabas on their apostolic travels to preach about Jesus.

When Paul wanted to go to Asia Minor, Mark returned to Jerusalem. No one knows why. Maybe Mark found the journey too hard. Maybe he was homesick! Whatever the reason, Mark's decision upset Paul. Later, Mark wanted to travel with them again. But Paul refused to take Mark with him! So Paul and Barnabas parted ways. Barnabas and Mark went to Cyprus to preach about Jesus there. However, Paul and Mark's friendship in Christ was stronger than any quarrel. Mark was in Rome when Paul was in prison for preaching the Gospel. Paul was lonely in prison and wrote to his student Timothy about Mark: "Get Mark and bring him with you, for he is helpful to me in the ministry" (2 Timothy 4:11).

Later, Mark became the bishop of Alexandria in Egypt. Church tradition says that he was martyred and buried there. St. Mark's symbol is the lion. You often see him in artwork pictured with the other Evangelists; he is always the one with the lion next to him. St. Mark, help me to pay attention to the readings at Mass!

St. Mark the Evangelist

April 25

© Sophia Institute Press

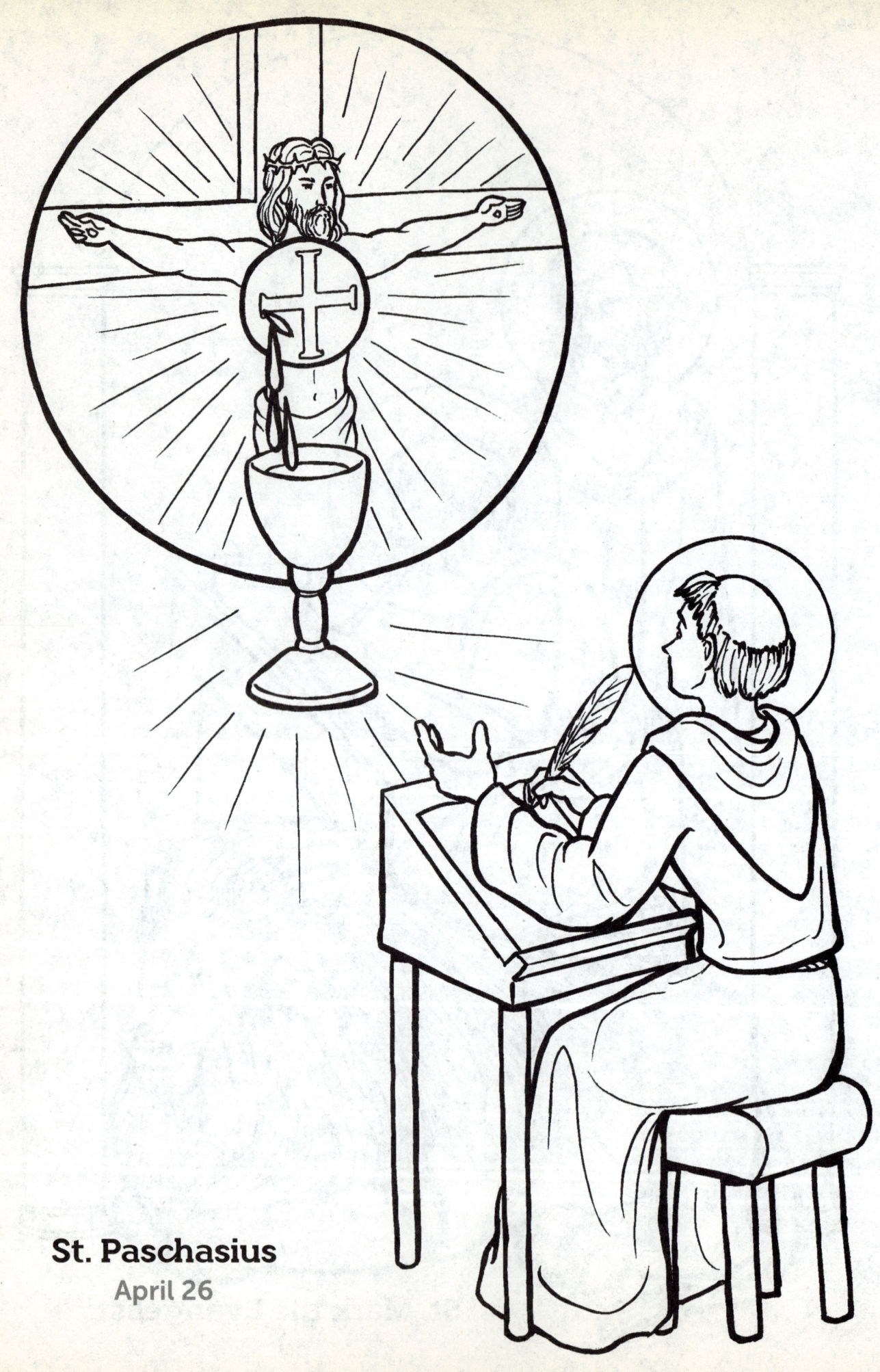

St. Paschasius
April 26

St. Paschasius

785–865 • France

An abandoned baby boy wailed on the steps of the convent of Notre-Dame de Soissons. His piteous cries drew the portress to the door where she discovered the unhappy infant. With pity in her heart, she gathered the baby boy in her arms and brought him inside where he was raised by the nuns of the convent. The sisters named the boy Paschasius, and the Abbess Theodrara became like a mother to him.

When Paschasius grew too old to live at the convent, he went to serve the Abbot Adalard of Corbie Abbey, who was the brother of the Abbess Theodrara. Paschasius spent his time in the abbey studying and teaching. He would often turn in prayer to the Blessed Sacrament and meditate on Jesus's words in Scripture: "This is my Body" and "This is my Blood." He must have marveled over how Jesus had offered His Body and Blood on the Cross out of love for every single person, even those who had been abandoned like he was.

Paschasius journeyed with the Abbot Adalard to Saxony to help him found the monastery of New Corvey. While he was there, Paschasius continued writing and teaching. His most famous work is about the Eucharist—how the bread and wine are truly Jesus's Body and Blood. His writings helped the faithful better understand the Eucharist.

After many years, Paschasius returned to Corbie and became its abbot. He governed Corbie Abbey for seven years before he resigned and left for a nearby monastery, where he dedicated his life to prayer and study. He returned to Corbie Abbey in old age and died a holy death. His body was buried in the Church of St. John of Corbie, where many miracles were reported at his tomb.

St. Paschasius, please help me to honor and worship Jesus in the Eucharist!

St. Louis de Montfort

1673–1716 • France

Louis de Montfort had a deep devotion to Jesus and Mary from the time he was young. He desired to become a missionary priest and bring many souls to Jesus. A benefactor recognized Louis's priestly vocation and paid for Louis to attend the most famous seminary in Paris, the Seminary of Saint-Sulpice. Desiring to begin his missionary vocation immediately, Louis walked to Paris on foot and gave away all of his money to the poor people he met on the road.

As a priest, Louis became a great preacher. His words touched others' souls and converted the most hardened hearts. Once, he preached to a garrison of soldiers, and by the end of his sermon, every soldier's eye was wet with tears. Barefoot, the soldiers formed a procession, holding a banner high and marching with crucifixes and rosaries.

Louis visited Pope Clement XI in Rome, and the pope declared him an apostolic missionary to France. Louis then formed a group of missionary priests called the Company of Mary. They strove to be faithful to Christ through devotion to His holy mother. Louis also founded an order of nuns called the Daughters of Wisdom, who sought to imitate the wisdom of the crucified Jesus by following Mary. Louis knew that Mary wants to bring all her children to her Son. No one loves Jesus more than Mary does, and if we imitate her perfect love for Jesus, then Mary will help make our love for Jesus perfect, too.

But Louis's success made him enemies. He had religious rivals who did not agree with what he preached. They even went so far as to try to murder him! One of his enemies slipped poison into his drink. Louis unknowingly drank from the poisoned cup and fell violently ill. Even though an antidote was given to him, he struggled with the effects of the poison for the rest of his life. Another enemy once lay in wait to ambush Louis at the end of an alley. But Mary and his guardian angel watched over him. He sensed the harm waiting for him and took another way.

Louis served Jesus and Mary as a priest for sixteen years. Finally, he died a holy death, worn down by illness. Thousands flocked to his burial, and there were many miracles reported at his tomb. St. Louis de Montfort, help me go to Jesus through Mary!

St. Louis de Montfort
April 27

St. Peter Chanel

April 28

St. Peter Chanel

1802–1841 • France

When Peter was young, no one would have guessed that the little French shepherd boy would became a brave martyr for the Faith. But there was something special about him. The local priest saw that Peter was meant for more than the life of a shepherd. So the priest convinced Peter's parents to let their son attend the little school he had started. At school, Peter read letters written by missionaries in America. Inside his heart was born the dream to become a missionary himself. And so Peter joined the seminary and became a priest.

Even though Peter wanted to be a missionary more than anything, he had to wait. The Marist congregation that he joined had him teach at the seminary for five years. Those years seemed long for Peter, but he learned to be patient because he knew that he was doing God's will. Finally, he was sent as a missionary to the Pacific Islands. He journeyed from island to island until he finally landed on the island of Fotuna to stay.

At first, missionary life was a struggle. Peter had to learn the language of the native islanders, and he suffered from hunger and poverty. While the king of Fotuna, Niuliki, was friendly to Peter, very few of the natives listened to Peter's words or believed in Jesus.

Then one day, an islander heard Peter's preaching and asked to be baptized. This islander was the king's own son, Meitala. The king was furious. Whatever friendliness he felt for Peter disappeared. He did not want his son to become a Catholic!

The king of Fotuna ordered his chief warrior, Musumusu, to get rid of Peter. So Musumusu came up with a plan.

First, he challenged Meitala to combat. The two warriors fought and Musumusu was wounded. Then, Musumusu went to Peter and asked him to dress his wound. While Peter tended to Musumusu a group of warriors attacked Peter's house, and Musumusu lifted his axe and slew him. Even though Peter Chanel had been killed, his mission to spread Jesus's Gospel to the island did not die. The islanders were inspired by his death, and, within two years, the entire island became Catholic and remains so to this day.

St. Peter Chanel, help me to fulfill the mission Jesus has for me!

St. Catherine of Siena

1347–1380 • Italy

Six-year-old Catherine and her older brother were walking on the road to their home. Without warning, the young Catherine froze and gazed up at the sky. Her brother grabbed her hand, and Catherine burst into tears. Moments before, the glorified Jesus had appeared to her in a vision, along with many saints. When her brother took her hand, the beautiful vision had disappeared! This vision of Jesus forever changed Catherine's life, and only a year later, she promised Jesus that she would give her life completely to Him.

When Catherine turned sixteen, her mother wished her to marry. But Catherine knew that she could love no man but Jesus. She refused to marry and cut her beautiful, long, golden hair. Her parents were angry at first, but when they realized that Catherine was determined to dedicate her life to God, they allowed her to join the order of Dominican tertiaries. Catherine lived in a tiny room in her house, prayed, offered sacrifices, and did penances. She only left her small room to go to Mass.

Jesus appeared to the nineteen-year-old Catherine on the day before Ash Wednesday. He gave her a ring, which she described as her wedding ring to Jesus. It was invisible to everyone but her. Jesus told Catherine that her time alone was over and that she was now ready to serve others. And that is what she did. She nursed the sick in the hospitals and fed the poor in their homes. During a terrible plague not only did she take care of the sick, but she buried the dead with her own hands.

One day, when Catherine was praying in a church, rays shot forth from the crucifix and pierced her hands, feet, and side. She fainted, and, when she regained consciousness, she saw that she had received the stigmata, which means that her body now bore the five wounds of Christ. The stigmata were invisible during her life but became visible after her death.

Because of her wisdom, Catherine was an adviser for two popes. For many years, the popes had lived in Avignon, France, instead of Rome. This caused much turmoil in the Church. Catherine convinced Pope Gregory XI to return to Rome. Gregory's successor, Urban VI, asked Catherine to move to Rome and act as his adviser. Only two years later, Catherine died a holy death at the age of thirty-three. St. Catherine of Siena, show me how to deepen my love for Jesus!

St. Catherine of Siena
April 29

Pope St. Pius V

April 30

Pope St. Pius V

1504–1572 • Italy

Pope St. Pius V was the 225th pope. He was born to a noble but poor family and was called Michele Ghislieri. When he grew up he became a Dominican priest. At that point in history, the Church was under attack from both inside and out. Princes and monarchs were converting to the new Protestant religions and separating their countries from the Roman Catholic Church. The Muslims from the Ottoman Empire in the east were fighting for control of the Mediterranean and did not allow Christians to practice their Faith freely. But the Church was suffering even more from within. The clergy and religious were not following the rules of the Church. They were too attached to wealth, vice, and power.

Michele was dismayed at all the terrible things happening to the Church. He refused to live in luxury but would fast, stay up late in prayer, and make journeys on foot without his cloak. When the pope died, the cardinals elected Michele pope, and he took the name Pius V. With tears in his eyes, Michele had begged not to be pope. He knew how hard it would be to defend the Church. But he accepted God's will and immediately set to work reforming the Church from within. He banished luxury from the papal court, sat at the bedside of the dying, gave the Church's money to the poor, and kissed beggars' feet.

Then he sought to defend the Church from without. He supported the Catholics persecuted in Protestant countries. He also formed the Holy League, a naval fleet to combat the forces of the Ottoman Empire. Soon, a great battle would be fought by the Holy League called the Battle of Lepanto. The outcome of the battle would decide whether Europe would remain Christian or be taken over by the Ottoman Empire. Pius V urged the faithful to offer Rosaries to Our Lady of Victory for the success of the fleet. On the day of the battle, Pius V was working hard with his cardinals. Suddenly, he ran to the window and gazed out into the sky.

"A truce to business," he cried. "Our great task at present is to thank God for the victory which He has just given the Christian army." The outnumbered Christian forces had defeated the Ottomans in Greece, and Pius V miraculously knew of their victory on the same day many miles away in Rome. In thanksgiving, he instituted the first Sunday of October as the feast of the Rosary. For the rest of his life, Pius V sought to defend the Church and safeguard her teaching of the Gospel of Christ until he died a holy death. Pope St. Pius V, please protect the Church from within and without!

St. Joseph the Worker

Feast of St. Joseph

Joseph paused a moment to gaze at Jesus working beside him and was filled with great love and wonder. Jesus was Joseph's foster son—for Jesus's true father was God the Father in heaven—and Joseph loved Him with all his heart.

Joseph was a carpenter. He spent his days working hard to take care of Jesus and Mary. He would rise early in the morning before the sun and work hard the long day. Mary would draw water from the well in Nazareth and make bread for their meals. Together they worked hard as a family.

When Jesus was old enough, Joseph taught Him how to be a carpenter. At first, Jesus's little hands were clumsy with the tools. Joseph was patient and showed Jesus how to hold a chisel and carve the wood. As Jesus grew older, He grew stronger, and Joseph and Jesus worked together side by side. Joseph's work felt lighter because Jesus was with him. Those precious hours working beside Jesus were treasured moments in his heart.

Jesus, Mary, and Joseph would rest from their work on the Sabbath Day. God had worked to create the world in six days, and on the seventh day, the Sabbath, He rested. This day of rest was a day of blessing on all of creation. The Sabbath was dedicated to God, so the Holy Family would go to the synagogue on that day to pray. In his heart, Joseph would thank God the Father for giving him Mary and Jesus to watch over. He would pray to God for the strength to take care of them.

As the years passed, Joseph watched Jesus become a strong young man. But as time went on, Joseph also grew older and weaker. Now Jesus was the one watching over him. Soon Joseph was so weak that he knew that he was dying. He lay in bed, and Jesus and Mary sat beside him, each holding his hand. Love shone from their eyes and Joseph's heart was filled with peace. Joseph died in Jesus's and Mary's loving embrace.

St. Joseph, help me to work hard on the tasks God gives me!

St. Joseph the Worker
May 1

St. Athanasius

May 2

St. Athanasius

c. 296–373 • Egypt

When Athanasius was a young man, the bishop of Alexandria in Egypt recognized in Athanasius someone who would serve the Church. He ordained Athanasius a deacon and made him his personal secretary.

In those times, a man named Arius was spreading a false teaching about Jesus. Arius claimed that Jesus was not equal to the Father and not fully God. Many people began to believe this false teaching (called Arianism because Arius taught it). The Church was troubled and divided. In 325, the Emperor Constantine called together a council of bishops so that they could bring peace back to the Church and explain the truth about Jesus. The bishop of Alexandria went to the council, and he brought with him his secretary Athanasius.

At the council, Athanasius bravely defended the truth that Jesus is fully God. Athanasius shined in the debates—his words were clear and full of energy. All that watched him knew that he would become a strong leader in the Church.

His words convinced the bishops at the council that Arius's teachings were false. And so, the council of bishops declared that Jesus is fully God and equal to the Father. This important council was called the Council of Nicaea, and from it we receive the Nicene Creed that we pray today at Sunday Mass.

Soon after the council ended, the bishop of Alexandria lay on his deathbed. He called Athanasius to him to say goodbye. The rest of the bishops gathered to elect someone to replace the dying bishop. The people surrounded the church in which they were gathered and cried out, "Give us Athanasius!" The bishops knew that Athanasius would defend the Faith, so they agreed to make him the next bishop of Alexandria. Athanasius was only thirty years old.

At first, Athanasius did not want to be bishop. He knew that his life would be full of struggles. Even though the Church had declared that Arianism was wrong, many powerful people still believed it. These people spread lies about Athanasius, and the Emperor Constantine believed those lies and banished Athanasius from Alexandria. When the emperor died, Athanasius returned; but he was exiled from his city five more times because he defended the truth about Jesus. But Athanasius never stopped teaching the truth to the Christians under his care, and he died a holy death.

St. Athanasius, help me never to be afraid to stand up for the truth!

Sts. Philip and James

Biblical Figures

Jesus called Philip to be one of his disciples. He said to Philip, "Follow me," and Philip chose to follow the Lord. Not only that, he brought his friend Nathanael to Jesus, and Nathanael also became one of the Twelve Apostles.

One day, a large crowd of more than five thousand people came to listen to Jesus. Jesus asked Philip, "Where can we buy enough food for them to eat?" Jesus already knew what He was going to do, but Philip did not know what Jesus was thinking. He did know, however, that they did not have enough money to buy food for so large a crowd. He said to Jesus that he could work outside for two hundred days straight and still not earn enough money to buy everyone food.

But then Jesus's disciple Andrew brought a boy to Jesus who had five loaves and two fish, though Andrew knew that so little food could not feed so many people. Jesus told the disciples to have everyone sit down. He then took the loaves, gave thanks to God, and gave pieces of the loaves and the fish to the crowd. The five loaves and the two fish multiplied so that everyone could eat as much as they wanted! There was even enough bread left over to fill twelve wicker baskets. Philip and everyone else were amazed at this great miracle!

It is said that after Jesus's resurrection Philip preached the Good News of Jesus to the Greeks in the city of Hierapolis. There, he was crucified upside down and became a martyr for Jesus.

Two of Jesus's Apostles were named James. This James was a relative of Jesus and just a few years older than Him. Known as a just man, he prayed so much on his knees that they grew as tough and hard as a camel's hooves.

After Jesus died and rose from the dead, James became the bishop of Jerusalem. He cared for the Jewish Christians, baptized them, and taught them about Jesus. He wrote a letter in the New Testament called The Epistle of James, which you can read in the Bible. James, too, was martyred for his witness to Jesus.

Sts. Philip and James, help me to answer Jesus's call!

Sts. Philip and James
May 3

The English Martyrs

May 4

The English Martyrs

1534–1680 • England

The punishment for treason is death. Treason is an act of disloyalty to your country. Queen Elizabeth I declared it treasonous to be Roman Catholic in England. This was the same crime for which the Roman emperors had sent the early Christian martyrs to their deaths. The Roman emperors believed they were gods, and so if Christians did not worship them, they were seen as disloyal to the empire and the empire's religion. Elizabeth did not think she was a god, but she did think she was the leader of the Church of England.

Queen Elizabeth's father, the violent Henry VIII, had broken with the Catholic Church in Rome and started his own church. Elizabeth was his daughter, and she became the leader of that same English church. She believed that if someone did not belong to her church, then that person was disloyal to her kingdom and her kingdom's religion. And so Roman Catholics were sentenced to the cruel and public death of being hanged, drawn, and quartered. But like the Roman martyrs before them, the English Catholics were not afraid of death. They died knowing they had done the right thing, willingly giving up their lives for the true Faith so that they could rejoice with Jesus in heaven.

The most famous English martyrs are St. Thomas More and St. John Fisher, but there are over three hundred English Catholics who died for their Faith. Among the many martyrs, let us remember a few of their names: Bl. Nicholas Horner, a simple tailor who kept Catholic priests hidden and safe; Bl. Robert Bickerdike, a Yorkshireman arrested for the simple and kind act of buying a priest a drink; Bl. William Gibson, a Scottish nobleman arrested for being Catholic; Bl. Robert Nutter, an English Dominican priest who returned to England even though he knew it would be dangerous; Bl. William Carter, a printer who published Catholic books forbidden by the Crown; Bl. Thomas Bullaker, a priest arrested for saying Mass in London; and Bl. Henry Heath, a college librarian in Cambridge who became a Franciscan priest. These brave English martyrs gloriously went to their deaths out of love for Jesus and the Roman Catholic Church.

Martyrs of England, help me to love Jesus and the Catholic Church more than my life!

St. Nunzio Sulprizio

1817–1836 • Italy

Nunzio's childhood was full of sorrows. His father died when he was three years old, and his stepfather either ignored him or treated him badly. Nunzio found comfort at a school run by a local priest. There the priest not only taught Nunzio how to read and write, but he also taught him to love and serve Jesus. When he was only six, Nunzio's next great sorrow came with his mother's death. His grandmother loved him dearly, and so he went to live with her. His days with his grandmother were happy. Together they would laugh, pray, and go to Mass. At Nunzio's school, the priest would take the children to worship God in the Blessed Sacrament. Nunzio longed to receive Jesus, but he was too young. In his town in Italy, children were not allowed to receive First Communion until they were fifteen years old.

Sorrow struck again when Nunzio's grandmother died. Nunzio was not yet nine years old, and he must have felt that all the people he loved in the world had left him. Nunzio's uncle, a blacksmith, took him in, but his uncle was a hard man. He took Nunzio out of school to work in his smithy. If he thought Nunzio did not work hard enough he starved him and sometimes even beat him. He forced him to run distant errands carrying loads that were too heavy for a nine-year-old boy. But Nunzio remembered Jesus's sufferings and all of the terrible beatings He endured. He offered his own sufferings to Jesus.

One winter day, when he was fourteen years old, Nunzio injured his leg as he was running errands for his uncle. It quickly became infected and was so painful that he could barely stand. His uncle told him that if he could not run errands then he would work the bellows. The infection grew worse and worse. Nunzio would dip his leg in a nearby stream, and the cool, running water cleansed and soothed his hot, infected leg. He would pray his Rosary by the stream, offering his pain to Jesus on the Cross.

Finally, Nunzio was sent to the hospital. The priest there asked him what he wanted most of all. He replied that it was to make his First Communion, which the priest gave to him. For the next few years, Nunzio helped take care of patients in the hospital. He comforted them and told them to offer their pain to Jesus. Nunzio contracted bone cancer in his leg and died at the age of nineteen, offering all of his sufferings to Jesus to the end. St. Nunzio, help me offer my sufferings to Jesus on the Cross!

St. Nunzio Sulprizio

May 5

St. Benedicta

May 6

St. Benedicta

d. 550 • Italy

St. Benedicta was a nun in Rome and a dear friend of Galla, a holy widow and the founder of her convent (who would also one day be a saint).

Near the end of her life, Galla suffered from cancer. She had two candles lit at the foot of her bed because she loved the light. One night, as she lay in her bed, worn down by her sufferings, the Apostle Peter appeared between the two candlesticks and gazed at the suffering nun with kindness.

Without fear, Galla asked the Apostle Peter, "What is it, my lord? Have my sins been forgiven?"

The Apostle Peter gave a gentle nod of his head and said, "They are forgiven. Come."

Galla felt a surge of joy. If her sins were forgiven then that meant she would be in heaven with Jesus soon. Then she thought of her dear friend, Sr. Benedicta. She wanted Sr. Benedicta also to share in her happiness in heaven. So Galla dared to ask the Apostle Peter a favor, "I beg you to let Sr. Benedicta come with me."

St. Peter replied, "Sr. Benedicta will follow you in thirty days." Then he vanished.

Now Galla could rest in peace knowing that her dear friend would also go to heaven. Galla told her mother superior exactly what happened and of St. Peter's promise. Three days later, Galla passed away, with her sufferings ended as she rejoiced eternally in heaven. Then, just as St. Peter had promised, Sr. Benedicta also died in Christ exactly thirty days later. The nuns were all amazed that Sr. Benedicta had followed Galla to heaven, exactly as St. Peter had promised she would. It was a miracle! Now they knew that Sr. Benedicta, too, was a saint.

The nuns kept this miracle fresh in their memory and told it word for word to the young nuns who entered the convent. The young nuns told the miracle to Pope St. Gregory the Great, who wrote the miracle down in a book.

Because of the love St. Galla bore her friend Sr. Benedicta, we know that Sr. Benedicta is also a saint in heaven!

St. Benedicta, help me to be a good friend!

St. Flavia Domitilla

First Century • Italy

The sea breeze caught the tendrils of her braided hair as Flavia Domitilla gazed over the water and thought of the life she once had. She was the niece of the Roman emperor Domitian, and her husband, Flavius Clemens, had been the emperor's cousin. Her two sons were the emperor's heirs. As wealthy and important Romans, Domitilla and Clemens had thought their life happy, but, still, Domitilla had known that something was missing.

Both Domitilla and Clemens had heard about a new religion called Christianity. The Roman empire persecuted Christians because they did not worship the emperor as a god. But one day, Domitilla and Clemens met with the Christians. They learned all about a Jewish man named Jesus. He was the Son of God and had died and risen from the dead to save all the world from its sins. These words about Jesus burned in Domitilla's heart. She knew that she had found the *something* that had been missing. Jesus was the only one who could give true happiness and teach her how to live. Both Domitilla and Clemens believed and were baptized.

Domitilla knew that their life would now change. Clemens was a consul, an important Roman official, and his job required him to do things that were against his new Faith. He stopped doing those things, and his fellow Romans thought he was a terribly lazy and irresponsible man. But some knew he behaved this way because he was a Christian. Domitilla admired her husband for doing what was right and also did her part to help her new brothers and sisters in Christ. Domitilla owned a large estate, and she turned her land into a secret burial ground for Christians. Domitilla wondered, however, what her uncle Domitian would do now that she and her husband had become Christians.

She did not need to wait long to find out. One fateful day, soldiers came to their door and arrested Domitilla and Clemens for being Christians. The Emperor Domitian ordered Clemens to be put to death, even though Clemens was his cousin; Domitilla he banished. Clemens and Domitilla parted with sorrow, but they knew this sorrow would someday turn to happiness. Before, this life was all they would have had together; but now they would spend eternity together in God's joy.

Standing on the shore of the island of her banishment, Domitilla's lips formed a quiet prayer. She prayed for the souls of her husband, her family, and all persecuted Christians. She would remain faithful to Christ until the day of her death. St. Flavia Domitilla, help me remain faithful to Jesus!

Pope St. Boniface IV

May 8

Pope St. Boniface IV

d. 615 • Italy

St. Boniface IV turned a temple for ancient gods into a church that instead honored Mary and the martyrs of Rome.

Boniface IV was the sixty-seventh bishop of Rome and pope—the head of the Catholic Church and Jesus's representative on earth. Once, the great city of Rome was the capital of the pagan Roman Empire. Now the city of Rome had accepted the truth of Christ into her heart, and all of her empty pagan temples were falling to ruin.

The most magnificent of these temples was the Pantheon, with its soaring domed ceiling. Boniface IV did not want to see such a beautiful building fall to ruin. So he had an idea: why not turn the building into a Catholic Church? Then such a glorious work by human hands could give praise to the true God, the God who created us and loves us!

But first, Boniface IV had to cast out demons from the temple. The temple had been built to worship false gods, and these false gods were actually demons ready to tear souls away from God.

Boniface IV threw out everything in the Pantheon that belonged to the false pagan religion. He blessed the temple, and all of the false demons lurking inside were banished away. Boniface renamed the Pantheon the Church of the Virgin Mary and All the Martyrs. He brought the bones of the Roman martyrs buried in the catacombs and placed them in a basin of red stone under the high altar. Now people could come to this beautiful church and worship Jesus in the company of Mary and the saints.

Boniface IV believed that God's churches should be magnificent and sacred places of worship to honor God. He himself, however, lived in holy simplicity. Even though he was pope, Boniface lived in humble poverty and prayer, and he gave everything that was best to God. He led the Church of Christ with holiness and wisdom until he died a holy death.

St. Boniface IV, help me to give everything that is best to God!

Bl. Maria del Carmen of the Child Jesus

1834–1899 • Spain

When Maria was a young woman of twenty-two, she married Joaquín Muñoz del Caño. But her marriage was not a happy one. Joaquín was a sinful and unfaithful man. But she chose to be true to her vows as a wife and offered her suffering for the conversion of her husband.

For twenty years, Maria prayed and prayed that her husband would come to love Jesus. God heard Maria's prayers and rewarded her patience and the fact that she never stopped praying. God's grace transformed Joaquín's soul. He turned to God and begged for Maria's forgiveness. Maria's husband lived as a faithful Christian until his death four years later.

Maria and Joaquín did not have children, and now Maria was a widow. Her heart went out to her neighbors' children. She saw in their faces the face of the Child Jesus. But she was sad because many of these children were poor and did not go to school. Most of all, she was sad because these children were not taught how much Jesus loved them.

Out of love for these children, Maria opened a small school in her home. There, children would be taken care of and given the gifts of both education and Faith. Maria del Carmen changed these children's lives with her love of Jesus.

Some women came to help Maria run her school, and together they went to live in a convent. This small community of women was the start of a new religious congregation that would grow into the Franciscan Sisters of the Sacred Heart. Maria became Mother Carmen and opened eleven houses dedicated to the education of children and adults, as well as a resting place for the sick. The sisters' most important work was to teach others to "know and love Christ."

Mother Carmen served her new order until she died a holy death. Bl. Maria del Carmen, help me to bring others to Jesus!

Bl. Maria del Carmen of the Child Jesus

May 9

St. Damien of Molokai
May 10

St. Damien of Molokai

1840–1889 • Belgium

More than anything, Damien wanted to be a missionary. His older brother had joined the order of the Congregation of the Sacred Hearts of Jesus and Mary, and Damien followed in his brother's footsteps and also joined the order. He continued to pray hard to be a missionary, but it was his older brother who was selected to go on a mission to Hawaii. It seemed as if Br. Damien's prayer would not be answered. Then, right before he left, Br. Damien's older brother fell sick, and Br. Damien asked to go in his place. Permission was granted, and Br. Damien set sail for Hawaii.

Soon after Br. Damien landed in Honolulu, he was ordained a priest. There was an outbreak of leprosy in the kingdom of Hawaii. At that time, leprosy was an incurable disease that damaged the skin and the nerves. The Hawaiians were so afraid of leprosy that they quarantined the worst cases in a colony on the island of Molokai. Not even doctors and nurses went to Molokai because they were afraid of catching leprosy, too. Fr. Damien saw that that the lepers of Molokai needed a priest to share the love of Jesus with them and give them hope. And so he volunteered to go to Molokai.

Fr. Damien was tough, brave, and determined. He took care of the lepers' bodies as well as their souls. He dressed their sores; constructed coffins and dug graves; and built them a school, a church, and many homes. Fr. Damien said Mass for the lepers and heard their confessions. He told them that their lives were precious in the eyes of God. He spent many years comforting them and teaching them the Faith.

One evening, Fr. Damien was preparing his bath, and the water was so hot that it was scalding. He accidentally stepped into the hot water—but his foot felt nothing. Fr. Damien knew that he had caught leprosy. The nerves in his foot were so damaged by the illness that he felt no pain from the burning water. But leprosy did not stop Fr. Damien. His illness only made him work harder because now he knew he had less time to take care of his beloved lepers. He dragged his bandaged foot behind him as he traveled from sick bed to sick bed. Eventually, a nun traveled to Molokai to take care of him as he lay dying. The nun's name was Sister Marianne Cope. She, too, was a missionary and would also become a saint. She promised to carry on Fr. Damien's work and watched over him until he died a holy death. St. Damien of Molokai, help me never to be afraid to take care of others!

St. Matthêu Lê Văn Gam

1813–1847 • Vietnam

Matthêu's parents raised their son as a Catholic in Vietnam. To live their Faith, Matthêu and his family had to be very brave. At that time, it was dangerous to be a Catholic in Vietnam, since the emperor did not like Catholics.

As a young man, Matthêu wished to be a priest and was a seminarian (someone who is training to be a priest) for a short time. But he was also his parents' eldest son, and so he had to return home and take on the responsibilities of his house.

Matthêu married and had four children. He and his wife brought up their children in a Catholic home. In 1846, the Emperor Thiêu Tri began arresting and punishing Vietnamese Catholics. The seminarians in Vietnam were especially in danger because the emperor wished to put to death any Vietnamese priests. Matthêu knew he had to help the seminarians escape from Vietnam.

Matthêu was a skilled sailor. He sneaked a group of seminarians onto a ship and sailed across the seas to Malaysia, where the seminarians could not be captured by Vietnamese officials. The authorities were suspicious of Matthêu's trips back and forth over the sea. One July, they caught him as he once again tried to help seminarians escape aboard his ship.

For ten months, Matthêu was kept in prison and tortured. But Matthêu refused to give up his Faith. Finally, the Vietnamese officials tried to force Matthêu to reject Jesus by stepping on a cross. But Matthêu would not step on the cross. Nothing could convince him to deny Jesus, whom he loved more than his life. Matthêu was put to death and became a glorious martyr for the Faith.

St. Matthêu Lê Văn Gam, help me to serve those who are being persecuted for Jesus!

St. Matthêu Lê Văn Gam

May 11

St. Pancras
May 12

St. Pancras

c. 289–c. 303 • Phrygia (modern-day Turkey)

St. Pancras was a bold young martyr for the Faith, though not much is known about his life. It is said that he died for Jesus when he was only fourteen years old!

Legends say that Pancras was born in Phrygia and that both of his parents were Roman citizens. His mother died giving birth to him, and his father died when Pancras was only eight years old. After his father's death, Pancras went to live with his uncle Dionysius.

Sometime later, both uncle and nephew moved to Rome, the capital of the empire. There, Dionysius and Pancras met Christians living in hiding because of the emperor's persecution. The Good News about Jesus touched their hearts. Both Pancras and his uncle became baptized Christians.

At that time, the Emperor Diocletian was brutally persecuting the Christians. He hated them because they would not worship him as emperor and a god. They would worship only the one, true God.

Even though he was only fourteen years old, Pancras was unafraid of death. When the Roman soldiers found out that he was a Christian, they took pity on him because he was young, and they tried to convince him to sacrifice to the Roman gods.

But Pancras refused: he would never deny Jesus. Pancras knew that if he died Jesus would bring him to heaven. Angry that Pancras would not give up, the Roman soldiers killed him with their swords. The Christians stole away his body and buried him in the catacombs. St. Pancras's brave death inspired many Christians. A great church was built over his tomb almost two hundred years later.

St. Pancras, help me to be brave and never to deny Jesus!

Our Lady of Fatima

1916 • Portugal

Three shepherd children were watching their flock in the hills near Fatima, Portugal. The children's names were Lucia, Francisco, and Jacinta. An angel appeared to them, calling himself the Angel of Peace. He appeared to them three times, and, on the last visit, he gave them Holy Communion.

Almost eight months later, the three children were on a slope called the Cova da Iria with their flock. They were praying the Rosary when a flash in the clear sky startled them. Another flash of light revealed a beautiful lady, shining brilliant as the sun. It was Our Lady, and her presence filled the children with joy. She asked the three children if they were willing to suffer to make up for the sins that offend God and for the conversion of sinners. The three children said "yes." Before she left, Our Lady promised that she would appear to them on the thirteenth day of the month for the next six months.

Every month, crowds followed the children to the Cova. The people could not see Our Lady, but some saw a strange light, others a gray cloud. Our Lady told the children to pray for sinners and showed them a frightening vision of hell, where poor sinners go—many because no one prayed for them. Our Lady also promised the children that, in October, she would perform a great miracle.

When October came, thousands of pilgrims visited the Cova to see Our Lady's promised miracle, even though it had been raining and water soaked the ground. Our Lady appeared and told the children that she was Our Lady of the Rosary and that they should pray the Rosary every day. Then she lifted her hand up to the dark sky. Suddenly, the sun burst through the clouds, spinning like a silver disk. The crowd gasped as the sun twirled and danced. Then it seemed to fall from the sky, and the people shrieked and fell to their knees. They thought the world was ending. But the sun returned to the sky, and the people found that the soaked earth was now completely dry.

While all this was happening, the children saw a different vision: Jesus and Joseph appeared, as well as Our Lady of Sorrows and Our Lady of Mount Carmel. In the vision, Jesus blessed the whole world with the Sign of the Cross.

Today, Fatima is a famous pilgrimage site that spreads Mary's message to pray the Rosary for the conversion of sinners and peace in the world. Our Lady of Fatima, bring peace to the world!

Our Lady of Fatima
May 13

St. Matthias

May 14

© Sophia Institute Press

St. Matthias

Biblical Figure

Matthias had been a follower of Jesus ever since He started preaching. Matthias was there at Jesus's baptism in the river Jordan. He followed Jesus during the three years when He preached in Galilee about God's Kingdom. He marveled over Jesus's great miracles.

Then Judas, one of the Twelve Apostles, betrayed Jesus. Judas was a thief. He secretly stole from the Apostles' moneybag. The Pharisees paid Judas thirty pieces of silver to betray Jesus. Judas took the silver and led soldiers to where Jesus was praying in the Garden of Gethsemane, and there they arrested Jesus. When Matthias heard the news that the Romans had crucified Jesus, his heart broke. But when he heard the news that Jesus had risen from the dead, his heart rejoiced!

After Jesus ascended into heaven, Peter—the leader of the Twelve Apostles—called together 120 of Jesus's followers. Peter declared that one of Jesus's disciples, someone who had followed Jesus since He started preaching, should take Judas's place as one of the Twelve. The 120 men thought, prayed, and recommended two men: a man called Barsabbas and Matthias. They then prayed, "You, Lord, who know the hearts of all, show which one of these two You have chosen."

After the prayer, they cast lots (which are sticks or stones with markings) to select the person to replace Judas. They did this so that God would be the one to choose between Barsabbas and Matthias. The lot with the right mark fell to Matthias, and the men welcomed him among the Apostles. They knew he was a good man and would preach about Jesus to the ends of the earth!

And that is what Matthias did. He baptized believers in the name of the Father, and of the Son, and of the Holy Spirit. He preached the Good News of Jesus's resurrection. It is said that he was martyred for his Faith.

St. Matthias, help me to be ready to serve God whenever He calls me!

St. Isidore

c. 1070–1130 • Spain

Isidore was a farmer who worked on the land of a wealthy man named Juan de Vargas. Isidore knew that his farm work was important. He had a deep love for the land and for animals. But he knew that God was even more important than his work. After all, God created the earth and all the animals that live on it! Isidore would often pause in the middle of his work to pray. He also would go to Mass in the mornings.

Because Isidore went to Mass each morning, he was late to his work in the fields. The other farm laborers became angry at him. They thought he was being lazy and not doing his fair share of work. The farmers reported to their master that Isidore was always late. Juan de Vargas decided to see for himself if what the farmers said about Isidore was true.

Early one morning the master went out to the fields. He watched as Isidore left behind his ox and plow to go to Mass. But what he saw next struck him with amazement.

An angel took up Isidore's plow and started doing the farmer's work for him! Even though Isidore went to Mass, the farm work was still miraculously getting done.

Juan de Vargas realized that Isidore was a holy man, and he allowed Isidore to go to Mass and pray as often as he liked. He knew that his farm would be blessed by God if Isidore worked on it.

Isidore was married to a holy woman, Maria Toribia. Together, they served God. Even though they were poor, Isidore would bring beggars and others even poorer than they were to their home for dinner. Maria would feed everyone stew.

One day, Isidore brought so many people home that Maria ran out of stew. When she told her husband, he asked her to check her pot again. She checked the pot, and more stew had appeared! She was able to feed everyone enough so that they all had their fill.

Even though the couple was so blessed by God, they also had their suffering. Their only child tragically died. Both Isidore and Maria decided that they must offer up their sorrow to God and dedicate their lives to Him with prayer and serving others.

Isidore died a holy death after a life filled with prayer and work. St. Isidore, please help me to dedicate my work to God!

St. Isidore
May 15

St. Brendan the Navigator
May 16

St. Brendan the Navigator

484–577 • Ireland

Brendan was a monk and a brave traveler. All throughout Ireland, he founded monastery after monastery so that the Faith could flourish in Ireland. Then he set sail for Britain and navigated the seas to the cliffs of the Welsh shore. For three years, Brendan founded more monasteries in Britain before returning home to Ireland. From his many travels sprang the legend of his great sea voyage to find the Blessed Land of Paradise.

When Brendan and his monks were at prayer, a man stumbled upon them and, with great tears and sighs, told them that he had been to the Blessed Land of Paradise. Brendan and his monks were amazed and determined that they, too, would go on a great voyage to find this blessed land. Brendan and fourteen of his monks set sail, and they had many adventures as they journeyed from island to island.

One night, after many years of wandering, Brendan saw the scales of a great sea monster gleaming in the dark ocean. Rather than being frightened, Brendan sailed right up to the sea monster and landed his boat on top of its back! Bravely, Brendan stepped onto the sea monster's silver scales, and his monks followed his lead. All through the night, they sang hymns to God under the stars on the back of the sea monster. Together in the morning, they said Mass. When Mass was finished, the silver scales shivered beneath them, and the monster began to move. The monks were startled and fearful, but Brendan called out to them not to be alarmed, as they would ride the sea monster to the nearest island.

After the monster left them on the island shore, they filled their boat with many supplies because they knew they would soon reach the Blessed Land of Paradise. When they did arrive there, they saw a land full of the richest fruits and green trees and grass, and they heard running streams and birdsong. An angel appeared and told them to collect the rich fruits and the precious stones sparkling on the shore. They must now return to Ireland because they had been wandering for seven years.

After his return, Brendan founded the great Monastery of Clonfert. Because of Brendan's fame as a traveler by land and by sea, many monks and students also traveled far and wide to study there, and the monastery became famous for holiness and learning. When Brendan died a holy death he was buried at the Monastery of Clonfert. St. Brendan, help me seek God in my journey through life!

St. Giulia Salzano

1846–1929 • Italy

A warm smile bloomed across Mother Giulia's wrinkled face. Her young students had worked so hard at memorizing their catechism, and she was proud of them. One of her students fumbled over the words, and Mother Giulia patiently explained not only what the catechism was saying, but why it was important.

Teaching the catechism was Mother Giulia's life's work. She had once said, "While I have any life left in me, I will continue to teach the catechism. And then, I assure you, I would be very happy to die teaching the catechism."

This was because she knew that learning the catechism was important. The catechism is a book that explains what Catholics believe. When we learn our catechism, we learn what Jesus taught.

Mother Giulia did not only teach the catechism to her students, she also explained how Jesus's Sacred Heart was on fire for love of them; everything that we do should be for the glory of Jesus's Sacred Heart. That was why, when she founded her order of sisters to teach the catechism, she called them the Congregation of the Catechetical Sisters of the Sacred Heart.

Mother Giulia's life had not been easy. Her father died when she was four, and she had been raised in an orphanage. The sisters who educated her in the orphanage had been kind. When Giulia left the orphanage, she knew that she wanted to teach children the catechism. Later, she founded an order of nuns for this very purpose. Her love for the Blessed Virgin Mary and the Sacred Heart guided her on her path.

She taught the catechism to children until the end of her life, just as she had wanted. Right before she died at the age of eighty-three, she reviewed the catechism for about one hundred children before they received their First Holy Communion.

St. Giulia Salzano, help me learn about my Faith.

St. Giulia Salzano
May 17

Pope St. John I
May 18

Pope St. John I

d. 526 • Italy

Pope St. John was the fifty-third pope. While he was pope, King Theodoric ruled over Italy. King Theodoric was an Arian, which meant that he did not believe the truths of the Catholic Faith. His rival was Emperor Justin, who was a faithful Catholic and the ruler of the great Byzantine Empire.

The Emperor Justin passed a law that took away the churches and positions of the Arian bishops. This made King Theodoric furious. He threatened the lives of the Catholics in his kingdom if the emperor did not change his law. Because of the king's violent threats, Pope John I agreed to Theodoric's order to travel to Constantinople (the capital of the Byzantine Empire) to try to change Emperor Justin's mind. The pope knew that, if he did not go, King Theodoric would persecute the Catholics in Italy and throughout the rest of his kingdom.

When Pope John I landed on Constantinople's shore, Emperor Justin and the crowds of Constantinople marched twelve miles to meet him. They carried crosses and candles, and Emperor Justin was dressed in his finest robes. The emperor bowed deeply to Pope John I, doing him great honor. The crowds of Constantinople cheered. Later, the emperor held a magnificent ceremony where the pope re-crowned him as emperor. This showed Emperor Justin's alliance with the Roman Catholic Church.

Pope John I discussed with the emperor the things that King Theodoric had asked. Though he did not wish to have the law overturned, he did convince Emperor Justin to treat the Arians in his kingdom kindly.

The pope sailed back to Italy to report back to King Theodoric. But when he arrived, he received a very different welcome from King Theodoric than he had received from Emperor Justin.

Instead of dressing himself in his best robes, King Theodoric dressed the pope in chains. Instead of throwing a joyous celebration, the king threw the pope into prison. While in prison, Pope John I was mistreated, and he soon died as a holy martyr.

Pope St. John I, help me to endure what I suffer in Jesus's name!

Sts. Dunstan, Æthelwold, and Oswald

Tenth Century • Britain

Dunstan was born to a wealthy family and decided to become a monk. He built a little room only five feet long and two feet deep. There he prayed and played the harp. Metalworking was his hobby, and he would craft beautiful bells and chalices. Legend says that one day, while Dunstan was hard at work with his hammer and anvil, the devil snuck into his cell and tried to tempt him. In response, Dunstan grabbed the devil's cloven foot and nailed a horseshoe onto it as the devil howled in pain!

Dunstan became a wise adviser to the king and was named archbishop of Canterbury. Under his rule, many reforms were passed in the Church.

Archbishop Dunstan had two students who supported him in his reforms, Bishop Æthelwold of Winchester and Archbishop Oswald of York.

Bishop Æthelwold cast out of the churches clergy who were leading sinful lives and replaced them with virtuous monks. He believed that priests should strive to lead holy lives. Because of his reforms, he was called the "Father of Monks."

Archbishop Oswald was a friend and supporter of Dunstan. He founded churches and also encouraged monks to lead holy lives. The poor had a special place in his heart. Every day during Lent, he would wash the feet of the poor. It was as he was performing this very act of service one day that he died.

Sts. Dunstan, Æthelwold, and Oswald, help me to lead a holy life!

St. Bernardine of Siena

1380–1444 • Italy

When he was only six, Bernardine's parents died. His aunt took him into her home and taught him his prayers and all about God. Bernardine loved God so much that he became a Franciscan priest. Soon after, the missionary preacher Vincent Ferrer came to Italy. Vincent was famous for his miracles and was so holy that he, too, became a saint. When Bernardine went to hear him preach, Vincent prophesied that someone listening at that moment would someday take his place and preach to the people of Italy. No one, not even Bernardine, knew that Vincent was talking about him.

Years later, when Bernardine did start preaching, he became one of the greatest preachers of his time. His style was different from the other preachers of his time. Usually, sermons were prepared in advance and simply read aloud in church. But Bernardine traveled from city to city by foot, preaching to people where they worked and shopped; and he spoke about how they could make their everyday lives holy. His words drew such large crowds that the townspeople would erect a pulpit for him to speak from in the middle of the marketplace.

At that time, Italy was corrupt, violent, and full of distractions. Bernardine preached peace and repentance. To spread his message, he created a banner with the letters IHS in the middle of a blazing sun. IHS are the first three letters of Jesus's name in Greek. Soon, everyone in Italy was buying holy cards with the image of Jesus's name on the blazing sun. Bernardine's enemies went to the pope and accused Bernardine of spreading false teachings. The pope ordered him to stop preaching until he had been investigated. Bernardine humbly obeyed and handed over to the pope written copies of his sermons. It quickly became obvious that Bernardine's enemies had lied. The pope declared Bernardine innocent and even invited him to preach in Rome!

Three times the pope asked Bernardine to become a bishop, but Bernardine refused because he knew he could win more souls for Christ by preaching. After forty years of preaching, he died on the eve of the Feast of the Ascension. Because he refused to be made bishop three times, Bernardine is often portrayed in art with three bishop's miters (a tall hat) at his feet. St. Bernardine, help me to honor Jesus's holy name!

St. Cristóbal Magallanes and Companions

1869–1927 • Mexico

Less than a hundred years ago, the Mexican government persecuted Catholics. It was a crime to be baptized and for priests to celebrate Mass. The government banished many priests, but some bravely refused to leave their parishes, risking their lives to serve the Mexican people. One of these brave priests was Fr. Cristóbal Magallanes.

The Mexican government had outlawed the training of priests. Fr. Cristóbal knew that priests were necessary to help the people live Catholic lives. Only a priest can say Mass, absolve sins in the Sacrament of Confession, and change bread and wine into Jesus's Body and Blood. Fr. Cristóbal opened a seminary and trained men for the priesthood. Twice the government shut down his seminary, and twice he reopened it. After it was closed for the third time, he went from home to home to train priests in secret.

The Mexican people loved their Catholic Faith, and they loved their priests. Some started a rebellion. They were so angry at the government for persecuting Catholics that they were willing to kill and be killed. But Fr. Cristóbal knew that bloodshed was not what Jesus would have wanted. He preached against violence to his people and to his priests-in-training.

One day, on his way to say Mass, soldiers arrested Fr. Cristóbal. The government had made up charges against him, claiming that he supported the rebellion and preached violence. They didn't care that Fr. Cristóbal was a peacemaker. They just wanted an excuse to get rid of as many priests as they could. And so they sentenced Fr. Cristóbal to death without a trial.

Fr. Cristóbal was flung into prison. He patiently waited four days for his execution. He even gave away his few belongings to his jailers. Just like Jesus, he forgave his executioners, declaring, "I am innocent, and I die innocent. I forgive with all my heart those responsible for my death, and I ask God that the shedding of my blood serve the peace of our divided Mexico." He was martyred by a firing squad. Twenty-one other brave priests and three lay companions were also killed by the Mexican government and became martyrs for Jesus. St. Cristóbal and Companions, help me to defend my Faith with peace!

St. Cristóbal Magallanes and Companions

May 21

St. Rita of Cascia
May 22

St. Rita of Cascia

1386–1456 • Italy

Rita lived in a tumultuous time in Italy. People from rival families would kill each other in cold blood. Even though Rita wanted to be a nun, her parents arranged her marriage into one of these fighting families. Rita's new husband, Paolo, had a short temper and was often unkind to Rita. But the more she prayed for him, the more Paolo changed. He grew kind and took his Faith seriously. He even gave up fighting against a rival family. But even though Paolo tried to live peacefully, those in the rival family did not. Paolo was cruelly murdered, and Rita became a widow.

Sorrowing over her loss, Rita prayed for her husband's soul. Now more than ever, she believed in peace instead of violence. She did not want her sons' lives to be ruined by murder and revenge. But the boys' uncle had other ideas. He took Rita's sons away from her and raised them with thoughts of revenge. When, in a few years' time, both of her sons died of illness, Rita sorrowed over their loss. Her only consolation was that they had escaped lives of violence and murder.

Now that her family was gone, Rita was free to become a nun. But the convent refused to accept her. Even though she had forgiven the rival family that had murdered her husband, that did not mean the fight was over. The nuns were afraid the rival family would harm them if Rita entered their convent. They told Rita that she could become a nun on one condition: she must make peace between her family and the family that had killed her husband.

After much prayer, Rita told her husband's family that they must let God's peace enter their hearts. She pointed to Jesus on the Cross and reminded them that Jesus had forgiven His enemies. Her words touched their souls, and they forgave their enemies for Paolo's murder. The two rival families chose to live in peace.

Now Rita was free to enter the convent. She would pray before her favorite image of the suffering Christ. Because of the sorrows in her own life, she felt deeply in her heart all of Jesus's sorrows. Her heart wept over the crown of thorns pressed into Jesus's head and the cruel nails in Jesus's hands and feet. One day, she felt so sorry for Jesus's wounds that she begged Him to let her share a little in His suffering. A small, open wound, which seemed to have been made by a thorn, miraculously appeared on her forehead. Jesus had shared with her the pain of His crown of thorns, just as she had begged of Him. Rita bore the open wound upon her forehead until she died a holy death.

St. Rita of Cascia, help me to offer my sufferings to Jesus!

St. Euphrosyne

1110–1173 • Belorussia (modern-day Belarus)

Ever since she was a little girl, Euphrosyne loved to read and pray. Her father was a prince in Belarus, so Euphrosyne received many marriage proposals. But Euphrosyne did not want to marry. She wanted to serve God in a convent. So she turned down each and every marriage proposal and ran away to join her aunt's convent, the name of which was Holy Wisdom.

At the time when Euphrosyne lived, books had to be carefully written out by hand because there was no such thing as a printing press. Euphrosyne loved books, and so she would spend much of her time copying out holy texts with quill and ink. If she sold any of her books, she would give the money to the poor.

After many years, the bishop asked Euphrosyne to found her own convent. Euphrosyne set out, taking only her holy books, and founded the convent of the Holy Savior. She taught her nuns how to read and write and sing holy hymns.

At her request, the patriarch (head bishop) of Constantinople sent her a copy of a miraculous image of Mary and Jesus. Euphrosyne would meditate and pray before the holy image of the Mother of God holding her son close to her heart.

Near the end of her life, Euphrosyne went on pilgrimage to the Holy Land to visit all the important sites where Jesus once had lived. She died a holy death in Jerusalem at the monastery of Mary, the Mother of God.

St. Euphrosyne, help me to grow close to Jesus and His Mother Mary!

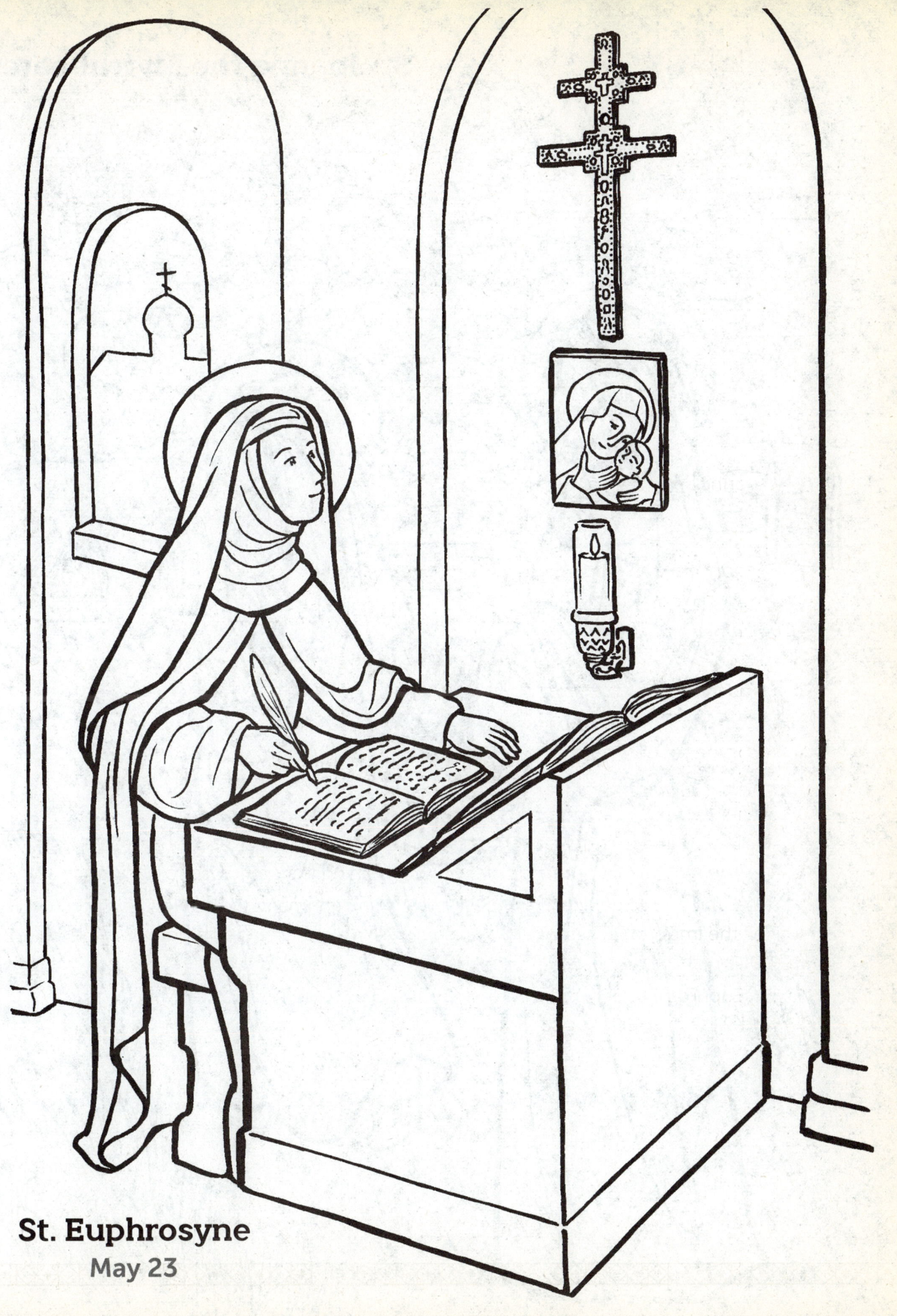

St. Euphrosyne
May 23

© Sophia Institute Press

St. Joanna the Myrrhbearer
May 24

St. Joanna the Myrrhbearer

Biblical Figure

As Jesus traveled through Galilee and preached the Good News of the Kingdom of God, there were women who followed Him. One of these women was Joanna, the wife of Chuza, King Herod's steward. Joanna would give of her money, time, and food to make sure that Jesus and His disciples were properly taken care of. When she heard that Jesus was arrested, she trembled in fear for Him. She wept when she saw Him carry His heavy wooden Cross. Her heart broke as, from a distance, she watched Him breathe His last upon the Cross.

After Jesus's death, Joseph of Arimathea, one of Jesus's disciples, placed His body in a new tomb. Joanna and the other women followed Joseph and marked the tomb where Jesus was laid. They returned to the city and prepared myrrh, perfumed oils, and other spices so as to honor and anoint Jesus's body. At daybreak on the first day of the week, Joanna, Mary Magdalene, and Mary, the mother of James, gathered the oils and spices. Joanna's heart cried as the spiced scent of myrrh floated up to her. Myrrh was a holy oil used in worship at the Temple. This was the oil she would use to anoint Jesus's bruised body.

The women reached the tomb and found, to their surprise, that the heavy stone at its entrance was rolled away. Warily, they went inside, but they could not find Jesus's body. Joanna and the two Marys stared at each other, wide-eyed in fear. Had someone stolen Jesus's body?

Without warning, two men in dazzling white garments flashed into their presence. These men's appearances were so strange and wondrous that the women knew they were no earthly creatures, and they bowed to the ground with fear. The men spoke in thunderous voices, "Why do you seek the living one among the dead?" Then the two angels explained that Jesus had risen from the dead as He had promised (Luke 24:5–7).

Joanna's heart filled with joy. The Master whom she loved had defeated death and was risen! Joanna and the two Marys rushed to the eleven Apostles and told them the joyous news that Jesus was alive. At first, the Apostles did not believe the women, but soon Jesus would appear to them, too, and so they believed. Joanna and the two Marys were the first messengers of Jesus's Resurrection. St. Joanna, help me rejoice in Jesus's resurrection!

St. Bede

c. 673–735 • England

Bede entered a monastery when he was a boy. When a terrible plague broke out in the monastery, many monks died, and many became too weak to sing their prayers. Only two monks were strong enough to chant their prayers in a clear and low song. One of these was the fourteen-year-old Bede.

Bede lived a quiet life of study and prayer. We would not know anything about him if he had not written so many important books. Bede knew that God had given him the talent of writing. And so he used his talent as best as he could for the glory of God.

Bede's most famous book is about the Catholic Faith in England. Stories about English saints and heroes, kings and queens, leapt from his pen to the page. He described how St. Augustine of Canterbury braved the ocean to bring the Faith to the English shore, and the mighty battle in which St. Oswald defeated a pagan tyrant.

All of his writings showed his deep love of God, and he wrote up until the day he died. His last book was a translation of the Gospel of John. On the day of his death, his helper Wilbert, told him, "There is still one sentence, dear master, which is not written down." Bede dictated to Wilbert the last line, and the boy wrote it down. Wilbert declared that now the book was finished. Bede agreed with him and said, "Thou hast spoken truth. It is finished." Bede did not only mean that the book was finished, but also his life. He asked Wilbert to help him lie down, and Bede sang in a low, clear voice his favorite prayer: "Glory be to the Father and to the Son and to the Holy Ghost." Then he peacefully gave his soul to God.

St. Bede, help me to use my talents for God's glory!

St. Bede

May 25

St. Philip Neri
May 26

St. Philip Neri

1515–1595 • Italy

Philip was a funny, cheerful boy, and his family nicknamed him "Good Little Phil." His uncle ran a successful business in Florence, and, when Philip was a young man, he worked for his uncle. His family hoped that one day he would take over this family business. But God had other plans for Philip. One day at prayer, Philip had such a deep mystical encounter with God that his heart was filled with joy and love. He had to share his joyful love of God with others!

Philip moved to Rome. Rome is where the pope lives; it is the heart of the Church. But the people in Rome were taking their Faith for granted. Both the priests and the people had stopped trying to live holy lives. Philip wanted to rekindle the Church's heart with the same fire of love that filled his own. He would wander the streets of Rome and start conversations with strangers. Everyone liked talking to him because of his good cheer. During conversations he always asked the same question: "Well, brothers, when shall we begin to do good?" And then he would take that person to a hospital to serve the sick, or inside a church to pray. He made it possible for people to start serving God right away.

One Pentecost Eve, a globe of fire appeared before Philip's eyes. The blaze entered his mouth, and so great a love for God overwhelmed him that it was more than he could endure. He cried out to God, "Enough, enough, Lord, I can bear no more." After he recovered, he felt his chest. There he found a swelling right over his heart, almost as if his heart had grown larger out of love for Jesus.

Soon after this experience, Philip became a priest and founded the congregation of Oratorians. He kept his cheerfulness and sense of humor even when hearing confessions. For a proud man's penance, Philip made him carry Philip's own fat old dog in his arms through the city streets. This was to teach the man humility. Philip also laughed at himself. He would wear his cloak inside out, or he would intentionally mispronounce Latin words to keep others from admiring him too much.

The people of Rome grew to love their cheerful priest. His joyful love for God renewed their love for God, too. Philip died a holy death at eighty years of age after a full day of hearing confessions. His congregation of Oratorians continue his work to this day with a joyful spirit. St. Philip Neri, enflame my heart with love for God!

St. Augustine of Canterbury

d. 604 • Italy

Far from Rome, in England, was a people ready to receive the gift of faith. Ancient Romans once lived in England. They built wide roads, great cities, and Christian churches. But the Romans had left long ago, and their cities and churches were now ghostly ruins, and ancient Christianity in England nothing more than the whisper of a memory.

Pope Gregory the Great, in Rome, knew that it was time for Christianity to live in England once again. Æthelberht, the noble and pagan English king of Kent, had married the Christian princess Bertha. Gregory believed Æthelberht would kindly receive Christian missionaries from Rome in honor of his queen.

Pope Gregory chose Augustine, the prior of the Abbey of St. Andrew's in Rome, to lead a group of monks to England. The journey would be dangerous. Sailing the ocean could mean storms and shipwreck. But the monks were even more frightened of living in a barbaric land. They were afraid the English pagans would hunt and kill them. They were so frightened that, right before they set sail for England, they sent Augustine back to Rome to beg the pope to let them return home. But the pope sent them a letter full of encouraging words. "They must be brave!" he said. "They must preach the Good News of Christ to the English!"

Augustine and his monks landed on the English shore. King Æthelberht arranged a meeting under an oak tree. Augustine and his men met the king, chanting prayers and holding high an image of Christ. King Æthelberht saw that Augustine and his men came in peace. He allowed them to preach the Catholic Faith in England and gave them a home in Canterbury, his capital city.

In Canterbury stood the ruins of St. Martin's Church, a church built by the Romans of the past. Now Augustine and his men from present-day Rome gathered at St. Martins and said Mass. Augustine and his monks lived lives of poverty and prayer. Their holiness was so inspiring that the king's heart was drawn to Jesus.

Augustine baptized King Æthelberht within the year after he had landed. Ten thousand of the king's subjects were also baptized with their king. Now Augustine and his men could preach Christianity all throughout the country. Because of Augustine, the Catholic Faith lived in England once again. Augustine served the growing English Church until he died a holy death.

St. Augustine of Canterbury, help us bravely go to wherever God sends us!

St. Augustine of Canterbury

May 27

Bl. Margaret Pole

May 28

Bl. Margaret Pole

1473–1541 • England

A member of the English Royal Family, Margaret was married to the king's cousin, Sir Richard Pole, and had five children. She was a fine lady and deeply devoted to her Catholic Faith. When Catherine of Aragon, the Spanish princess, came to England to marry the heir to the English throne, Margaret Pole became her lady-in-waiting, and a friendship blossomed between them. Sadness touched Margaret's life when her husband died. But when Catherine of Aragon and Henry VIII married and soon became king and queen of England, they made sure that Margaret was well taken care of. Henry VIII thought Margaret the saintliest woman in England. So when he and Catherine had their first child, the princess Mary, the king made Margaret the princess's godmother and governess. Margaret dearly loved her little goddaughter, and these were happy times for her and her family.

But as the years went by, Catherine still had not given birth to a son. Henry VIII wanted a male heir, so he decided to divorce Catherine and marry another woman named Anne Boleyn. It is against the Catholic Church's teachings to divorce and remarry, but Henry did not care about what was right or wrong. He started a new church, the Church of England, so that he could do whatever he wanted. Margaret sorrowed for her friend Catherine, and she worried about little Mary because the king declared that Mary was no longer a princess, since he had divorced her mother. Because Margaret was loyal to Catherine, Mary, and her Catholic Faith, Henry banished her from the court.

Margaret had a son, Reginald, who was a cardinal in the Catholic Church. Cardinal Reginald now wrote to Henry and told him that what he was doing was wrong. Henry was furious and wanted revenge. He executed two of Cardinal Reginald's brothers and imprisoned his mother, Margaret, in the Tower of London. There Margaret suffered for nearly two years. It was cold and damp in the tower. The winter nights were long and her clothes too thin to keep her warm. Rebellions broke out because of Henry's tyranny, and Margaret was blamed. Even though she was innocent, Henry ordered her execution. She did not even receive a trial. But Margaret was not afraid. She knew that God would take care of her soul. She walked calmly to the executioner's block and bravely died for her faith in Jesus and His one true Church. Bl. Margaret Pole, help me to be true to the Faith, even when those around me are not!

St. Conan and Son

d. 275 • Lycaonia (modern-day Turkey)

Conan's wife had died, and he lived with his young son in Iconium. Conan's son was also named Conan, and so the father was known as Conan the Elder, and his son as Conan the Younger.

To grow closer to God, Conan the Elder gave away all of his comforts and earthly possessions and lived as a hermit. The young son shared in his father's deep faith. Conan the Younger dedicated himself to the service of the Church in Iconium and served as a lector at the age of twelve years old.

The Emperor Aurelian passed a decree that pronounced death to Christians that did not give up their Faith. Conan and his son were among the first Christians rounded up and presented to the Roman officials in Iconium. They stood tall and straight, their eyes bright and unafraid.

The official asked the father and son if they were both Christian. Both father and son declared that they were with strong, unwavering voices.

The official asked them if they would give up their Christian Faith.

Both father and son refused. Conan the Elder declared that he was willing to give up a short life on earth for eternal life in heaven. Conan the Younger nodded his agreement.

The Roman official had no pity in his heart. He declared that both father and son should be roasted over a fire.

The father held his son in his arms amid the scorching flames. Conan the Elder knew that he had taught his son the most important thing of all—he had taught him to love God and to love his Faith. Together father and son breathed their last. Now they would both go to their Father in heaven and spend forever together in the company of the other glorious martyrs for the Faith.

Sts. Conan the Elder and Younger, help me to love God and to love my Faith!

St. Conan and Son

May 29

St. Joan of Arc

May 30

St. Joan of Arc

1412–1431 • France

The sun glinted off the young maid's sword, held high before the walled city of Rheims. If her army took this city then the French king would be officially crowned, and the long Hundred Years' War—the war that had cost numberless French and English lives—would soon be ended. The army waited for her signal and then surged forward with great cries and the clash of armor. The maid rushed into the fight with her army, though she never took a life.

The young maid's name was Joan of Arc, and she changed the course of history. She led a broken-down army that no one else could lead, fought battles that no one else would fight, and won a war that no one else could win.

Joan was born in the tiny village of Domrémy and was known for her gentleness and goodness. At thirteen, she heard the voices of St. Michael the Archangel, St. Catherine, and St. Margaret, telling her to lead the French army to victory. At first Joan was frightened, but she trusted God. She understood that God had chosen a young and defenseless girl to win victory for France because He chooses the weak to humble the proud. God would save France, not Joan— she was only his humble servant.

Joan went to the French court to meet the king. To test her, the king disguised himself and hid in the crowd. Immediately, Joan identified him even though she had never seen him before. She told him that God wanted her to lead his army. The king realized that Joan had been sent by God and did as she wished. And that is how Joan led the French army and pushed the English out of France.

Even though victory would soon be France's, there were still small battles to fight. In one of these battles, Joan was captured and put on trial by Church officials who worked for the English, not the pope. Joan declared that the voices she heard were from God and that she had been doing His will. It was a corrupt and unfair trail, and the judge condemned Joan as a witch, sentencing her to burn at the stake. At her execution, Joan's lips kissed the crucifix, and her eyes never left it as she called out the name of Jesus. The pyre was set on fire, and Joan knew that soon she would be with God and the saints in heaven. St. Joan of Arc, help me to do what God asks me to do!

The Visitation of the Blessed Virgin Mary

Marian Feast Day

A soft breeze cooled Mary as she strained up the steep hill at the end of her journey to visit her cousin Elizabeth. Her hand rested on her belly, and she remembered the angel Gabriel's words to her: "Behold, you will conceive in your womb and bear a son, and you shall name him Jesus" and "Behold, Elizabeth, your relative, has also conceived a son in her old age, and this is the sixth month for her who was called barren; for nothing will be impossible for God" (Luke 1:31, 36–37). Mary reached the crest of the hill, caught sight of her cousin, and called to her in greeting.

Elizabeth was drawing water from the well in the courtyard. When a bright and joyful voice called out to her, a sudden pressure bounded in her womb. Her baby boy inside her body had leapt in recognition of the voice! The words the angel had spoken to Elizabeth's husband, Zechariah, about her baby flashed across her mind. "He will be filled with the Holy Spirit even from his mother's womb," the angel had said, "and he will turn many of the children of Israel to the Lord their God" (Luke 1:15–16).

Elizabeth turned and sought the one who had called her. When her gaze lighted on Mary, she brightened with joy. The Holy Spirit flooded Elizabeth, and she cried out, "Most blessed are you among women, and blessed is the fruit of your womb." She stretched out her hands, and Mary and her cousin Elizabeth held each other close. "How does this happen to me;" Elizabeth continued, "that the mother of my Lord should come to me? For at the moment the sound of your greeting reached my ears, the infant in my womb leaped for joy" (Luke 1:41–44).

Elizabeth's words filled Mary with a deep peace. She praised God who had blessed her, for she was a small and humble woman; a nobody in the eyes of the world. She had done nothing to make herself worthy of God's favor. But the Father had chosen her to be the mother of His Son. Mary's words spilled over with joy and love of God: "My soul magnifies the Lord; my spirit rejoices in God my Savior" (Luke 1:46–47). And she proclaimed a great prayer in praise of God's glory.

Mary stayed with her cousin until Elizabeth gave birth to her son. Afterward, she returned to her home in Nazareth. Dear Mary, help my soul magnify the Lord!

The Visitation of the Blessed Virgin Mary
May 31

St. Justin Martyr
June 1

St. Justin Martyr

100–165 • Samaria

Justin was a pagan philosopher who wanted more than anything to find out the truth about God. He studied under teacher after teacher, and none of them could tell him what the truth was.

One day, Justin strolled by the sea, lost in thought. Then he noticed an old man walking beside him. The old man smiled and asked Justin what he was thinking about. Justin explained that he was trying to find out the truth about God. The old man's smile grew wider. He told Justin that he was a Christian. He explained to Justin that we cannot figure out who God is on our own: God is too great, and we are too small. Instead, God must tell us about Himself. The man then explained how the prophets foretold the coming of Jesus Christ, and that Jesus was God, and that Jesus teaches us the truth about Himself; to know Jesus is to know the truth about God.

The old man's words touched Justin's heart and set him thinking. But Justin was not ready to become a Christian yet. He kept the old man's words in his mind, thinking about them, wondering if what he had said was true.

Christians at that time suffered terrible persecution because they would not sacrifice to the Roman gods. Now, Justin paid attention to these Christians. He saw their courage and their joy. He saw that they were not afraid to die for Jesus. They would not die with such courage and joy if what they believed was not true, Justin thought. The martyrs' blood gleamed as an unarguable witness to truth, and Justin became a Christian.

Justin dressed in the philosopher's robe and staff and moved to Rome. There he taught and wrote the truth about God: that Jesus is God.

Justin and another philosopher in Rome, named Crescens, held a public philosophical debate in which Justin soundly defeated Crescens's arguments. Furious and spiteful because he had lost, Crescens denounced Justin as a Christian to the Roman authorities. Soldiers arrested Justin, and the Roman official warned him that he would receive no mercy if he did not sacrifice to Roman gods. Justin shook his head. He declared that he would go to heaven if he died for Jesus. So the Roman official ordered Justin's beheading. Justin became a martyr for Jesus, his blood a gleaming witness to the truth.

St. Justin Martyr, help me to bravely seek out the truth about God!

Sts. Marcellinus and Peter

d. 304 • Italy

An older man was speaking to a gathering of Christians. He was telling the story of how he came to the Faith of Christ. A young boy in the crowd, his eyes shining bright, hung upon every word the man spoke. The man explained that, before becoming Christian, he had been a Roman executioner. One evening, two men had been cast into prison: one man—named Marcellinus—was a priest, and the other—Peter—was an exorcist, someone who casts out demons. The executioner could tell they were different from his usual, violent prisoners. Both had spirits of peace and joy. When they saw him, they smiled. The executioner was shocked: how could these two men smile at him when they knew he was going to kill them?

Marcellinus and Peter spoke to their fellow prisoners about a man named Jesus. The executioner could not help but draw closer. They spoke the name of Jesus with such love and joy! They explained that Jesus had been crucified and had risen from the dead to save all people from their sins. When they died, they would rise from the dead and be with Jesus. The two men turned to the executioner. Jesus had died to save him from his sins, too, they explained. The executioner's heart leapt at their words. Could his terrible deeds truly be forgiven? He dared not believe it.

The day arrived for Marcellinus's and Peter's executions. Soldiers took them to a field far away from the city and ordered them to clear the thorns and brambles from where they would be buried. The executioner watched in amazement as Marcellinus and Peter cleared the field quickly and cheerfully. Nothing disturbed their trust in Jesus. Then it was the executioner's turn to do his job. He saw the joy in the two men's eyes because they knew they were going to heaven to be with Jesus.

Soon after the execution, the executioner became a Christian. He knew that Marcellinus and Peter had forgiven him, because it was through their prayers that he received the grace to love Jesus.

The young boy listening never forgot the words of the former executioner. He grew up and became Pope Damasus I. As pope, he wrote down the stories of Sts. Peter and Marcellinus so that their lives could also inspire others to love Christ. Sts. Marcellinus and Peter, help me to bravely and cheerfully follow Jesus!

Sts. Marcellinus and Peter
June 2

**St. Charles Lwanga
and Companions**
June 3

St. Charles Lwanga and Companions

d. 1886 • Uganda

A group of priests called the White Fathers traveled to Uganda in Africa, and King Muteesa, the Ugandan king, received them with friendliness and kindness. Charles Lwanga, a twenty-five-year-old page in the king's court, listened to the White Fathers' message and became a catechumen (someone who is preparing to be baptized).

King Muteesa died, and his son, King Mwanga, took the throne. The new king was a cruel and sinful ruler who persecuted Christians. The head of the king's pages was a Catholic, and he begged the king to stop his persecutions and to give up his sinful life. Furious, the king had him beheaded. Charles Lwanga took his place as the head of the king's pages. He knew that all the Christians at court were in danger. Even so, that very night, he sneaked out of the palace and went to the White Fathers to be baptized. Then he watched over the secret instruction in the Catholic Faith of the young pages at court.

One day, the king discovered one of the boys studying his catechism. Immediately, he ordered all of the pages in the court to gather before him. Then, in an ominous voice, he ordered all the Christians to reveal themselves.

Fifteen boys—including Charles Lwanga—stepped forward. The youngest of the boys, Kizito, was only thirteen years old.

King Mwanga asked the boys if they planned to remain Christians.

"To death!" all fifteen cried.

The king's eyes flashed. "So be it!" he cried. And he ordered their execution.

Soldiers marched Charles Lwanga and his companions thirty-seven miles to their place of execution. Charles Lwanga held his head high, and little Kizito joked and laughed. They were not afraid to die for Jesus.

When they arrived at their place of execution, the prisoners built their own funeral pyre. A soldier wrapped Charles Lwanga in a mat of sticks and set his feet on fire. His last groan was a prayer to God. The rest of the boys were martyred for refusing to give up their Faith. They all became glorious martyrs in heaven.

St. Charles Lwanga and Companions, help me to be brave for Jesus!

St. Petroc

d. 594 • Britain

Petroc was the youngest son of King Glywys of Wales. When his father passed away, the people begged him to take the crown and rule over a part of the kingdom with his older brothers. But Petroc did not want an earthly kingdom, he wanted to share in the Kingdom of God. So Petroc gave up the crown and traveled to Ireland to become a hermit.

Petroc grew in wisdom and holiness, and he traveled to Cornwall and founded a monastery. He would often stay up late into the night in prayer and offered great sacrifices to God to grow in holiness. He only ate bread during the week, but he did allow himself a small treat on Sunday to celebrate the Lord's feast.

Desiring to grow even more in holiness, Petroc went on a pilgrimage to Rome for many years. But despite all of his work to become holy, Petroc still was a bit proud.

When he returned home from Rome, it started to rain. Petroc stared up into the heavens and declared that God would make the rain stop.

The rain did not stop.

In fact, it continued to rain for three days. Petroc realized that he had tried to predict the weather out of pride. He had presumed that he could know how God would act.

Repenting of his pride, Petroc went straight back to Rome on another pilgrimage. He realized that he still had a long way to go to become holy.

Because of his quest for holiness, many legends sprang up about Petroc. It is said that after his return to Rome he went on to Jerusalem, and finally India. In India, he met a wolf and tamed it. From then on, the wolf stayed always at his side and returned with Petroc to Cornwall. In another legend, there was a neighboring king who used a mighty serpent to devour his enemies. Petroc defeated this terrible beast so that it could never harm anyone again.

Petroc was also known for many miracles, including healing the sick and those who were injured. Near the end of his life, he founded a second monastery, and he died on the road during his travels.

St. Petroc, help me to give up those things that stop me from being holy!

St. Petroc
June 4

St. Boniface

June 5

St. Boniface

c. 675–754 • England

An abbot from England, Boniface had a strong desire in his heart to convert the German peoples. The Germans were pagans, which means they worshipped many false gods. Boniface wished to teach the Germans about the one, true God and how He sent His only beloved Son to save us from our sins. Boniface traveled to Rome to request permission to preach from the pope. When the pope met Boniface, he saw that the abbot was strong in the Faith. The pope gave him permission, and so Boniface preached in Germany. Later, the pope would make Boniface bishop of all of Germany.

In the dark German forest was a tall and mighty oak tree. It was so ancient, tall, and strong that the Germans believed it was sacred to their false god, Thor. Boniface knew that if he chopped down the "sacred" oak, the Germans would see that the true God was mightier than their false god. So he gathered the Germans in the forest, around the oak, and proclaimed he would chop the tree down.

The Germans' hearts were wrathful. They yelled and cursed this enemy of their god but waited to see what would happen. They believed that Thor would send a lightning bolt to strike Boniface down for threatening his sacred tree. Boniface raised his axe. Some in the crowd yelled louder. Some held their breath. With a powerful stroke, Boniface struck the bark of the oak, but his single blow left only a small notch in the thick trunk. He raised his axe to strike again. All of a sudden, a great rush of wind blasted the tree. The massive oak toppled over with a mighty crash. The onlookers gasped. Then their angry cries turned into cheers: St. Boniface's God had destroyed the sacred oak! The Christian God was the true God! The German pagans were then baptized and became Christians.

Boniface took the wood of the great oak tree and used it to build a church to St. Peter. Then he preached the Gospel all throughout Germany, founding monasteries and convents. For many years he taught the German people about Jesus, just as his heart desired. Even as he grew older, his heart still burned to bring the Good News of Jesus to pagans who lived even farther away in the deep, dark forests. At seventy-nine years of age, he embarked on another missionary trip. On the way, he was attacked by raiding pagans who mistook his chests of books for gold and silver. He and his companions were killed, earning the crown of martyrdom for Jesus.

St. Boniface, help me to share the love of Jesus with those who do not know Him!

St. Norbert

c. 1075–1134 • Germany

Norbert rode on his fine horse without a care in the world. Even though he was a deacon in the Church, he was very rich. He was part of the German king's court and lived a life of luxury. Norbert did not care about God; he cared only about himself and led a sinful, greedy life. As Norbert continued to ride, the air became heavy. A dark, threatening cloud appeared in the sky. Sensing a terrible storm was coming, Norbert spurred his horse to a run. He did not want the rain to ruin his fine robes! But the storm was faster than he was. Sheets of rain beat down as Norbert's horse streaked down the road. Thunder growled in the sky, and then a great thunderbolt blasted the ground right before the horse's feet. The terrified horse reared up on its hind legs and threw Norbert to the ground. Norbert did not get up. He lay on the ground as though dead.

An hour later, Norbert regained consciousness. He could have died from the fall! He recognized that his fall had been a warning from God. If he had died, his soul would not have gone to heaven, because his heart was full of sin. He thanked God for giving him a second chance.

Norbert knew he had to change his life, so he became a priest. He spent part of his fortune to found a monastery, and he gave the rest to the poor. He traveled barefoot throughout the country and preached about Jesus. Followers joined him, and he started several religious orders at the pope's request. As Norbert preached from town to town, he performed great miracles in the name of Jesus. In one town, he restored sight to a blind woman. The townspeople were amazed and wanted to make him their bishop! Norbert sneaked away from the city in secret. He was now a humble man and did not want such honor. But he could not avoid it for long. Soon, the pope made Norbert an archbishop.

To his great sorrow, Norbert saw that many men who belonged to the Church still lived sinful lives like he once had. He sought these men out and spoke to them about Jesus's love and begged them to live holy lives. Some of the men's hearts were touched by Norbert's words and they changed their ways. But others' hearts became hardened. Some of them even plotted to kill Norbert. Three times they tried to murder him, but each time he escaped their vile plans. Norbert continued to serve the Church until he grew old and died a holy death. St. Norbert, help me to turn away from anything causing me to sin!

St. Norbert
June 6

St. Robert of Newminster
June 7

St. Robert of Newminster

d. 1159 • England

A monk named Robert heard of a new group of Cistercian monks who lived lives of sacrifice in order to become holy. His heart leapt with joy at the news. He knew he was meant to join them so that together they could live lives of sacrifice and make their souls holy for God.

So Robert set off to join these monks, traveling through the northern country by foot in the cold winter. Near the banks of the river Skell, he found them living in small huts of woven sticks and mud, with roofs of turf and grass.

The Cistercian monks welcomed Robert, and together they offered their sacrifices to God. Stories of their holiness spread far and wide. A wealthy man wished to give up the world and follow their example, so he joined the Cistercian monks and gave all of his money to his new community. His wealth was used to build the great Fountain Abbey, with its soaring columns and arches and a gray bell tower.

After a time, Robert left Fountain Abbey to start the Abbey of Newminster with a group of monks. Robert became the Abbot of Newminster, and he lived a life of great sacrifice to be a good example for the monks under his care. Beloved by his monks for his kindness and holiness, he spent long hours in prayer and his writing. His life of holiness and sacrifice was such a good example to the other monks that, within ten years, three groups of monks left Newminster to build new monasteries so that even more monks could live lives of holiness, sacrifice, and prayer.

During his time as abbot, Robert was friends with a hermit named Godric, who would also one day become a saint. When Robert died, the hermit Godric had a vision in which he saw bright angels take Robert's soul, appearing like a globe of fire, through the gates of heaven.

St. Robert, help me to desire a life of holiness and sacrifice!

St. Melania the Elder

c. 350–c. 410 • Spain

Melania entered the olive grove at the top of the hill. The silver green-olive leaves shimmered in the noon sun. This olive grove was the Garden of Gethsemane, also known as the Mount of Olives. It was here that Jesus had prayed the night before He was crucified, and He had asked His three disciples, Peter, James, and John, to keep watch with Him in the night. It was here that Jesus had wept tears of blood that had fallen on a large rock in the garden.

It was here that Melania knew she would found a convent.

Melania had been born to a wealthy family in Spain and had married a prominent official and moved to Rome. In Rome, she became a Christian. But Melania was widowed at a young age, and from then on she dedicated her life to serving the poor and making sacrifices in the pursuit of holiness. After making sure that her only living son was well-taken care of, she traveled to Egypt to study under the best theologians so she could better understand the Faith. Late into the night, she would read the sacred texts, captivated by their wisdom and beauty.

But she did not go to Egypt only to study. From her own wealth she provided for those who chose to be poor for Christ. In Egypt, there is a tradition that she fed 5,000 persecuted Christians for three days.

Later she traveled to Jerusalem, the holy city where Jesus preached and died, and Melania knew that there, at the Mount of Olives, she would found a convent for women dedicated to serving pilgrims. For twenty-seven years, Melania remained at the monastery, hosting pilgrims and performing good works, dedicating her life to sacrifice and prayer.

At around the age of sixty, Melania returned to Rome, the home of her youth. There she visited her son and her granddaughter, Melania the Younger (who would also become a saint). Soon after, she returned to Jerusalem and her beloved convent, where she died a holy death.

St. Melania, help me to use my gifts and talents to serve others!

St. Melania the Elder
June 8

St. Ephrem the Syrian
June 9

St. Ephrem the Syrian

306–373 • Mesopotamia (present-day Turkey)

Ephrem grew up Nisibis, a city often besieged, attacked, and passed from ruler to ruler as the Romans and Persians struggled for power in the region. Now it was a time of peace in Nisibis. The Romans were in control, and people of many different religions lived in the city.

Ephrem was a Christian teacher and deacon. Because he was a teacher, Ephrem wanted to do his part to teach people of different religions about Jesus. He loved God so much that he wanted others to love God, too.

Ephrem's love for God overflowed into song. He wrote beautiful hymns: chants soft and low, powerful and glorious, joyful and sad. He knew that beautiful music touches the heart.

Everyone who sang and listened to Ephrem's words learned the truth about Jesus. He wrote hundreds and hundreds of hymns—each one a little lesson in praise of God.

But peace in Nisibis did not last. The king of Persia threatened to conquer the city, and the new Roman emperor hated the Christians and refused to help them so long as they remained true to Christ. After many attempts to take the city by force failed, the Romans agreed to give it to the Persians to stop the war. The Persian king cruelly persecuted the Christians, forcing them to flee Nisibis if they wanted to remain safe. Ephrem and other Christians found refuge in the city of Edessa. There, too, Ephrem found much work to do as a teacher. Many more people needed to learn the truth about Jesus!

Ephrem continued to write hymns. He led a choir of female singers in the middle of the market square. The shoppers would stop to listen to the beautiful voices and come away praising Jesus in their hearts.

Near the end of his life, a terrible famine struck Edessa. Ephrem spoke to the wealthy of the city and convinced them to give food to the poor and starving. Soon he withdrew to a cave and died a holy death in prayer and solitude.

St. Ephrem, help my love for God be a song in my heart!

The Angel of Portugal

1916 • Portugal

We all know the story of how Our Lady of Fatima appeared to three shepherd children as they were watching their flock. She told them to pray the Rosary for peace and to pray for sinners no one else would pray for. Our Lady even made the sun dance in the sky so that the world would believe in her message. But did you know that before Our Lady appeared to the three children, an angel appeared to them first?

It was a spring day when Lucia, who was nine, and her two cousins, Francisco and Jacinta, ages eight and six, were in the hills watching their sheep as they did every day. A drizzle of rain sent them to a nearby olive grove, where they rested, ate their lunch, and prayed the Rosary. A strong wind stirred the trees. The children looked up and saw a white light approaching them. It was in the form of a young man, bright and transparent as crystal in the sun's rays. The children were astonished. When the man of light was near enough, he said, "Do not be afraid. I am the Angel of Peace. Pray with me." Then he bowed down, and the children did the same. They repeated after the angel three times the following prayer:

My God, I believe, I adore, I hope, and I love You. I ask pardon for those who do not believe, do not adore, do not hope, and do not love You.

Then the angel disappeared, and the children were flooded with feelings of peace and joy. The angel appeared to them two more times. In his second visit, he taught them the importance of patiently offering their sufferings for sinners and to make up for sins that offend God. He also told them that he was the guardian angel of Portugal and that their sacrifices would bring peace to their country.

In the angel's third visit, he held a golden chalice. Above it floated the Blessed Host, which is the Body of Christ. Red drops of blood fell from the Host into the chalice. The angel bowed before the Host and chalice, led the children in prayer, and gave them Holy Communion. To Lucia he gave the Host to eat; to Francisco and Jacinta he gave the wine of the Blood of Christ to drink. When the angel disappeared, the children were filled with the sacredness of what had just happened. Little did they know that the angel's visit was preparing them for an even greater visit—one from the Queen of Peace, Mary, the Mother of God. Angel of Portugal, help me to offer my sufferings to God for peace and for poor sinners!

The Angel of Portugal

June 10

St. Barnabas

June 11

St. Barnabas

Biblical Figure

A Jewish man named Saul zealously persecuted Christians. One day, as he was heading to find and arrest more Christians, a flash of light blinded him, and he heard Jesus ask why he was persecuting Him. After he was miraculously healed and able to see again, Saul became a Christian. But because he had hunted down and put to death so many followers of Jesus, the Christians did not trust him and were afraid of him.

Barnabas believed in second chances. He decided to trust Saul and introduced him to the Twelve Apostles. He knew that, from now on, Saul would do his best to make up for his mistakes and to share his faith in Jesus. And so Barnabas and Saul became friends.

Many people were converting to Christianity in the city of Antioch. The Apostles decided to send Barnabas to serve the Christians there. But Barnabas knew that he would need help. He could think of no one better to bring with him than his friend Saul (soon to be known as the Apostle Paul). John Mark, Barnabas's nephew, also joined them. John Mark would later be known as Mark the Evangelist and would write the Gospel of Mark in the Bible.

Barnabas and the Apostle Paul traveled from city to city, proclaiming that Jesus had died and risen to save us from our sins. In a city called Lystra, Paul healed a man who could not walk. The people thought that Barnabas and Paul must be gods in human disguise because they had performed so great a miracle. They did not understand that it was Jesus who had performed the miracle through them. The people tried to worship Barnabas and Paul. The two Apostles were terribly upset. They tore their clothes in grief, declaring that they were only human and that their God was the only true God.

Later, Paul asked Barnabas to go on another journey to preach the Faith. Barnabas wanted to bring along his nephew, John Mark, but Paul did not trust John Mark. John Mark had traveled with them before and had abandoned them, perhaps because he was homesick. But just as he had with Paul, Barnabas believed in second chances. So Paul and Barnabas parted ways, and Barnabas took John Mark with him as he preached about Jesus. Even though they no longer traveled together, Barnabas and Paul remained brothers and friends in Jesus Christ. St. Barnabas, help me be wise in giving others second chances!

Pope St. Leo III

d. 816 • Italy

When Pope Adrian I died, Leo III was elected pope on the same day. But some of Adrian I's relatives did not like that Leo was the new pope. So they plotted against him.

One day, as Leo led a procession in honor of St. Mark, his enemies attacked him. They tried to gouge out his eyes and pluck out his tongue. If he did not have eyes and a tongue, then the rules were that he would have to resign as pope. Leo was rushed to a monastery where his eyes and tongue miraculously healed. But the pope knew he was still in danger. His enemies would attack him again. He needed to have a powerful ally, someone who would support him and the papacy. So he decided to go to the kingdom of the Franks, where the great Charlemagne ruled. Charlemagne was a just king who spread the Catholic Faith throughout his kingdom and who had shown himself to be a supporter of the Church.

Pope Leo escaped from Rome and traveled through mountains and forests to the kingdom of the Franks, where he met Charlemagne and explained to him what had happened. Charlemagne promised his support for the pope, and, a month later, Leo returned to Rome with Charlemagne's men. The people of Rome rejoiced that their pope had returned, and his enemies no longer dared act against him for fear of making an enemy of the king of the Franks. The next year, Charlemagne himself visited Rome, and a trial was held in which Pope Leo swore an oath against any wrongdoing, and his enemies were condemned to death. But the pope pleaded for their lives to be spared, and so his enemies were sent into exile instead.

During Mass on Christmas Day in St. Peter's Basilica, Charlemagne knelt before the altar and Pope Leo III placed a great jeweled crown on his head. In this grand ceremony, the pope made Charlemagne the Holy Roman Emperor in the West. From that time on, only the pope could crown the Holy Roman Emperor. Charlemagne was now the protector of the Roman Church. Together, Pope Leo and Charlemagne defended the Church from pagan invaders and false teachings. Once Charlemagne died, Pope Leo's enemies again plotted against him. But this time the pope was prepared. He heard of the plot and stomped it out before he could be harmed. He governed the Church until he died a holy death. Pope St. Leo III, please protect the Church against her enemies!

Pope St. Leo III
June 12

St. Anthony

June 13

St. Anthony

1195–1231 • Portugal

In a town in Italy, a group of Dominican friars were visiting a group of Franciscan friars for Mass. But there was a mix-up, and no one knew who was supposed to preach the homily! The abbot asked a young Portuguese friar to preach the homily, even though the friar had nothing prepared. The young friar's name was Anthony. Anthony stepped up to the pulpit. The other friars felt sorry for him because he had not had time to get ready. But when Anthony began to speak, the friars were astounded—he preached one of the best sermons they had ever heard!

Soon Anthony went out to preach about the greatness of Jesus throughout Italy. In one city, the people ignored him because they led busy, sinful lives. Some even made fun of him. So Anthony declared that if they would not listen to him preach, he would preach to the fish instead! Anthony marched to the seashore, and a few curious onlookers followed him. Standing on the sand, arms outstretched, Anthony proclaimed God's great love for Creation. As he preached, first one fish swam close to the shore, then another, and soon schools and schools of fish were listening to Anthony by the shore. The onlookers were amazed. They rushed back to the town and gathered the townspeople to watch the miracle. The people gasped as the fish bobbed their heads out of the water and listened to Anthony's powerful words. When Anthony finished his sermon, the fish darted away in flashes of silver. The townspeople begged Anthony's forgiveness, and from then on they listened to his preaching.

Anthony continued to preach throughout the country and brought many people closer to Jesus. But then he became sick, and so he retreated to a small home under a walnut tree to offer up his suffering to Christ. A passerby saw a burning light shining from the window of Anthony's cell. He burst into the room, afraid that there was a fire, and saw the wondrous sight of Anthony holding the Child Jesus in his arms. Anthony begged the man not to reveal what he had seen until after Anthony's death. Knowing that his death approached, Anthony traveled to Padua and died a holy death in a nearby convent at the age of thirty-five. St. Anthony of Padua, help me to carry the child Jesus in my heart!

St. Lidwina

1380–1433 • Holland

The girls laughed as they skated on the ice on that clear, cold winter day. The fifteen-year-old Lidwina and her friend glided and spun, carefree and joyous. Then Lidwina's skate slipped, and she fell hard onto the ice. Immediately she had to be taken home, her right rib cracked. But doctors then did not know how to treat Lidwina's wound, and so it became infected, and the infection spread all throughout her body. Lidwina suffered intense pain.

Ever since she was little, Lidwina had liked to sneak into the church and pray before the image of the Blessed Virgin Mary, sometimes even for entire nights. Through her prayers, Our Lady revealed to her that she would live a life of suffering. Now that life of suffering had begun.

Lidwina was bedridden for the rest of her life, her body racked with pain, the infection spreading sores all over her. Some people thought the devil had cursed her, but others recognized that she suffered with holy patience. Lidwina offered all of her sufferings to Jesus, and the only food that she ate was Jesus's Body and Blood in Holy Communion.

God allowed Lidwina's pain to be a source of miraculous healing for others. Once, Lidwina prayed for a woman suffering from a head-splitting toothache, and the toothache disappeared. Another woman placed her young boy, who was crying in pain, at Lidwina's bedside. Not only did the boy's pain disappear, but when he grew up he became a priest.

God also gifted Lidwina with visions. Jesus showed her His suffering on the Cross. After her vision, marks from Jesus's crown of thorns appeared on her forehead, and her arms were full of wooden splinters from the Cross. In another vision, a rose bush appeared before her that was not yet in bloom. Lidwina heard the words, "When this shall be in bloom, your suffering will be at an end."

In the spring of her fifty-third year, the rose bush of her vision blossomed. On Easter Sunday, Jesus appeared to her and gave her the Sacrament of the Anointing of the Sick to strengthen her soul for the next life, and she died a holy death.

St. Lidwina, help me to be patient in my suffering!

St. Lidwina
June 14

St. Germaine Cousin
June 15

St. Germaine Cousin

1579–1601 • France

The peal of the bells for Mass called to the soul of a shepherd girl watching her sheep in a field near the woods. So she planted her staff into the ground, and her sheep gathered around it. Then she set off for Mass, her rosary held in her misshapen hand. At her return, she found that not a single sheep had wandered off or fallen victim to the wolves. From then on, the girl went to daily Mass, and she never lost any of her sheep.

The shepherd girl's name was Germaine, and she watched the sheep far from home because her stepmother could not stand the sight of her. Germaine's right hand was crippled, and she had sores on her neck from disease. Some of her stepmother's children had died after birth, and the woman could not bear that her children had died while the disfigured Germaine had lived. Her disgust for Germaine grew into hatred. She forced the young girl to sleep in the barn, dressed her in rags, and gave her scraps for food. She forced Germaine to weave wool even though her fingers were crippled, and sometimes she even beat her. Germaine's father stood by and did nothing. Instead of becoming bitter over her treatment, Germaine offered all of her sufferings to Jesus and prayed for her stepmother's soul.

The village children loved Germaine. They did not mind that she was disfigured. After school, they would run to the fields looking for her, and she would tell them about her deep love for Jesus. The children told their parents about how holy Germaine was, but no one believed them because her stepmother had spread lies about the shepherd girl all throughout the village. Then something happened that changed the villagers' minds about her. The stream Germaine usually crossed to get to Mass was flooded. The children on the opposite side of the bank yelled warnings to Germaine that crossing was too dangerous. To their astonishment, she made the Sign of the Cross, and the waters parted, leaving a dry path for her. Other miracles happened around Germaine, and soon everyone realized how holy the shepherd girl was.

One night, a priest traveling to the village saw a bright light in the sky, and a young girl wearing a crown was being carried to heaven by angels. The next morning, he told the villagers what he saw. They rushed to Germaine and found that she had died in her sleep with an angelic expression on her face. St. Germaine, pray that my suffering brings me closer to Jesus!

St. Richard of Chichester

c. 1197–1253 • England

Richard was the second son of a gentleman farmer. Both of his parents had died, and the family land was falling into ruin. He worked so hard on the farm that he saved the family land. In gratitude, his older brother offered to give him the farm. But Richard refused this kind offer. His dream was to become a scholar at Oxford University.

And so Richard went to Oxford. There he studied under Edmund of Abingdon, who was a holy man and would later become a saint. Richard did so well at Oxford that eventually he became the head of the university. By that time, his tutor, Edmund of Abingdon, had become archbishop of Canterbury. Archbishop Edmund had made enemies with the king of England because he resisted the king's control of the Church. The king sent the archbishop into exile, and Richard followed him. He remained with Edmund until he died, and afterward Richard became a priest.

Only two years after being ordained, Richard was elected bishop of Chichester. Because he, too, resisted the king's control of the Church, the king did not accept Richard as bishop and refused to give him the land that belonged to him as bishop. So Richard lived in a local parish church and visited the people of his diocese by foot. When he needed rest from his work, he grew fig trees. Perhaps the sweet taste of figs reminded him of his time on the farm as a boy. Finally, after two years, the king—under threat of punishment from the pope—gave Richard his land.

At that time, many bishops wore furs and rich jewels; but Richard wore a simple wool tunic and an itchy hair shirt. He gave much of his wealth to the poor and established holy rules for his priests to follow. Once during Mass, he accidentally knocked over the chalice that contained the Blood of Christ, but not a single drop was spilled. The people celebrated this miracle, realizing that their bishop was a holy man.

Near the end of his life, Richard preached in support of the Crusades, so that pilgrims could travel to the Holy Land without risk to their lives. He died on the road as he was traveling to dedicate a church to St. Edmund. His body was taken back to Chichester, where he was buried at the cathedral. St. Richard of Chichester, pray that nothing will stop me from living out God's will in my life!

St. Richard of Chichester

June 16

© Sophia Institute Press

**Bl. Ranieri
Scacceri**

June 17

Bl. Ranieri Scacceri

1117–1161 • Italy

Ranieri liked a good party—the music, the excitement, the dancing. His parents had tried in vain to get him to focus on his studies. They had sent him to a good tutor and warned him that he was wasting his years, that anything important in life could only be gained through hard work. But Ranieri did not listen. Late into the night, he played his fiddle, drawing in the crowds and drinking with his friends. The drinking led to sin, and he never prayed, but Ranieri did not care.

One evening, Ranieri was playing his fiddle at a grand party when he spotted a man passing by, wearing a long robe. Ranieri grinned. This man obviously needed to be taught how to have a good time. Ranieri sauntered up to the man, fiddle in hand, but when he came near, his grin disappeared. Something about the man's peaceful face and the dignity of his bearing made it so that Ranieri could not tease him. Instead, Ranieri found himself earnestly talking to the man. He learned that the man had once been rich but had given everything away to the poor and dedicated his life to the things of God and the soul.

Ranieri returned home, the man's words burning in his heart. He realized that what his parents had said and what the man had said was all true: he had been wasting his life and ignoring the only thing that was truly important—the state of his soul. From then on, Ranieri was determined to do better. He burned his fiddle, worked hard as a merchant in his father's business, and saved enough money to make a pilgrimage to the Holy Land. He put on an itchy hair shirt and wandered barefoot to all the holy sites where Jesus once had lived. Many years he spent praying at the Church of the Holy Sepulcher, the church built over the place where Jesus was buried. When Ranieri returned home, he joined a Benedictine monastery.

Ranieri still knew how to draw in a crowd, but now he drew them in with his preaching instead of his music. God also allowed Ranieri to perform healing miracles in His name. Ranieri would anoint the sick with holy water and make the Sign of the Cross, and they would be healed. The people loved Ranieri and continually brought him their sick for healing until he died a holy death. Ranieri became known as the troubadour who had traded his music for God. Bl. Ranieri, help me to pay attention to what is most important—the state of my soul!

Bl. Hosanna

1449–1505 • Italy

A little girl skipped along the bank of the river Po. She paused to wonder at the beauty of the river scene, the shimmer of water beneath the tall trees and the bright sky. Then something even more bright and beautiful appeared. A splendid angel stood before her and whisked her soul up to the heavens, where she saw a vision of the choirs of angels and the Blessed Trinity. The almost painful wonder and awe of the Trinity's sacred beauty pierced her soul. Then the Child Jesus appeared before her, carrying His Cross. When the little girl returned home, she knew that she belonged to God forever.

This girl's name was Hosanna, and all through her childhood she continued to see visions of Jesus. But when she told her father she wished to be a nun, he refused to let her enter the convent because he wanted her to marry. So when she turned fourteen, she visited a Dominican convent and returned home wearing a nun's habit. If she could not enter a convent, then she would live and pray like a nun at home. When she turned eighteen, Jesus gave her a spiritual wedding ring to show that her heart was united to His heart.

When Hosanna was still young, her parents passed away. Now she could not enter the convent because she had to take care of her younger siblings. She managed the household and gave much of the family wealth the poor. But even though she was so busy, she still dedicated much time to prayer, and Jesus continued to appear to her. In her prayers, Hosanna begged to share in Jesus's pain on the Cross so she could offer her suffering for the Church. Jesus answered her prayer when she turned thirty. He gave her the wounds from His crown of thorns on her forehead, His lance mark on her side, and His nail marks on her feet. Sometimes the wounds on her feet were so painful that she could not walk. But all these sufferings she received with a glad heart because she suffered them out of love.

News of Hosanna's holiness spread, and many people visited her to ask for spiritual advice. They found Hosanna always joyful and kind, and her words wise and true. A few months before her death, Hosanna was finally able to say her vows as a Dominican religious, and she died a holy death. Bl. Hosanna, help my heart always be united with Jesus's heart!

Bl. Hosanna

June 18

St. Romuald
June 19

St. Romuald

c. 951–1027 • Italy

Romuald lived the worldly life of a nobleman in Italy. He did not think much about God because he was busy thinking about pleasure and wealth. One day, when he was about twenty years old, Romuald's father asked Romuald to accompany him to a duel in which his father would fight. With growing horror, Romuald watched each deadly clash of steel as his father fought his enemy. Finally, Romuald's father slew his enemy. And the realization flashed upon Romuald that his father had just become a murderer. Romuald knew he was walking the same path and that someday he, too, might commit such an unspeakable act. Immediately he knew he must change his life, and so he fled to a monastery.

Romuald wished to transform his life completely and live a strict life of prayer and penance, but many other monks in the monastery did not follow the rules. So Romuald began pointing out when they broke the rules. The other monks did not like this new monk telling them what to do. And Romuald realized that even though the monks should be living better lives, he was not the one who should be correcting them. He received permission to move to a hermitage in Venice, where he was able to live a strict life full of prayer.

For five years, Romuald lived a life of great prayer and sacrifice. He desired to give himself to God completely and to dwell on the things of God. Many disciples gathered around him, wishing to live as he did. They continually meditated on the psalms, the beautiful hymns of praise in the Bible, so that their whole life was a prayer to God.

Eventually, the news came to Romuald that his father had also repented of his sins and became a monk. His father, however, was wrestling with doubt, unsure if a monk's life was the sort of life God had called him to live. Romuald rushed to his father, and together they lived a life of prayer and sacrifice until his father's doubts were lifted and he committed his life to God.

For the next thirty years, Romuald wandered around Italy and founded many monasteries. During this time, a nobleman named Maldolus had a vision. In his vision, monks in white garments ascended a ladder up to heaven. Maldolus decided that his vision was telling him to give land to Romuald on which the holy monk could build a monastery. This monastery became the main monastery for Romuald's new order. Many monks joined the order and lived holy lives of prayer and sacrifice. Romuald died peacefully, alone in his cell, praying to God.

St. Romuald, please help me offer prayers and sacrifices to God!

St. Alban

c. 304 • Britain

Alban might not have been a Christian, but he did not want to see someone killed for being a Christian either. The governor of his town was persecuting Christians, so when a cleric ran to his house and begged for a place to hide, Alban took him in. Alban was curious about why this man was willing to risk his life for this Faith. So he began to ask the cleric questions about Christianity. The cleric told Alban about Jesus's life, death, and resurrection. The more Alban heard, the more interested he became. What had started off as curiosity had turned into a desire to know and love Jesus. Alban decided to become a Christian, and the cleric baptized him in his home.

News came that soldiers were coming to search Alban's house for the cleric. They would be there any moment. Alban took the cleric's cloak and wrapped it around himself. When the soldiers arrived, he told them that he was the cleric they were looking for. The soldiers dragged Alban before the governor, who immediately saw that Alban was not who he said he was. Furious, he told Alban that if he did not reveal where the cleric was hiding, then he would suffer the cleric's punishment as if he were a Christian. Alban declared that he was, indeed, a Christian and was willing to suffer for his Faith. And so the governor condemned him to death by beheading.

The executioner marched Alban toward the hill where he would die. Onlookers crowded up the side of the hill and on the bridge over the river, blocking Alban and the executioner's path. Alban lifted his eyes to heaven, said a prayer, and the water parted, leaving a dry path to the other side. At this, the executioner dropped his sword, refused to carry out the execution, and believed in Christ. They had to find another executioner to behead Alban.

Alban continued up the hill, followed by the crowd. When he reached the top, he wished to show one more miraculous sign to the people that God was watching over him. He prayed to God for water to drink, and a fountain of water bubbled up at his feet, so that he quenched his thirst. Now that God's glory had been revealed to all, Alban was ready to die. The executioner who killed Alban immediately went blind after committing the terrible deed. News of all of the miracles at Alban's death reached the governor's ears, and he stopped his persecutions. He did not want to risk the anger of God. And so Alban's glorious martyrdom saved other Christian lives. St. Alban, help me to be a brave witness for the Faith!

St. Alban
June 20

St. Aloysius de Gonzaga
June 21

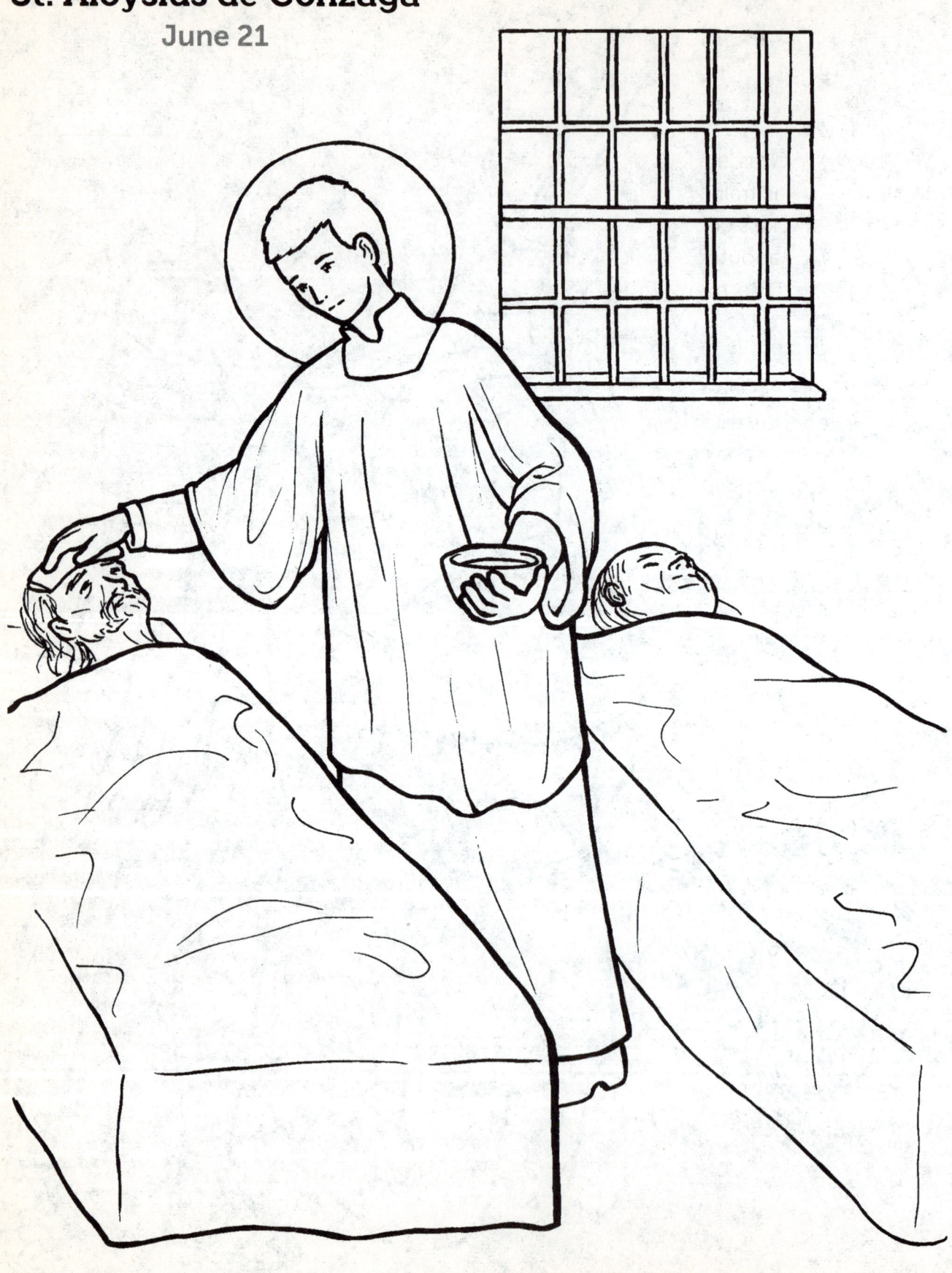

St Aloysius de Gonzaga

1568–1591 • Italy

Aloysius was the oldest son and heir of the noble house of Gonzaga, and his father was training him in the art of war. At the age of eight, he was sent to the grand duke's court to continue his training. There, he fell sick. To pass the time, he read about the lives of the saints, especially the brave Jesuit missionaries in India. The more Aloysius read, the more he realized that he did not want to live the life of war his father had chosen for him. He wanted to save souls, not destroy them. When he turned nine, Aloysius made a vow never to marry, because he wanted to give his entire life to God.

Aloysius told his parents that God was calling him to be a Jesuit priest. His mother was happy at the news, but his father was furious because Aloysius was supposed to be his heir. He was so angry that he did not give his permission, and Aloysius had to wait until he was eighteen to give up his inheritance and enter the seminary in Rome. He still dreamed of becoming a missionary, but ever since he had fallen sick as a boy, he had struggled with weak health. He was not strong enough to travel to India. This made Aloysius sad because he wanted to be brave and save souls. But he knew that God would show him what He wanted him to do.

When Aloysius was twenty-two, the Archangel Gabriel appeared to him in a vision. In the vision, the angel told him he would die within a year's time. Aloysius knew he must make ready for his death and do his best to become a saint. The next summer, a terrible plague broke out in Rome. The Jesuits opened a hospital for the victims. Aloysius knew that this was his chance to be brave for God just as he had hoped he could be. He searched for the sick in the streets, carried them to the hospital, and tended to their wounds. He knew that when he served the sick, he served Jesus.

Then came the day when Aloysius caught the plague. Aloysius knew that the angel's prophecy was coming true and he would die soon. In another vision, he learned the exact day of his death: June 21, eight days after the Feast of Corpus Christi, which is the glorious feast day celebrating the Body of Christ. On the day he had predicted his death, Aloysius became terribly weak, and he received the Sacrament of the Anointing of the Sick. Right before midnight, he gazed at the crucifix in his hands and breathed the name of Jesus as he died. St. Aloysius, help me to save souls for God!

Sts. John Fisher and Thomas More

d. 1535 • England

Henry VIII was the king of England. He wanted to divorce the queen, his wife, because she had not given birth to a son and heir. Then he wanted to marry a new queen. But Henry was a Catholic king, and Catholics are not allowed to divorce and remarry. Jesus taught that God joins a husband and wife in marriage, and so it cannot be undone. Henry didn't care. He thought he was more important than God. He decided he would stop being Catholic and start his own church. That way, he could make all the rules. Henry proclaimed that all of England would have to belong to his new church, too. Everyone would have to sign an oath to stop being Catholic and to follow him instead of the pope. If they did not, he would have them killed. Many signed the oath out of fear. But some brave Catholics refused. Two of these brave Catholics were John Fisher and Thomas More.

John Fisher was a cardinal and the queen's strongest defender. He declared that the divorce would go against God's law, and he refused to sign the king's oath. So Henry ordered his execution. John Fisher marched to his beheading with calm dignity, and all who saw him were amazed by his bravery. Immediately after his death, English Catholics declared him a martyr for the Faith.

Thomas More was the king's chancellor, his highest adviser. More than that, he and the king were friends. But although he loved his king, Thomas More loved God more. He refused to sign the oath against the Catholic Faith, and so the king imprisoned him in the Tower of London. Many people visited Thomas More and tried to convince him to sign the oath. They did not want to see him die. Still he refused, knowing that eternity in heaven is more important than a long life on earth. In prison, he wrote a book about the sorrows of Jesus, offering all of his suffering to Christ. Finally, Thomas More stood trial. Though he was innocent of treason, the jury found him guilty because that was what the king wanted.

On the day of his execution, Thomas More climbed the scaffold and declared, "I die the king's good servant, but God's first." The executioner knelt before him, begging his forgiveness for what he was about to do. Thomas More forgave his executioner, said his prayers, and became a martyr for the Faith. Sts. John Fisher and Thomas More, help me to live as God's good servant!

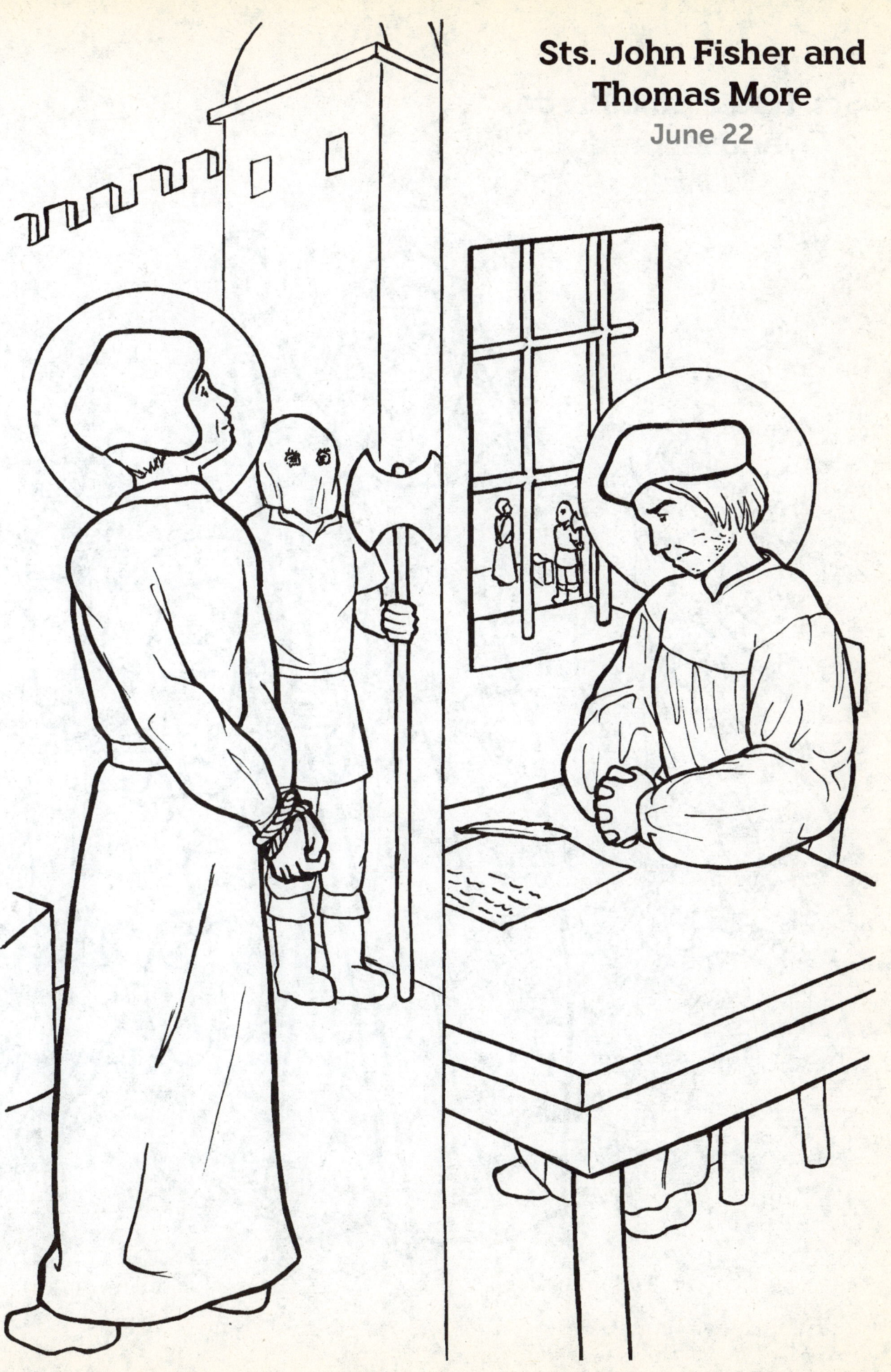

Sts. Hilda, Etheldreda, and Mildred
June 23

Sts. Hilda, Etheldreda, and Mildred

Seventh Century • Britain

St. Hilda founded the great monastery at Whitby, a city by the sea. Both monks and nuns at Whitby dedicated their lives to the study of Sacred Scripture. Many famous bishops first studied at the monastery, and so Whitby became famous for holiness and learning. Hilda's wisdom was known across the land, and people rich and poor came to her for advice.

For seven years before her death, a fever burned in Hilda's body. Doctors could not banish the fever, so Hilda patiently endured the suffering, the aches and the chills. But nothing could keep her from her holy work, not even illness. She continued to lead the monastery at Whitby until she died a holy death.

St. Etheldreda was promised in marriage when she was very young, but the man died before the marriage could be fulfilled. Next, her family forced her to marry the king of Northumbria for a political alliance. But by this time Etheldreda knew that God did not want her to marry but to be a nun instead. She convinced her husband to let her live in a convent. After twelve years, he came to carry her off, but she ran away with two other sisters as her companions.

The king's soldiers close behind, Etheldreda and her nuns took shelter on a cliff. There the tide rose so high that the king and his soldiers could not reach her. The high tide lasted for seven days, and finally the king promised Etheldreda that she could remain a nun. She and her nuns then traveled to the Island of Ely and founded a monastery. Etheldreda ruled over monks and nuns with great wisdom and holiness. She would spend the nights in prayer and would only eat one meal a day as a sacrifice to God. She predicted her own death by plague and died a holy death.

St. Mildred had a saintly mother, Lady Eafe. Eafe's two brothers had been murdered, so the king offered her some land on the Isle Thanet to make amends. She said she would take as much land as her pet deer could encircle. The king agreed, and her deer ran around half of the island. On this land, Eafe founded a monastery. Her daughter, Mildred, became abbess of the monastery after her. Mildred was kind and gentle, noble and wise. She cared for the poor and ruled over her monastery with great virtue until she died a holy death.

Sts. Hilda, Etheldreda, and Mildred, help me to live with wisdom and holiness!

Nativity of St. John the Baptist

Biblical Figure

The priest Zechariah watched with joy in his heart as his wife, Elizabeth, held the miracle of their newborn son in her arms. Their younger cousin, Mary, stood beside her. She had helped Elizabeth all through the birth with her strong and gentle care.

Even though Zechariah was bursting with happiness, he could not speak. He remembered the day, nine months before, when the Archangel Gabriel had appeared to him, a bright and wondrous messenger of God. The angel had told him that Elizabeth would bear a son, whom they were to name John, and that he would turn many people to God. But Zechariah had doubted the angel's words. He and Elizabeth were old; she was past child-bearing years. He had thought that the miracle would be impossible for God. Because of Zechariah's doubt, the angel had taken away his ability to speak. He would not be able to talk again until the angel's words were fulfilled. Now the miracle of his son's birth had come true. But there was something else that still had to happen before the angel's words were completely fulfilled—Elizabeth and Zechariah had to name their son.

Elizabeth declared that they would name the child John. Their neighbors and relatives were confused: it was part of Jewish tradition to name a child after a family member. But no one in their family was called John. The neighbors and relatives went to Zechariah. Surely, they thought, he would give a different name to his son. Zechariah signaled for a tablet. On it he wrote, "John is his name." The people were amazed.

With the naming of the baby, the angel's words had come to pass. Suddenly, Zechariah could speak again! He gave great shouts of joy and praise to God. Now the people's amazement turned into curiosity. What great things would baby John do when he grew up, they wondered, since God was surely with him?

Zechariah sang a song in praise of God for the birth of his son: "And you, child, will be called prophet of the Most High, for you will go before the Lord to prepare His ways" (Luke 1:76). As he sang, Mary and Elizabeth gazed into each other's eyes, Elizabeth holding John in her arms, and Mary's hand resting on her belly. They knew that John would prepare the way for Mary's son, who was the Messiah. John would be a voice calling out in the desert of Galilee, "Make straight the way of the Lord." St. John the Baptist, help my heart to be always ready for Jesus!

Nativity of St. John the Baptist
June 24

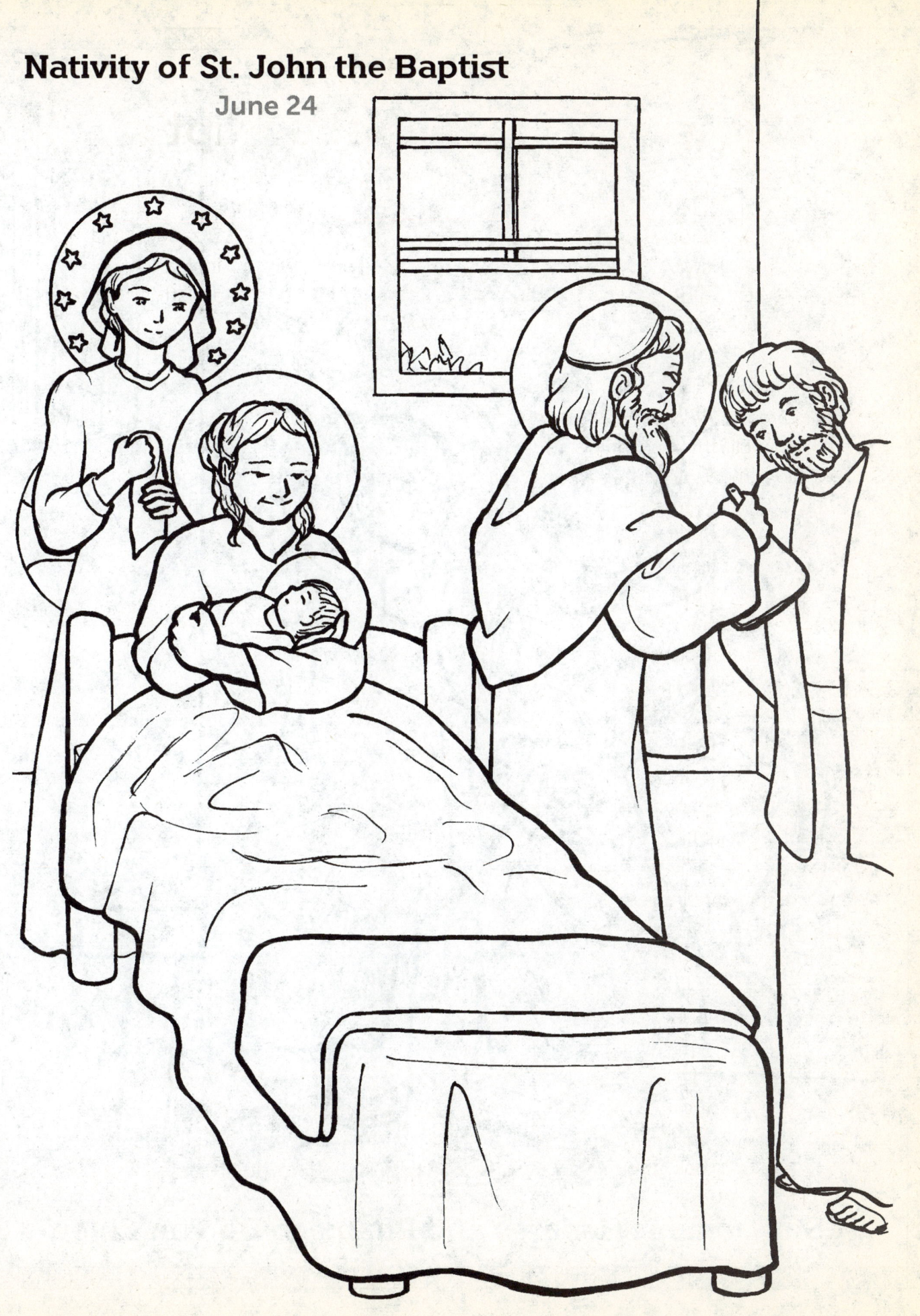

Sts. Dominic Henares and Phanxicô Đo Van Chieu

June 25

Sts. Dominic Henares and Phanxicô Đo Van Chieu

d. 1838 • Spain and Vietnam

Bishop Dominic Henares taught at the seminary at Vietnam. He was a Spanish missionary at a time when it was very dangerous to teach the Faith in Vietnam because the Emperor Minh Mang persecuted Catholics. But the emperor's persecutions did not stop Bishop Dominic Henares from sharing his love for Jesus. He knew how important it was to educate Vietnamese men to be priests. One of his most faithful students was Phanxicô Đo Van Chieu, a catechist who taught the Catholic Faith.

It was becoming dangerous for Bishop Dominic Henares to stay in Vietnam, but he refused to leave. Phanxicô Đo Van Chieu, his faithful catechist, remained with him. Soldiers came to their village, and the two men hid in a small boat. But the boat's owner was so nervous that the guards immediately knew he was hiding something. They searched the boat, discovered the bishop and his companion, and imprisoned them. The judge ordered Phanxicô Đo Van Chieu to be scourged mercilessly. But no matter how cruelly the soldiers treated him, he refused to give up the Faith.

Soon it was time for the executions of the bishop and his faithful catechist. A large crowd gathered to watch. Three Vietnamese soldiers, who were Christians and so had also been imprisoned, were dragged out to watch the execution as well. The judge wanted the three soldiers to despair, seeing the deaths of Bishop Dominic Henares and Phanxicô Đo Van Chieu. But when their death sentences were read aloud, the bishop and his catechist showed such joy that the crowds were amazed. They knew that soon they would be with Jesus in heaven because of their faithfulness to Him. Because of their joy, the three Christian soldiers did not despair. Instead, they called out to the bishop and begged him to pray for them.

Bishop Dominic Henares and Phanxicô Đo Van Chieu became glorious martyrs for the Faith. The three Christian soldiers who were inspired by their example soon also shared in their martyrdom and their glory in heaven. Sts. Dominic Henares and Phanxicô Đo Van Chieu, help my love for God inspire others to love God too!

St. Josemaría Escrivá

1902–1975 • Spain

Something unusual in the snow caught the sixteen-year old boy's attention—footprints made by bare feet. The boy realized that these footprints were made by a friar without shoes walking in the cold snow. The friar had not worn shoes, even though it was winter, because he was living a life of poverty as a sacrifice to God. The boy thought that, if other people make sacrifices for God, should not he offer something to God as well? With this thought, God was preparing the young boy—whose name was Josemaría Escrivá—to become a priest and later a saint.

When Josemaría told his father that he wanted to become a priest, tears fell from his father's eyes. It was the only time Josemaría saw his father cry. His father told him that he would not stop him, but he begged his son to think about his decision carefully. He told Josemaría that being a priest would be difficult. A priest does not have a home like other people; instead, he is called to be a saint.

That was exactly what Josemaría wanted. He felt the call to the priesthood as a special blessing from God.

He wanted to be a saint.

Three years after he became a priest, Josemaría was deep in prayer. A sudden sight came to him, and he realized that God was giving him a special mission: to spread the message that all people can be holy in their everyday work.

So he started a group for men and women that helped people dedicate their work to God. This meant that a doctor, a farmer, a mother, a father, an artist, a teacher could make a promise to give their life and work to God and spread the message of God's love while still being a part of the everyday world. Josemaría called this group Opus Dei, which in Latin means "work of God."

Josemaría spent his life teaching the mission of Opus Dei. Groups spread across Spain and then the whole world. Josemaría wrote many books, which have sold millions of copies. Throughout his work and travels, Josemaría kept a spirit of humility and a deep love of God. He died a holy death in his workroom—giving his final glance to a picture of Mary.

St. Josemaría Escrivá, help me give all of my work to God!

St. Josemaría Escrivá

June 26

St. Cyril of Alexandria
June 27

THEOTOKOS

St. Cyril of Alexandria

376–444 • Egypt

Cyril was the patriarch of Alexandria, which means he was the leader of the Church in Alexandria. He was a man of strong faith and strong temper.

There was a priest named Nestorius who denied that Mary was the Mother of God. Nestorius had many followers, and his false teaching was confusing Christians. Cyril was outraged. He knew that if someone was denying that Mary was the Mother of God, they were also denying that Jesus was fully God and fully man. By attacking Mary, Nestorius was also attacking Jesus!

The leaders of the Church called together a council to declare the truth about Jesus and Mary. Because the false teaching concerned Mary, they decided to hold the council at Ephesus. Ephesus is where John, Jesus's beloved disciple, had lived. John had taken Mary into his home as Jesus had asked at His crucifixion. Mary and John had both lived in Ephesus until Mary fell asleep to be assumed then into heaven by her son, Jesus. There was no better place for the council to be held.

Cyril was in charge of the Council of Ephesus. He declared that Mary was the Theotokos. *Theotokos* means "God-bearer" in Greek. By giving her the title of Theotokos, Cyril was declaring that Mary was the Mother of God. The council condemned Nestorius's false teaching and declared that Mary was the Mother of God because Jesus is both fully God and fully man.

Now Christians everywhere knew what to believe about Jesus and Mary because Cyril had defended the truth!

St. Cyril of Alexandria, help me to grow in greater love for Mary, the Mother of God.

St. Irenaeus

c. 130–202 • Asia Minor (present-day Turkey)

Irenaeus lived in Smyrna and learned all about Jesus from St. Polycarp. St. Polycarp was a disciple of the Apostle John (also known as St. John the Evangelist), who wrote the Gospel of John in the Bible. This means that everything that St. Polycarp learned about Jesus came from someone who had seen Jesus, talked with Jesus, and had known Jesus best. All his life, Irenaeus remembered everything about St. Polycarp—his voice, what he looked like, and, most importantly, every word he said about Jesus.

Irenaeus became a priest and served under the bishop of Lyons, France. There Irenaeus served God and his bishop with all his heart. The bishop trusted Irenaeus so much that he asked Irenaeus to carry a letter from him to the pope in Rome.

While Irenaeus was in Rome, a terrible persecution broke out in Lyons. The Roman emperor's soldiers killed the bishop. Irenaeus received the news with great sorrow. He knew that God had spared his life by sending him far away from the persecution. He also knew it was his duty to return and serve the Christians in Lyons as best he could. The pope appointed Irenaeus the next bishop of Lyons.

There were many pagans in Lyons and throughout France who had never heard of Jesus. Not only that, there were many false teachers who taught lies about Christianity. Irenaeus knew it was his job to share his love for Jesus with his Christian flock. Also, he would send missionaries all throughout France so that everyone could learn about Jesus and go to heaven.

Irenaeus wrote an important book called *Against Heresies*. In it, he wrote down the truth of the Catholic Faith as he had heard it from St. Polycarp, who had heard it from St. John, who had heard it from Jesus. Many saints and theologians learned the truth of what Jesus had taught by reading Irenaeus's book. Irenaeus served Jesus and his flock until the end of his days.

St. Irenaeus, help me learn about Jesus by reading Scripture and the holy writings of the saints!

Sts. Peter and Paul
June 29

Sts. Peter and Paul

Biblical Figures

Peter was the leader of the Apostles and had founded the Church in Rome, the capital of the empire. There the murderous Emperor Nero hunted down Christians. He enjoyed having them thrown into the arena and ripped apart by wild beasts or setting them on fire at night. Peter was now an old man, and he fled from Rome to save himself from the mad emperor. He was escaping on the Via Appia, the road that leads from Rome, when suddenly Jesus appeared before him, carrying His Cross back toward Rome.

Peter called after him, "Where are you going, Lord?"

Jesus responded, "I am going back to Rome, to be crucified again."

Peter understood that Jesus wanted him to return to Rome. The time of his death had come. But instead of fear, Peter felt peace. He was joyful that he was to follow in Jesus's footsteps and carry his own cross. He would die for his Master, and Jesus would raise him from the dead.

When Peter returned to Rome, he comforted the Christians in hiding from the Roman soldiers. But soon Peter was discovered and sentenced to die the same way his Master had died: on a cross. Peter did not feel himself worthy to die the same way that Jesus had. So he asked that his cross be planted in the ground upside down. The Roman soldiers did as he asked, and Peter was martyred hanging on an upside-down cross.

No one worked harder to spread the Faith of Jesus than St. Paul. He had traveled far and wide to preach the Good News of Jesus to the Gentiles. The Gentiles were the non-Jewish people, and Paul knew that Jesus died for all people, not just the Jews. But certain Jews did not like Paul. They had him arrested, and Paul knew they meant to kill him. Because he was a Roman citizen, Paul appealed to the emperor, which meant that he would be safe under Roman protection until the emperor heard his case. But even though he was safe, he was kept in prison and taken to Rome. St. Paul wrote letters under house arrest and preached to the Roman Church for two years from his home.

Eventually, the merciless Emperor Nero sentenced Paul to death for being a Christian. St. Paul was beheaded by the sword, his martyr's blood a witness to the Faith.

Sts. Peter and Paul, help me serve the Lord!

The First Martyrs of Rome

First to Third Century • Rome

A terrible fire raged in Rome for nine days. More than half of the city burned down. As the flames engulfed his city, the Emperor Nero strummed his lyre and sang before the red horizon. He was a cruel man and thought the bright flames a magnificent display: after all, he could use the new space to build himself a Golden House. But then the people of Rome blamed Nero for the fire. This frightened him. The people might riot, or, even worse, try to kill him! He needed someone else to blame for the fire.

There was a new group of people in Rome that no one knew much about. They did not worship the Roman gods, and they called themselves Christians. Nero decided that he would blame the Christians for the fire. He didn't care that the Christians were innocent; he just wanted to shift the blame from himself to someone else. Nero ordered his soldiers to hunt down all the Christians, be they children or elderly, slaves or Roman citizens. The Romans made Christian executions into a great show. They threw them into a great arena and had them attacked by wild beasts while the Romans watched. But the Christians were steadfast and brave. They loved Jesus more than their bodies and their lives. They wanted to be with Him in heaven, and so nothing could make them deny Jesus.

After Nero, many other Roman emperors persecuted the Christians because the Christians only worshipped one God. The emperors thought they themselves were gods, so if the Christians did not worship them, they called them traitors. But the persecutions did not stamp out Christianity as the emperors hoped. The persecutions, in fact, did the opposite. Christianity spread!

The heroic, joyful, and peace-filled way the martyrs met their deaths inspired many to become Christians themselves. Not only that, the martyrs now live in heaven and are even more powerful. Their prayers before the throne of God showered many graces on the early Roman Church. For many of the Roman martyrs, we know their life stories. For many others, we only have their names because they were etched into their graves. Still many other Roman martyrs remain nameless. But whether we know the martyrs' names or not, all of their deaths shine as a witness to their love for Jesus and the truth of the Faith. First Martyrs of Rome, help me to remain brave and steadfast in my love for Jesus!

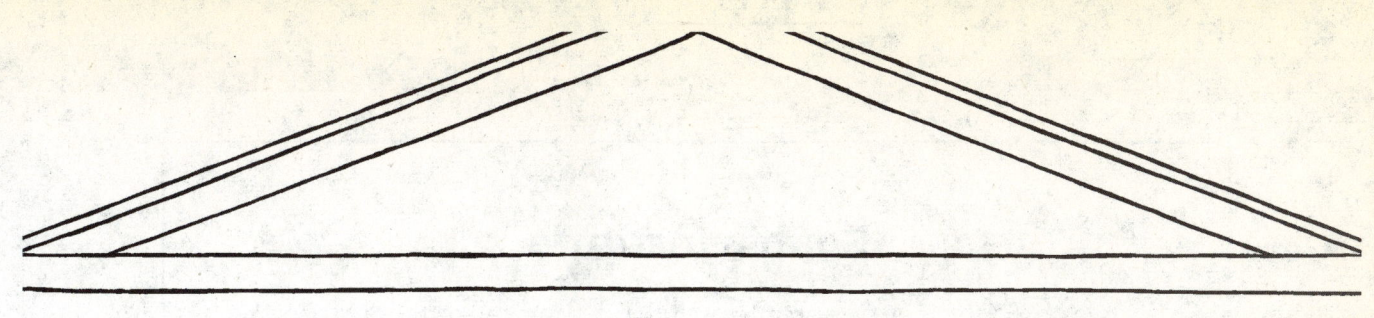

The First Martyrs of Rome

June 30

Sophia Institute

Sophia Institute is a nonprofit institution that seeks to nurture the spiritual, moral, and cultural life of souls and to spread the Gospel of Christ in conformity with the authentic teachings of the Roman Catholic Church.

Sophia Institute Press fulfills this mission by offering translations, reprints, and new publications that afford readers a rich source of the enduring wisdom of mankind.

Sophia Institute also operates two popular online Catholic resources: CrisisMagazine.com and CatholicExchange.com.

Crisis Magazine provides insightful cultural analysis that arms readers with the arguments necessary for navigating the ideological and theological minefields of the day. *Catholic Exchange* provides world news from a Catholic perspective as well as daily devotionals and articles that will help you to grow in holiness and live a life consistent with the teachings of the Church.

In 2013, Sophia Institute launched Sophia Institute for Teachers to renew and rebuild Catholic culture through service to Catholic education. With the goal of nurturing the spiritual, moral, and cultural life of souls, and an abiding respect for the role and work of teachers, we strive to provide materials and programs that are at once enlightening to the mind and ennobling to the heart; faithful and complete, as well as useful and practical.

Sophia Institute gratefully recognizes the Solidarity Association for preserving and encouraging the growth of our apostolate over the course of many years. Without their generous and timely support, this book would not be in your hands.

www.SophiaInstitute.com
www.CatholicExchange.com
www.CrisisMagazine.com
www.SophiaInstituteforTeachers.org

Sophia Institute Press® is a registered trademark of Sophia Institute.
Sophia Institute is a tax-exempt institution as defined by the Internal Revenue Code, Section 501(c)(3). Tax I.D. 22-2548708.